MW00614610

Good Monday Morning

Other Books by Denise Hildreth Jones

(fiction)

The Savannah Series
Savannah from Savannah
Savannah Comes Undone
Savannah by the Sea

Flies on the Butter

The Will of Wisteria

Hurricanes in Paradise

The First Gardener

Secrets Over Sweet Tea

(non-fiction)

Flying Solo: Divorce, Healing and a Very Present God

Reclaiming Your Heart: A Journey to Living Fully Alive
Reclaiming Your Heart Participant Guide
Reclaiming Your Heart Leader Guide
8-Week DVD Teaching Series

To watch the corresponding video devotionals for each week go to
https://www.reclaiminghearts.org/monday-musings/?y=2016

Good Monday Morning

52 DEVOTIONS FOR YOUR YEAR

DENISE HILDRETH JONES

D H J

For my mom...
the one who read to me from my first devotional.

Contents

Introduction

A few years back, my friend and mentor, Dr. Albert Lemmons, lent me his copy of a book called *The Valley of Vision*, a book of Puritan prayers and devotionals. When I recorded the very first Monday Musing video devotional in 2016, I mentioned that this book was borrowed from him. A few weeks later my own personal copy came in the mail. My neighbor, Sue, decided I needed my own. What a treasure. The prayer I read on that video was a prayer from the book that had cracked my heart open.

As you begin this journey with me for this next year, my prayer is that these devotionals along with your own digging and clinging and listening and learning and praying and leaning will break your heart wide open as well. So, that is why I wanted to offer this prayer to you as we begin our journey together. I encourage you to read it out loud before you begin this first Monday's devotional. May the Spirit of God, the "fountain of all good," reach to your deepest places, doing the work only He can do.

"Oh, fountain of all good, destroy in me every lofty thought. Break pride to pieces and scatter it to the wind. Annihilate each clinging shred of self-righteousness. Implant in me true lowliness of spirit. Abase me to self-loathing self-abhorrence. Open in me a fount of penitential tears. Break me. Bind me up. Thus will my heart be a prepared dwelling for my God. Then can the Father take up His abode in me, then can the blessed Jesus come with healing in His touch. Then can the Holy Spirit descend in sanctifying grace. O Holy Trinity, three persons in one God, inhabit me, a temple consecrated to Thy glory. When Thou art present, evil cannot abide. In Thy fellowship is fullness of joy. Beneath Thy smile is peace of conscience and by Thy side no fears disturbed, no apprehension, banished rest of mind:

With Thee my heart shall bloom with fragrance. Make me meek through repentance for Thine indwelling. Nothing exceeds Thy power, nothing is too great for Thee to do, nothing too good for Thee to give. Infinite is Thy might, boundless Thy love, limitless Thy grace, and glorious Thy saving name. Let angels sing for sinners repenting, prodigals restored, backsliders reclaimed, Satan's captives released, blind eyes opened, broken hearts bound up, the despondent cheered, the self-righteous stripped, the [formless] driven from a refuge of lies, the ignorant enlightened and the saints built up in their most holy faith. I ask great things of a great God."

Sweet friends, we have a great God and today we ask Him these great things. May this first of your year be blessed as God begins to write the next year in each of our stories.

Week 1

Setting the Table

Monday

Read: Matthew 6

Good Monday morning.

If you are like me, there is something exciting about picking up a new devotional at the beginning of the year. I've often wondered if God created calendars so we'd have a mental restart.☺ One of the ways I've grown to enjoy my devotionals is all the notes I write in them along the way. My *Streams In the Desert* devotional has been read and written in so many times it finally completely fell apart. Well, I think the fact that I ran over it contributed to that factor, too... So, as you pick this up I hope it will become that for you. A place to write your dreams, fears, joys and ways you are seeing God work in this year of your story.

So, we are just going to jump into the deep end. Why not! There is just more to experience there. Have you ever considered starting the New Year a different way? I'm not talking about a resolution that is forgotten or broken by February, I'm talking about doing something that will change your life. I do not say that flippantly. I say that as honestly as I know how to say it. For over a decade, I have spent the first part of each year recalibrating, if you will. Sloughing off the "stuff" of life that has crept in over the past year. So, the new year brings me back to the place my heart needs most, a deep intentionality to encounter the heart of my heavenly Father. I push aside the distractions of life and He becomes my focus. For three weeks it is He and I. Not that the rest of my year isn't His, but I shut myself away in this season. In fact, I have come to see this season as an "offensive posture" of spiritual warfare. As if this season prepares my heart and mind and spirit for both the vision and battles that lay ahead.

I listen differently, I seek differently, and I hear differently. I turn off the television and dig into the Word for longer stretches of time. I listen to some of my favorite teachers and preachers with notebook in hand instead of while I'm putting on my makeup. I push aside the foods that I love for the Savior I can't live without. And I say, "Search me, heal me, protect me, speak to me."

It has also become to me like a first fruits offering. Romans 11:16 (ASV) says, *"If the first fruit is holy, the lump is also holy. And if the root is holy, so are the branches."* I've operated this way in my life for a long time with both my resources and with my day... that if I give the Lord the first part, then it governs the whole and it makes the rest holy. My good friend and ministry partner, Ken Edwards, told me a few years back that at the beginning of his year he'll ask the Lord if He has a word for him for the year; and I've since then added this to my first of the year discoveries. It's been beautiful and I've definitely seen each year's word come to pass. One year I felt like the Lord gave me a phrase, which He'd never done before... but, thankfully, we can't put God in a box – He can do things differently than He's done in the past because He's God and He doesn't operate how we expect Him to.

The central story to all of our stories is the story of Adam and Eve. It is where our stories ultimately began. One piece of that story is that Satan used food as a tool of seduction. But if you then go to the gospel writers, right before Jesus began his public ministry and was sent to the desert to be tempted by Satan with the same things Eve was tempted with, the lust of the flesh, the lust of the eyes and the pride of life, what was Jesus doing? He had gone without food. He had been on a forty day fast. Jesus did the very opposite of what Eve chose to grab hold of. Yes, she was ultimately grabbing for self and power, but food was used as the vehicle. Jesus resisted the food for a season and accomplished in the Spirit what led to our ultimate deliverance. So, fasting for me has also become a part of this recalibration season. Whether a food group or a favorite item, a meal or a Daniel fast, each missed meal is an opportunity to spend that time being reminded that Jesus ultimately is the bread of life I need and the time is freed up to spend with Him.

As you enter this new year, what if you entered in a way you never have before? What if you considered taking some intentional time away from your normal routine in this first part of the year to ask God to come into your year in a deeper and richer way than years past? Maybe consider fasting breakfast, or lunch, or dinner for a set period of time. Consider turning off some of those shows you watch and instead going to your room and reading your Bible, or taking that time to read Bible stories or have devotions with your family. Cut off the noise in the car for a season and talk to the Lord or listen to some podcast messages or worship music. Then, in this season, pay attention to things you hear. Maybe you will hear the same "message," so to speak, multiple times. Maybe God will give you a word for your year. Maybe He will bring you some clarity for some decisions you need to make. Maybe He will ask some things of you that you might not have been able to hear otherwise. But what I can assure you will happen: He will be present in it. Every single time. *"Draw near to God and He will draw near to you."* James 4:8 (NKJV)

It was a first of the year fast and time with the Lord that prepared me for my divorce and the pain I would walk through. It was a first of the year fast that revealed to my husband a new way we needed to begin to give financially. It was a first of the year fast that gave me a word over my life that broke some things off of me that I needed to heal from. It was a first of the year fast that gave me some prophetic words for my bonus-children that I continue to watch Jesus fulfill. And I could tell you numerous other stories.

I believe calendars are God's gift to us. He doesn't need a calendar. But isn't it nice at the first of the year to look at this new, clean slate? Now, what if you looked at that clean slate with these questions in mind: "Father, what do You want to speak to me in this New Year?" "Father, what do You have for me in this New Year?"

Friends, when we love the Lord we can trust that He is in every detail of our story. So I want to encourage you. It's a new year -- set aside a week or a couple of weeks in this first part of it and ask the Lord if He has a word for you. I am confident that He will give you a word for this new year that will lead you deeper into what He is doing and desires to do.

What are some things that might have crept into your life over this past year that might need to be let go of? Wearing busyness as a badge of honor? Bitterness or resentment? Complacency? Anger? Fear? Pride? Unhealthy patterns of behavior?

_____
_____
_____

Spend some time this week asking God if He may have a word for your new year. Then, if He gives you one, look up all the scriptures you can find with that word in it.

Tuesday

Read **Romans 11:16**. What do you read this verse to mean?

_____
_____
_____

What are some ways you can apply it to your life, specifically?

_____
_____
_____

What impact could doing those things have on the outcome of your year? How could that change your year?

_____
_____
_____
_____

Wednesday

Many people have grown up their entire lives and never even heard lessons on fasting. However, I truly believe it is one of the least utilized weapons in the arsenal of a believer. Fasting was a practice by the "greats" of the Christian faith – and Jesus himself.

Read **Matthew 9:15.** What did Jesus say His disciples would do when He was gone? Who are His disciples today?

_____

_____

_____

Re-read **Matthew 6:1-18**. What are the three things talked about in these three sections? What is the word used before each one? So, what does that word indicate for our lives in regards to these things?

_____

_____

_____

What, if any, things have you ever been taught regarding fasting?

_____

_____

_____

Does the idea of fasting bring up any fears? What are they? Why do you think they are there?

_____

_____

_____

_____

Any time fasting is mentioned in scripture it is always the absence of food. Again, I believe this goes back to Eve's act in the garden. Because ultimately fasting is a denying of self in a way nothing else can be. That is why fasting is so powerful to discipline our flesh and lean into the power of the Holy Spirit that dwells in us and is able to supernaturally provide the strength that we need.

Fasting can be a meal or even a favorite food. I had a friend one time who fasted all fried foods, poor guy! I have fasted Coca-Cola before, often, because I know how much I enjoy it. I always tell Jesus, "If I am fasting Coke, you know I am serious!"

However, I have had seasons of fasting clothes buying, of fasting television and noise. And these, too, have allowed me to see Jesus in beautiful and intimate ways. So, ask Him. Ask Him what He is asking of you. He will tell you. Jentezen Franklin says often when he is writing or teaching on fasting, "If it means something to you it means something to God."

Thursday

Read **Matthew 6:16-18**. According to verses 17 and 18, how does Jesus say here we are to approach our times of fasting?

_____

_____

_____

Why might we be tempted to want to show others we are fasting?

_____

_____

_____

Read **1 Samuel 16:7**. What does it say God looks at and measures us by? Why is this important?

_____

_____

_____

Fasting is a good thing. We love being recognized for good things. But we aren't called to seek man's approval – our desire should be to please the Lord in what we do, first and foremost. He knows the motives and intentions of our hearts. May we pursue His heart with the purest of intentions this year together, friends…

Friday

I want to wrap up this week by passing along a couple of amazing resources on fasting that I've personally used and highly recommend: Jentezen Franklin's book called Fasting and then Fasting for Spiritual Breakthrough: A Guide to Nine Biblical Fasts by Elmer Towns are two of the best books on the topic of fasting I've ever encountered.

I also want us to look at a couple of other reasons of why someone would fast. Read the verses below and write down the reasons you find.

1 Samuel 7:6   Daniel 1:12, 10:2-3
Ezra 8:23   Luke 2:37
Esther 4   1 Corinthians 6:19-20
Psalms 35:13

_____
_____
_____
_____
_____
_____

Take a few minutes to reflect on all we've discussed this week. Do you still have questions about fasting? Do you feel the Lord leading you to take some time here at the beginning of the year and give up something for a short season in order to pursue Him differently? Use the space below to write out what you're thinking and feeling regarding this most holy of practices.

_____
_____
_____
_____
_____
_____
_____
_____
_____
_____
_____
_____
_____
_____
_____
_____
_____

Saturday Surrender

"Do you not know that your bodies are temples of the Holy Spirit, who is in you, whom you have received from God? You are not your own; you were bought at a price. Therefore honor God with your bodies."
1 Corinthians 6:19-20 (NIV)

You will hear me say this many, many times during our journey together this year: absolutely nothing is lost in surrender.

Fasting is a real act of surrender. I won't lie. It can be hard. But I can tell you this… it has been one of the most rewarding disciplines and invitations of love I have ever received from my Father, as I am so fully aware of how He has moved in and through my sacrifice and spiritual hunger.

There are things we know we're holding onto, trying to control, that we probably shouldn't be… our finances, a health crisis, the unhealthy eating patterns, an obviously bad relationship… and then there are things not so obvious that take a little digging into our hearts to realize they need to be given to the Lord. Once we realize our lives are not about us but everything, including our bodies, belongs to Him, it gives us an even greater depth of relationship with Him.

So I invite you this Saturday, like I will every Saturday, to spend some time asking the Lord what it is you may need to surrender to Him. Ask Him to reveal to you anything in your heart that you need to hand over to Him. I know for a fact that if we're willing to ask the tough questions, He's ready, willing, and able to provide a gentle, loving answer…

_____
_____
_____
_____
_____
_____
_____
_____
_____
_____
_____
_____

Sunday Sabbath

"By the seventh day God had finished the work He had been doing; so on the seventh day He rested from all His work. Then God blessed the seventh day and made it holy, because on it He rested from all the work of creating that He had done."
Genesis 2:2-3 (NIV)

Songs for Your Sabbath

Kurt Carr, *Just the Beginning*
Gateway Worship / Rebecca Pfortmiller, *We Cry Out*

If the omnipresent, omnipotent, almighty Creator of the heavens and the earth rested, how much more, then, do we need to?

Friends, the Sabbath was made holy for a reason. It was set apart from all other days as a day to reflect, to rest, to savor the presence of our heavenly Father. Do not miss the beauty of this gift the Lord has given to your heart.

Grab hold of it.

Savor it.

Fully experience everything it has to offer.

Maybe you need to revisit a conversation you started with Him earlier this week. Whatever you do, your God is inviting you to encounter His heart. Even if you have to shut yourself in your closet, do what you need to do to get quiet, get still, and rest in His sweet, sweet presence today…

Lord, I surrender this first part of my year to You. You know my needs. You know my desires. You know how I need You to move in my life. I thank You for giving me such clear direction in Your Word about how to encounter Your heart. My desire is to know more of You and to experience You in a new way like I never have before. I give this year to You. It is Yours. Lead me as I inquire you about fasting. Walk with me as I learn how to release things and truly surrender them to You. And thank You that Your presence is with me in any and every decision.

Week 2

I AM that I AM

Monday

⁂

Read: Exodus 3

Good Monday morning.

One of the hardest things in all of the world is to describe God. So, why not start with one of the hardest yet most beautiful things in scripture? God. He has so many attributes: Omniscient, All-Powerful, Creator, El-Shaddai… the list goes on and on. In fact, this is why we will spend eternity with Him, because even with eternity we will still be encountering more and more about Him. But when God describes Himself He does it in one very powerful moment and with five simple, but all encompassing, words. It happens in Exodus 3:13,14. God is about to ask Moses to go to Egypt and to, after four hundred years of slavery, deliver the children of Israel from Egyptian bondage. And so Moses asks Him, "Who do I tell them has sent me?" And God gives us a name for himself. He said, "You tell them, 'I am that I am' has sent you." Strong's commentary tells us that name 'I am that I am' is the name 'Yahweh'.

That word 'Yahweh' means "to exist" which emphasizes and confirms what theologians and scholars have said for years -- that God has existed from the very beginning. It's perplexing to our human minds because we only know of things that have a beginning, but God had no beginning. He was and is and is to come. He's also the one that holds all things together. So He is the one that keeps this world from coming off its hinges with the slightest tilt of an axis. He is the explanation to the things that defy explanation. He is The Great I Am. Isn't that a comforting thought in the chaos and mess of some of our own stories? It's also a comfort in the chaos of this world and the uncertainty of it... that there is One who has existed from the very beginning, before all time, before you and I were even a thought -- One who is so great He calls Himself, the I AM that I AM.

What a big God! So, when the enemy tries to make us believe anything other than the magnitude and majesty of our God, like he did when he introduced doubt into Eve's heart about God's reliability in Genesis 3:1, we can stand firm on the truth that He is who He says He is. Friends, from the beginning of time, God, Jesus, and the Holy Spirit existed and created all that was created. Our stories began with the ageless One. Yahweh. It is this truth that gives this Monday morning and all the Monday mornings that remain before He comes back for us hope. Because we need the I AM that I AM.

But before I leave you to go about the rest of your Monday, let's remember the words of that beautiful chorus that many of us have sung so often over the last few years:

Who is worthy?
None beside you, God Almighty
the
Great
I
Am.

"I AM" is your Father. That is a powerful thought. It is His breath that filled your lungs and gave you life. It was His willingness to sacrifice His son that gives you eternal life if you believe and receive. What in your life right now are you struggling to believe "I AM" is big enough for? Your marriage or children, or lack thereof? Your finances? Your job? Your health? Your past? If you could put honest words around your doubts what would they be?

_____

_____

_____

_____

As we start this journey together there is a powerful truth we need to realize, and that is how the enemy operates when it comes to our God. Read **Genesis 3:1-5**. What was the enemy's first weapon on the heart of Eve? And who was his assault against?

_____

Read **John 10:10**. And notice the progression. What is Satan described as? And what would he want to steal from you? What would he want to kill in you? And what would he ultimately want to destroy? Remember this fact as we go along: the enemy always comes at our heart to get us to believe a lie about God, our "I AM," because ultimately he is after destroying our faith in our God.

_____

_____

Author Jonathan Cahn in The Book of Mysteries says, "You have always said His name. It is woven into the fabric of existence that when you speak of yourself, you must say His Name... and you must always speak His Name first."[1] Isn't that powerful?! So whenever I say, "I am Denise," I am speaking the name of my Father first. Whenever I say, "I am not capable of doing that" or any of the other negative things I may say about myself, I start with His name. There is no need to elaborate. I'm sure this has already impacted you. I'd encourage you to meditate on this truth as you go throughout your day. Especially tomorrow as you dig in even deeper to all that this "I AM" truly is.

Tuesday

Look at the table below of the names of God in the Old Testament. Which of these do you need God to be for you right now? The scripture reference is where each name of God first appears in the Bible. Look up the verses of the ones that stand out to you and reflect on how God fulfilled that role then and how He's fulfilling that role even now for you.

_____

_____

_____

_____

_____

NAME OF GOD	SCRIPTURE	MEANING
El Shaddai	Genesis 17:1	Lord God Almighty
El Elyon	Genesis 14:18	Most High God
Jehovah Nissi	Exodus 17:15	The Lord My Banner
Jehovah-Raah	Psalm 23:1	The Lord My Shepherd
Jehovah Rapha	Exodus 15:26	The Lord That Heals
Jehovah Shammah	Ezekiel 48:35	The Lord is There
Jehovah Tsidkenu	Jeremiah 23:6	The Lord Our Righteousness
Jehovah Mekoddishkem	Exodus 31:13	The Lord Who Sanctifies You
El Olam	Genesis 21:33	The Everlasting God
Jehovah Jireh	Genesis 22:14	The Lord Will Provide
Jehovah Shalom	Judges 6:24	The Lord is Peace
Jehovah Sabaoth	1 Samuel 1:3	The Lord of Hosts

---

[1] Jonathan Cahn, _The Book of Mysteries_ (Frontlines: Charisma House Book Group, 2016), Day 2.

Wednesday

꧁

Read **Joshua 3:9-4:7**. Sit for a moment and really consider what has happened in this passage. The miracles. The power. The present I AM. Why did God do this?

_____

_____

Take some time today to recall some of the things you've seen the Lord do and be in your life. The table of the names of God on the previous page might be a good place to start.

_____

_____

_____

_____

_____

_____

How does remembering all you've experienced God do in your life affect your level of faith in Him moving forward?

_____

_____

_____

Thursday

꧁

On Monday, we talked about areas in our lives where we may be having a hard time believing God is big enough to handle our stuff. Look at the beautiful reminder we are given in **Deuteronomy 7:9**. What does it say about the Lord our God?

_____

_____

What are some ways God has shown Himself faithful to you? What are ways you have seen His faithfulness in your personal family generations behind you and the generations in front of you?

_____

_____

_____

In what ways can you, right now, show that you trust God with the areas of your life you're needing Him to be I AM in?

_____

_____

_____

Read **Isaiah 44:6, Revelation 1:8**. How does God describe Himself here? What does this tell you about who He is to you?

_____

_____

_____

_____

_____

Friday

Let's look back at Moses today. Read the following verses:

Exodus 3:11
Exodus 4:1
Exodus 4:10
Exodus 4:13

It's easy to hear so much about the miraculous things Moses was able to accomplish with God's help and begin to think he was some sort of superhuman. What do these specific verses show us about Moses, though?

_____

_____

Moses was a human, too. God didn't expect Moses to free the Israelites on his own power. God promised to be I AM for Moses, to equip him with resources to complete his calling. You're not expected to walk alone, either. In fact, in one of the future I AM statements we will study the passage "apart from me you can do nothing."[2] This is true for us now and it was true for Moses then. Apart from God, Moses was just a man wandering around the wilderness. But with God, he was a man able to set an entire nation free! Take a few minutes to think about the ways the Lord has equipped or is equipping you for all the things He has called you to; how is He being I AM for you? Or how do you need to allow Him to?

_____

_____

_____

Saturday Surrender

Exodus 13:17-14:31 is the account of God leading the Israelites out of Egypt. Tucked inside this passage is a short, yet oh so powerful verse. Moses encourages himself and his fellow Israelites in Exodus 14:14, "The Lord will fight for you; you need only to be still."

"…you need only to be still…"

How often can we truly say we let the Lord do the fighting and we let ourselves get still?
Not as often as we should, I'm sure. We believe another lie of the enemy about our God, that I AM needs us — He needs us to fix things, to hold things, to manage things, to start things… when, in reality, we're the ones that need Him. Like it says in Acts 17:24-25 (NIV), "The God who made the world and everything in it is the Lord of heaven and earth and does not live in temples built by human hands. And He is not served by human hands, as if He needed anything. Rather, He himself gives everyone life and breath and everything else."

Those areas in your life where you are having a hard time trusting that God is big enough, how might you be getting in the way of letting Him fix, hold, manage, or even begin? What would getting still look like for you? What would it allow Him to do?

_____

_____

_____

---

[2] John 15:5 (NIV)

Read **Psalm 131:1-3.** How is the picture of being still reflected in this passage?

_____

_____

_____

Let me say this to you as we begin this journey: nothing is lost in surrender. I want you to repeat that to yourself over and over as we walk through the remaining 51 weeks together.

Because Moses surrendered his desires, his will, and his insecurities, the Lord honored his obedience and was allowed to be all that He was capable of being. God would have only been limited by Moses' surrender, not by His ability. What became Moses' greatest desire as a result of his surrender? (Exodus 33:15)

_____

_____

Can you honestly say that God's presence, His glory, is your greatest desire right now in your life? If not, maybe there is something hindering you, something you need to release to God.

Use the space below to reflect on your heart's deepest desire right now.

Ask the Lord what you may need to surrender to Him during this season in your life and ask Him what it looks like to begin to release that to Him. Maybe you're afraid you'll lose something if you do let it go? What could you gain, though? What might God be able to do in your life if you were to surrender all things to Him?

_____

_____

_____

Sunday Sabbath

❧

"Remember the Sabbath day by keeping it holy. Six days you shall labor and do all your work, but the seventh day is a Sabbath to the Lord your God. On it you shall not do any work, neither you, nor your son or daughter, nor your male or female servant, nor your animals, nor any foreigner residing in your towns. For in six days the Lord made the heavens and the earth, the sea, and all that is in them, but He rested on the seventh day. Therefore, the Lord blessed the Sabbath day and made it holy."
Exodus 20:8-11(NIV)

Songs for Your Sabbath
Chris Tomlin, *Indescribable*
Phillip's, Craig and Dean, *The Great I AM*

There is nothing more beautiful than a Sabbath.

Today, simply find a quiet spot at some moment in your day and just let your heart sit in the truths God has revealed to you throughout this past week. Read a Psalm and a Proverb and reflect on those as well even in light of what you have studied this week. Sit in a worship song and let it saturate you. Enjoy this set apart day to encounter the heart of your heavenly Father.

Bring anything else you may need to bring to Jesus, but your heart needs this day and this moment.

Don't neglect it.

Don't rush past it.

Don't distract yourself from it.

The Sabbath was created just for you, friend…

Eugene Peterson, the author of The Message *Bible, said he and his wife learned to use their Sabbath as a time to "pray and play." I pray your heart will find some time to play as well.*

Lord, You really are the Great I AM. Forgive me for believing the lies of the enemy about You. Please help me to remain rooted in the truth that You really are who You say You are. And may my heart be reminded as I speak your name today of how intentionally You named yourself for my story. Thank you that you knew exactly what I would need… the Great I AM.

Week 3

I AM the Bread of Life

Monday

✦

Read: John 6:22-40

Good Monday morning.

To you and me it's an ordinary thing tossed on the table for free at most restaurants. To the Israelites it was the very provision and power of God. It went all the way back to the children of Israel, who Moses delivered. After they were delivered from Egypt God provided bread that rained down from heaven for them. Manna, it was called. So God knew bread. Bread mattered. A lot.

Now, God is about to give us greater revelation into what exactly I AM that I AM encompasses. Jesus said to Philip, "Anyone who has seen Me has seen the Father."[3] So, with these following statements Jesus is about to bring into clarity who He is and what God has revealed to us through Christ and relationship with Him.

This first revelation arrives as Jesus has just fed five thousand men including all of their wives and kids. He's given the ordinary through the extraordinary. Natural food by supernatural means. The next day this same multitude is looking for Jesus again. He knows they are there looking for bread you toss on a table. But He knows what they need is Him, the Bread of Life. They think they need natural bread but He knows they need a bread that will satisfy the deepest hunger of their hearts.

We're going to see this pattern played out over and over in each one of the I AM statements – an ordinary symbol used to describe the extraordinariness of Jesus.

"For the bread of God is He who comes down from heaven and gives life to the world. And they said, 'Lord give us this bread always; we want this bread'. And he said 'I am the bread of life." It's like He's looking at them saying, "I knew you would want this! That's why I did it this way. I've

---

3 John 14:9 (NLT)

27

just done for you in the natural to give you a picture of this supernatural bread that is only Me. I've quenched your human hunger to give you a revelation of who I am for your heart hunger. I am your bread. I am the bread that will give you real life."

We all know what it is to be hungry. Each morning we wake up and it starts the whole cycle again... we've just fed ourselves over and over the day before, but yet, we wake up hungry, by the middle of the afternoon we're hungry again (and if you're anything like me you're hungry like every two hours!). In our hunger God gives us a gift. Hunger makes us search for food. The hunger of our hearts will cause us to do the same.

Ecclesiastes 3:11 says, *"God set eternity in the hearts of man."* That means that God set us up with a holy hunger. All those times that we're reaching out for something: the next relationship, the next drink, the next piece of food, the next shopping trip, the next search for significance, whatever our "next thing" is, God is saying that this is a heart hunger. Your heart is hungry for Me and I am the bread of life. "He who comes to Me shall never hunger and he who believes in Me shall never thirst."4

Friends, God set you up to hunger for Him, the Bread of Life. Choose Him and you will never be hungry again.

Take a minute to think about those things, or maybe that one thing, you tend to turn to for satisfaction and comfort or significance. A relationship? Images on a computer screen? Your favorite candy bar? Alcohol? A new pair of shoes? An intense workout? The validation of others? What is that thing you may find yourself relying on instead of God?

_____

_____

What lie(s) about God might the enemy have you believing in those moments you choose to find fulfillment in something other than Him?

_____

_____

Friends, this week I encourage you to own who you are when you are in Christ. When you accept Him as the Bread of Life, you are a new creation, and you no longer have to live ruled by your flesh or its natural cravings.

Read **2 Corinthians 5:16,17** and **Romans 8:1-17.** When we have Christ's Spirit, the Holy Spirit, living in us, then what has our spirit now become dead to?

_____

---

4 John 6:35 (ESV)

When Christ's Spirit takes up residence in us we no longer have to live enslaved to our flesh. In fact, Christ has given us everything we need for victory over our flesh. It would be like a slave being given freedom yet still believing they are a slave. Friends, we are free in Christ! Free to live in the abundant life He has created for us. Free to live in freedom. When we accept Him as the Bread of Life He brings us into real life and is able, by the power of His Spirit and not our strength, to help us surrender those false satisfiers and to dismantle every lie of the enemy and make it bow its knee to the truth that is Jesus Christ and His Word.

Tuesday

Read **Exodus 16.** Why were they only allowed to gather enough manna up for each day?

_____

_____

Read **Matthew 6:11.** Why do you think Jesus taught us to pray only for our daily bread?

_____

_____

"For He satisfies the longing soul, and the hungry soul He fills with good things."
Psalm 107:9 (ESV, emphasis added)

What a beautiful picture that is. What a beautiful comfort that is. What a beautiful truth that is. Jesus is the one who fills. Jesus is the one who satisfies. Jesus is the one who makes sure we have enough for what we need each and every day. Jesus is the one who brings life. This passage also says that He fills our soul with "good things." What 'good things' has Jesus filled your soul with?

_____

_____

_____

Read **Galatians 5:22-23** and list the good things He desires to develop in you.

_____

_____

_____

_____

Wednesday

❧

We all have deep desires, things we are believing the Lord for... healing, restored relationships, a spouse, financial provision, the ability to conceive a child. Right now, in your current season, what is that deep desire in your heart?

_____

_____

According to **Psalm 37:4**, what must we seek to do first and foremost?

_____

_____

What does it mean to you to "delight yourself in the Lord?" Look up some of its definitions and write them down here. Then paraphrase what it means to you.

_____

_____

Hear me when I say, though, that this isn't a special fix-all formula: "take delight in God and He'll give you whatever you want." The beauty of this word _delight_ in Hebrew actually means "to be soft or pliable." So "delighting" means our will stays soft and pliable and surrendered, and then He can get what He has for us to us. Our desires begin to line up with His. And the "hunger" of this life falls away to the "hunger" of Him.

Thursday

❧

Read **Matthew 5:1-11**. What does Jesus say will be granted to those who hunger and thirst for righteousness?

_____

_____

The Amplified version adds the word "completely" to that promise.

What does it mean to "hunger and thirst for righteousness?"

_____

_____

Seeking and desiring to be completely right with God and 'morally right or justifiable', as Merriam-Webster puts it, isn't always at the top of our to-do lists. But may our prayers today be to have a heart hunger first for Jesus. Because remember, a heart that seeks after Him first has everything it needs. That kind of heart also desires to glorify and please our heavenly Father in all we say and do – when that's the root of our desires, He will satisfy them every single time…

Friday

Go back to **Exodus 16** and highlight anything that stands out to you in light of our study this week.

When some of the Israelites failed to follow God's directions for gathering the manna, how did God respond? Did He stop providing for them?

_____

_____

What does God's response say about His character?

_____

_____

How has the Lord extended similar grace to you?

_____

_____

_____

Saturday Surrender

"Do not be conformed to this world, but be transformed by the renewal of your mind, that by testing you may discern what is the will of God, what is good and acceptable and perfect."
Romans 12:2 (ESV)

As we've walked this week together since Monday when you wrote down those things you tend to seek to satisfy instead of your Creator, have you found yourself more mindful this week that in relationship with Christ those do not have to be your imitation sustenance? Did you give into the urge to cope or pursue satisfaction with a temporal thing like food, a relationship, alcohol, shopping, or recognition? This is not your portion my friend.

Have a conversation with the Lord right now about what real relationship with Christ affords you and ask Him to give you a clear understanding to walk in it. I encourage you to read Romans 8 as well as the book *Victory Over the Darkness* by Neil Anderson to get a life changing understanding of our identity in Christ. Ask Him to cultivate in you a "hunger and thirst for righteousness" so that His desires become yours.

Maybe you're not sure what it is you tend to turn to – just ask Him to reveal anything to you that you might be missing.

Sunday Sabbath

"Therefore I tell you, do not worry about your life, what you will eat or drink; or about your body, what you will wear. Is not life more than food, and the body more than clothes? Look at the birds of the air; they do not sow or reap or store away in barns, and yet your heavenly Father feeds them. Are you not much more valuable than they? Can any one of you by worrying add a single hour to your life?"
Matthew 6:25-27 (NIV)

Songs for Your Sabbath
Fernando Ortega or Danny Gokey, *Give Me Jesus*
Janet Paschal, *The Body and The Blood*

Just like you did last Sunday, carve at least a few minutes to steal away to a quiet spot to let that beautiful heart of yours sit in and reflect on the truths you walked through this past week.

Bring anything else to the Lord you may need to, or even continue a conversation with Him you started earlier in the week… just be sure to guard this precious time for you and God to enjoy each other this Sabbath. Remember, this Sabbath was made for you…

Lord, thank You for revealing Yourself to me as my Bread of Life. I know I tend to try satisfy my heart hunger in other ways – and for that I'm so very sorry. Please help me to remember to run to Your arms when I feel that hunger and longing for deeper satisfaction, knowing that You and You alone will provide what I'm really after: eternal fulfillment. I also pray Father for a truthful understanding of who I am in You. Of the freedom Jesus affords me. Of the victory He has given me to walk in where I will be ruled by Your Spirit and not by my flesh. That is my inheritance. May I enjoy the beauty and power of spending it here and now.

Week 4

I AM the Light of the World

Monday

Read: John 8:12-19

Good Monday morning.

Philly and I were traveling recently and staying in a hotel room. One night about the time he was coming out of the bathroom I turned the television off which made this unfamiliar room completely dark. And, of course, I hear a loud thud, poor guy, he runs into familiar things even with the lights on, and then a loud holler (as we would say in the South) and I got tickled because for whatever distorted reason that's what I do... I tend to laugh when he gets hurt... I know, it's horrible.

Oh, the power of light. And oh the power when Jesus illuminates Himself. Last week He described Himself as the bread of life and, this week, He reveals Himself as "the light of the world."[5] *Don't you just love that?* Now, think about this: the very first thing God said in all of scripture is, "Let there be light."[6] It was almost like He was identifying in that one singular moment what would be a perpetual need on this journey. The need for light.

God is a dispeller of darkness. Max Lucado says, "Every battle at its root is a spiritual battle." The battle between the darkness the enemy brings and the light that Jesus is. Yet, the power in our battle is that Jesus has already won it! The Word says, "I [Jesus] have already overcome the world."[7] The enemy is clamoring for his final say, but Jesus's love had the first word and His love will have the last word.[8] John 1:4-5 (NLT) says it this way, *"The word gave life to everything that was*

---

[5] John 8:12 (NIV)

[6] Genesis 1:3 (NIV)

[7] John 16:33 (NIV)

created and His life [the Word is Jesus in this scripture] brought life to everyone. The light shines in the darkness and the darkness can never extinguish it." So no matter how dark life may get, the darkness can never extinguish the light. Jesus isn't saying "I give light," He's saying "I AM light." This is a significant difference. The light can *never* be destroyed. Never... no matter how dark things may look.

Now consider what light does. First, it illuminates. My prayer is that you will be illuminated to your need for Jesus. You were not created to do life without Him. For some of us, He may illuminate some of our sin or some of the poor choices that we are making in order to convict us because His desire is always to take us to a deeper level of intimacy with Him -- like the Bible says, to grow us from "strength to strength."[9] Light also directs. Psalms 119:105 (ESV) says, *"Your Word is a lamp unto my feet and a light unto my path."* With Jesus we are not like Philly, stumbling around in the dark! When we walk in relationship with Jesus we can see clearly every step that is needed for this journey we are traveling when we need to see it. The Word of God brings such clarity to the hearts and steps of man. What a powerful promise!

And third, in John 9 we discover the Light won't be in the world forever; right after His "I am the light of the world" statement, He speaks to a blind man and says, "We must be quickly carrying out the tasks assigned to us by the One who sent us. The night is coming and then no one can work. But while I am here in the world, I am the light of the world."[10]

Friend, this is a sobering thought. If you do not have a personal relationship with Jesus Christ, and even for those of us that do, there will come a time there will no longer be the option to receive Him as our personal Lord and Savior. So for those of us who know Him, we have a great responsibility to be illuminating Him... in our neighborhoods, at our jobs, in restaurants, in our children's schools, around our own table, or on social media, no matter where we may be... we should be illuminating the light of Jesus Christ. "You are the light of the world, a city set on a hill cannot be hidden, nor do people light a lamp and put it under a basket."[11] The Light makes us light and we have a light that should be on full display. Friend, the world is getting darker, but the Light of the world is here. And if He is living in us, we have been given the great privilege and opportunity to offer Him with grace and love and compassion and truth in this season. The Light of the world Himself, Jesus Christ.

When you were a kid, were you afraid of the dark? Maybe when your kids were young they were or you have a little one now that is. What does it feel like to be completely surrounded by darkness or to encounter a child that is dealing with fear of being alone in the dark?

_____

_____

_____

[8] 2 Corinthians 5:14 (MSG)

[9] Psalm 84:7 (NIV)

[10] John 9:4-6 (NLT)

[11] Matthew 5:14-14a (NLT)

How do those feelings contrast with what it feels like to be surrounded by warm, peaceful, bright illumination, like the first moments of morning or when you turn the light on in a dark room?

_____

_____

What does it mean to you personally to know that Jesus is the Light of the World?

_____

_____

Tuesday

Oftentimes, there are places of darkness in our hearts, lies we may believe about God or others, unforgiveness we may hold, secret sin we may keep hidden, that prevent us from walking in the truth that Jesus has already overcome all of the darkness. What might some of those places be for you? An ongoing health battle? Bitterness? Anger? Financial turmoil? Marriage issues? Repeated disappointment?

_____

_____

_____

Other times we walk in seasons of darkness where we have trouble discerning what we should do in a given situation or in a given season. Are you struggling to find God's direction in a specific area? What are you needing to hear from Him?

_____

_____

Read **John 8:12**. What type of light does Jesus say we will have upon following Him?

_____

Now flip ahead a couple chapters and read **John 10:10** again. What kind of life did Jesus come for us to have?

_____

Do you see the connection there? Following Jesus and surrendering even the darkest places of our hearts will not only let us experience the light of life, but the light of abundant life, life to the full. I don't know about you, but I definitely don't want to miss out on that!

Read Psalm 85:13 in the English Standard Version, if you can. What does having a personal relationship with Jesus afford us in discerning where to walk and what to do?

_____

This is one of the many promises we have as believers in Christ. We are promised that His very footsteps will go before us showing us the way we are to walk. Anytime I'm in a season where I'm uncertain of what I'm to do next, I simply pray this passage, trusting that when I need to know, God will show me. I will not miss Him. Now, I may choose to disobey what He reveals, but He is faithful to reveal where I am to walk next. Sometimes, I am simply still and I wait. Other times I tell Him I'm going to move trusting that if this isn't Your plan, You'll make it clear. Sometimes He will stop my path and other times He will let me go. But what I am always confident of is God doesn't want me to miss Him, either. And if I keep my heart humble and seeking, He is faithful to speak.

Read **Psalm 119:105.** What does this passage say about light? How do you allow this lamp to be used in your life?

_____

_____

Wednesday

❧

As we've already uncovered, the enemy's ultimate goal is to make us believe lies about our heavenly Father. If the truth is that Jesus is the light of the world, some potential lies that we may find ourselves buying into could be:

o Things have always been this way. Nothing is going to change.
o I'm completely justified in feeling the way I do about him/her/the situation.
o It's all up to me to handle everything.
o Things will only get done and done well if I do them.
o I'm not worth being helped or healed.
o They don't want to hear the gospel. It will just make things uncomfortable.

These are just a few of the countless lies that the devil tries to feed us in order to make us live in darkness or not share the light. What are some of the lies that you've found yourself believing, keeping you in the darkness?

_____

_____

_____

_____

We are also living in a culture that doesn't just believe lies, it propagates lies. What are some of the greatest lies this culture is speaking to people's hearts today? What are some of the lies being spoken in the church?

_____

_____

_____

_____

Read **Matthew 5:14-16.** What is our responsibility as image bearers of the Light?

_____

_____

Thursday

Since you looked yesterday at the lies you've found yourself believing, let's investigate more of the truth that combats those lies. Refer back to the lie(s) you said your heart has believed. I want you to look up a few verses that proclaim the truth that proves that lie for what it is. And if those verses have pronouns in them, replace them with your name.

For instance, I'm tempted to believe the lie that I've got to juggle everything and keep all the balls in the air – that I need to do everything to make and keep everyone happy. The truth? I don't have to do that. I hold fast to the truth in Ephesians 6:7 (ESV) Serve wholeheartedly, Denise, as if you were serving the Lord, not people." When I realize that my only responsibility is to serve God from a pure place, then it removes from me a fear of people. Oh how freeing the truth is, friend…

So take some time to do that on this gift of a Thursday and see what truth your heart will uncover.

_____

_____

_____

_____

_____

_____

_____

Friday

A few years ago, I felt led to invite my neighborhood women to my home for dinner on a regular basis. I believed the main reason the Lord laid this on my heart was to create an atmosphere for them to encounter His presence. At those first couple dinners, I asked the ladies as we sat around the table to simply share their stories; the reaction to this simple request was surprising to me. Because I am so used to sharing my story and it's the first question I ask new people when I meet them, it was interesting how many of the women didn't even know what to do with this question... as if no one had ever asked them before. It also opened the door for me to share my story while being very transparent of the power of God in it while being vulnerable with my own failures and disappointments. I know it held great impact for many of the women who came and it was such an ordinary activity that created space for the holy.

What does **2 Corinthians 4:6** compare to the light?

_____

_____

And where does that light live, according to that same verse?

_____

For those that don't have the Light in them, though, what does that mean for them **(2 Thessalonians 1:9)**?

_____

_____

If you have the light of Jesus in your heart, what, then, are you supposed to do with it **(1 Peter 2:9)**?

_____

Be honest with yourself and with the Lord. On a scale of 1-10, how good of a job would you say you do with your life of "proclaiming the excellencies" of God or the good things He's done in your own story? Like the story I shared above, ask the Lord what are some specific ways you can share with others how good He has been to you.

_____

Saturday Surrender

"For God did not send His Son into the world to condemn the world, but in order that the world might be saved through Him."
John 3:17 (ESV)

This world is full of darkness. Our hearts can become places of darkness, too, if we let them. It would be so easy to become overwhelmed by all the evil things that happen. But we know we have hope; hope in the Light of the world. I hope you've fought for and found yourself seeking more truth and light rather than justifying the lies of the darkness this past week.

Have a conversation with the Lord right now about what it would look like to surrender any dark corners tucked away in your heart. You may know exactly what it is that needs some light shed on it; others may be completely unaware. Ask Him with all sincerity today to show you anything you may be needing to let Him take care of. Ask Him, as well, to begin to show you how to be a greater light bearer in your sphere of influence. Then spend time listening, journaling, and then acting on whatever He may speak.

Sunday Sabbath

"He makes wars to cease to the end of the earth; He breaks the bow and cuts the spear in two; He burns the chariots with fire. 'Cease striving and know that I am God; I will be exalted among the nations, I will be exalted in the earth.'"
Psalm 46:9-10 (NIV)

Songs for Your Sabbath
Michael W. Smith, *Light to You*
Hillsong, *Let There be Light*

Know on this sacred Sabbath day that despite all the evil and darkness in this world, we serve a God who is ultimately in control. And He has already overcome absolutely everything that has happened, is happening, and that ever will happen. Hallelujah!

So just like you did last Sunday, carve at least a few minutes to steal away to a quiet spot to let that beautiful heart of yours sit in and reflect on the truths you walked through this past week.

Bring anything else to the Lord you may need to, or even continue a conversation with Him you started earlier in the week… just be sure to guard this precious time for you and your God to enjoy each other this Sabbath…

Lord, thank You for revealing Yourself to me as the light of the world. Thank you for already overcoming the darkness that the enemy so desperately wants to engulf my heart with. Let me always be mindful of the beauty of Your light and the responsibility I have of reflecting that light to everyone I come in contact with. Allow your light to both search me and guide me. Thank you for the gift of this Light that has come into the world. And thank you that the darkness WILL NOT overcome it in Jesus name!

Week 5

I AM the Door

Monday

❧

Read: John 10:1-10

Good Monday morning.

Shortly after Philly and I got married, my youngest bonus daughter met me at the car one day: "Denise, you're not going to believe this, but _____ (she called her sister's name) slammed the door and it fell right off!" I walked in the back door and sure enough there sat one of the bedroom doors leaning up against the wall. Come to find out, the door was slammed and dad took the door off to remind the teenager that doors are a privilege, not a right, and that he was the owner of the house. I don't have to tell you how quickly she realized the value of a door. Doors grant access. Doors keep you safe inside and the bad guys outside. A lot like Jesus, huh? In fact, He even describes himself as door. In John 10:9 (AMP), *"I am the Door; anyone who enters through Me will be saved [and will live forever], and will go in and out [freely], and find pasture (spiritual security)."*

In case anyone has ever tried to tell you that there is another door to eternal life, that there is another way to get to heaven, or that there's another way to get to God, they have lied to you. Jesus is the only access to God and the only access to heaven. There's no other way. He's the one leading to eternal life. One of the greatest ways we can know this is the fact that He walked through a door no other professed messiah has ever walked through; He walked through the door of His own grave through resurrection power. Wouldn't it make sense, then, that the One who says He alone is the door to resurrection life would be the One who was able to walk through the door to His own resurrection? Every other professed messiah is rotting, even now, in his grave clothes. In fact, Jesus said, "All who came before Me [as false messiahs and self-appointed leaders] are thieves and robbers, but the [true] sheep did not hear them." (v. 8 AMP) So the true sheep, those who have a personal relationship with Jesus Christ, are able to discern the lies of the enemy when he comes professing another messiah.

It's interesting that this symbol of the door is also used in the Old Testament. When Noah told the people that there was going to be a flood, they didn't believe him — but they would soon discover the truth. When the rains began to come up from the earth and for the first time ever, down from the heavens, there was just one access to safety and it was the door to that ark.

We see the symbolism and foreshadowing of Jesus as the door yet again when Moses was trying to convince Pharaoh to let the children of Israel out of Egypt. God was sending miraculous signs, the very last one was called the Passover — the feast that is still celebrated today. God gave the Israelites specific instructions for everything they were to do for this Passover dinner. One thing was to slaughter a lamb and put the blood on the doorpost of each Israeli door. This would serve as a sign that when the death angel arrived to take the life of the firstborn son in each household, he would pass over the homes with the blood on the door. The blood on the doorpost kept the Israelite sons safe while the Egyptians fell to the power of the plague.

Friends, we've heard for years that there are many ways to get to God, but that is a lie -- there is only one. This Lamb, this Jesus, protecting us from the thief who comes to steal, kill, and destroy by trying to convince a culture that there are many ways to God. Jesus said, "I am the door… I have come that you might have life, enjoy life, and live it to the full." So I ask you today, have you walked through this door? And if so, do you at times give access to the door of your heart to anything or anyone else? I can tell you this: if you would trust THE Door, you will live the life you were created for.

Read **Hebrews 9.** Take a few minutes today to reflect on how access to God used to be granted and the freedom we now have because of Jesus. Have you ever thought about this? What does the revelation of it mean to you? How does it cause you to see Jesus as the door now?

_____

_____

_____

_____

_____

Tuesday

After my divorce, I wasn't sure if I would ever write books again. Then when the Lord began to stir a new story in me and I tried to get it published, my first two responses were rejections. I remember feeling worried, wondering if the door to publishing was now closed to me. I heard the Lord speak so clearly to my heart, "You only need one door. And the closed doors are protection." A few months later, when only one door opened, it was the perfect fit for my personality and giftings.

Let's take a closer look at part of the account of Noah in Genesis today. Read **Genesis 6:9-7:16** in the New Living Translation, if you can. Many people wonder about the details surrounding exactly how the animals knew to go to the ark and how they all fit in and how they didn't eat each other, but what it all points to is the supernatural power of the living God. And Ole Noah, as he rounded them all up, didn't seem to get overwhelmed with all the 'what ifs'. What does 7:5 say Noah did?

_____

Then what does verse 16 say God did?

_____

Noah did as he was commanded. God took care of the rest.

What value did a shut door on the ark have to Noah and his family?

_____

_____

_____

Is there a door that is currently shut for you that you wish was opened right now? What value could there be in this door being closed during this season? If you can't see the value in it, ask the Lord to show you what it could be. If He doesn't, trust that His ways aren't yours and some things we will simply never have the answers to.

_____

_____

Wednesday

Another Old Testament reference to a door is during the final plague on Egypt, the Passover. Read **Exodus 12:1-13**. Where was the blood applied? What value did the blood provide?

_____

_____

Read **1 Peter 1:17-21.** How is the Passover reflective of what Jesus would eventually come and do for us?

_____

_____

The lamb's blood over the Israelites' doors ensured safety of the firstborn males in each household from death in the Old Testament. Jesus' blood spilled in the New Testament ensures eternal safety for anyone who confesses and believes that Jesus died and rose again. [12] Hallelujah!

What a God we serve… that He would give us yet another foreshadowing of the sacrifice Jesus would eventually make just to be able to reconcile us to Him… meditate on that today, friend…

Thursday

How many doors do you have in your home? Probably an amount that would be annoying to count. Needless to say, there are most likely multiple routes in and out and around your home.

Look back at **John 10:9**. How many different doors or gates does Jesus say He is?

_____

He doesn't say He is "*a*" door, or "*one of the*" doors, or "*an optional*" door for salvation. He is THE door. What does that mean about the route for salvation?

_____
_____
_____

How does your heart respond to that truth? Does it make you anxious or nervous? Afraid? Safe? Comforted? Free?

_____
_____
_____

If it's not a source of comfort for you, you might need to have a conversation with the Lord about why that is and ask Him to help reframe the idea that Jesus is the only way to God in a way that brings joy to your soul.

Read **Revelation 4:1-5**. What was standing open in heaven?

_____

---

12 Romans 10:9 (NIV)

What is the "Door" that will give us access to that door like John had? We will not get through one without the other.

_____

Friday

❦

Let's look at a couple of contrasting characters today.

Read **John 10:1**. How does the person described there enter the sheep pen?

_____

Now look at **John 10:2-3**. How is the person who enters by the gate admitted?

_____

We see one that enters by trespassing and another that waits to be granted access through the proper channel. Friend, the enemy will stop at nothing to trespass his lies into our minds and hearts. Take a few minutes today and write about any area of your life where Satan might have tried to trespass and gain territory of your heart or mind through his lies. Anger? Disappointment? Shame? Fear?

_____

_____

_____

_____

Jesus patiently waits for you to recognize those points of access you've given the enemy, the places where he's jumped the gate to your heart. And Jesus desires so deeply to be granted access to do what He's so good at – removing those lies of the enemy and mending the wounded places where Satan has forced entry. Your sweet Savior will make sure that the enemy of your heart has no access unless you would grant it… all you have to do is let Jesus in…

Now look at **John 10:4-5**. What do the sheep know of their shepherd?

_____

Now look at **John 10:2-3**. How is the person who enters by the gate admitted?

_____

This passage debunks any thought that God doesn't speak to his children. David wrote in Psalm 34:4 *"I sought the Lord and He answered me and delivered me from all of my fears."*

Read **Revelation 3:20.** What is the "door" in this passage? Whose voice is being heard in this passage? What are some ways we hear God speak to us today? Take this time to look up some of your own scripture.

_____

_____

_____

_____

_____

_____

Saturday Surrender

"Submit yourselves therefore to God. Resist the devil, and he will flee from you."
James 4:7 (ESV)

We've reflected this week on things that we have granted access through the doors of our hearts other than the transformative love of God. We've meditated on the value that even closed doors add to our lives, despite how much we would want them to open. And we've spent some time thinking about how forceful the enemy is compared to how patient our heavenly Father is when it comes to gaining access to the valuable treasures that are our hearts.

James 4:7 is a scripture many of us often quote. However, look again at the first sentence. What are we to do before we resist the devil? First, we are to submit ourselves to God. Many of you might be wondering why the enemy isn't fleeing when you feel you are resisting; could it be that there is a surrender issue between your heart and God's?

So with all that in mind, have another conversation with your Father this Saturday about what it would look like to surrender those things that have taken up residence in your heart, remembering what we read about Noah in Genesis 7:5... he did all the Lord commanded him.

Sunday Sabbath

"But he who listens to me shall live securely and will be at ease from the dread of evil."
Proverbs 1:33 (NIV)

Songs for Your Sabbath
Kari Jobe/Gateway Worship, *Oh the Blood*
Chris Tomlin, *Jesus*

Yes, we have an enemy who is trying to force his way into our hearts in any way he can gain access.

Yes, there are doors that we so desperately want to fling wide open but they are closed and we may never know why.

But despite those bitter realities, we have an even greater truth – we can rest confident that our God is still God, He is still good, and He is still very much in control. Just like He was as He gathered those animals on the ark and just as He was when the death angel passed over the blood covered doorposts.

So just like you did last Sunday, carve at least a few minutes to steal away to a quiet spot to let that beautiful heart of yours sit in and reflect on the truths you walked through this past week.

Bring anything else to the Lord you may need to, or even continue a conversation with Him you started earlier in the week… just be sure to guard this precious time for you and God to enjoy each other this Sabbath…

Lord, I acknowledge that there is only one way to have access to You, through Your son, Jesus Christ. I give Him my complete heart. If there is any area of my heart that I have allowed the thief access to, please make it clear to me and I close that door now, in the name of Jesus. Thank You, too, for Jesus. For His willingness to become The Door for me. He didn't have to, but He chose to. And for that I am so grateful. My heart longs for the day I get to walk in the doors of heaven and be with You forever and ever.

Week 6

I AM the Good Shepherd

Monday

Read: John 10:11-18

Good Monday morning.

One of the songs that Philly and I asked to be sung at our wedding was a song called "You Are Good" by Kari Jobe. It simply says, "You are good, You are good, You are good, and your mercy is forever." Then came along this beautiful song, "Good Good Father," and it's almost like the heart of the worshipper in this season is trying to communicate that God is good. And He is. And Jesus wanted His people to know that.

One of the ways Jesus chose to describe Himself was as the Good Shepherd. Romans 2 says "it's the kindness of God that leads us to repentance."[13] And Jesus said, "if you've seen me, you've seen the Father."[14] Sometimes when we look at the world and the state that it's in, we think that there's no way we can have a *good* Father, but Jesus said I want you to know that your Father is good; if you've seen Me, and what I was willing to do for you, you have seen God and what He was willing to do for you. Remember, too, that each one of Jesus' I Am statements is another revelation of God's I Am statement. Jesus is allowing us to see who God truly is.

He declares this I Am statement in John 10:14-15 (NLT), *"I am the Good Shepherd. I know my own sheep and they know me. Just as my father knows me and I know the father. So I sacrifice my life for my sheep."* Friends, a shepherd is one who is willing to give his life for his sheep. And that is exactly what Jesus did for us. But not only that, think on this for a minute. Scripture tells us in Revelation that Jesus was the "lamb slain before the foundation of the world."[15] This means that when He had the opportunity to choose a different way, He still chose to sacrifice Himself for us in order that

---

[14] John 14:9

[15] Revelation 13:8

we would come into a love relationship with Him. Shepherds sacrifice their lives for their sheep. They'll stand in the gap between the adversary and the sheep. They'll leave the ninety-nine to go grab the one that got away and has been lost.[16] That's who our shepherd is, that's who our Jesus is.

Hindus work their way to a spiritual perfectionism.
Buddhists do it by self-discipline.
New-Agers by self-sufficiency.
Muslims do it by religious duties and good works.

Each one of these religions put the responsibility on the man. But Jesus became man, came to us and dwelt with us, then sacrificed Himself for us. He became the bridge that bridged the chasm of relationship. He came to us -- not the other way around. In fact, He came to us when there was nothing good in us. When every action deserved death, He came giving life. Now that, my friend, is good!

He also says in regards to us, His sheep, "I know them."[17] Is there anything more beautiful than being known? That's why I love talking about how God loves us in our details because it lets us know how well He knows us... our needs, our desires, our giftings, our temptations, our love language. He goes on to say in John 10:14, "and My sheep know me." This is another beautiful way that Christianity is so very different than other religions because in other religions, their god is some ethereal thing that can't be fully known. A god they are always having to work harder and harder to be recognized or validated by. But relationship with Jesus Christ brings us the opportunity to know Him. Every time I read His Word, I know Him better. Every time I quiet my soul in prayer, I know Him more. Every time I worship Him and sing in the car to the top of my lungs the way I love to do, I know Him better. Friends, this is the I AM we have. We have a good shepherd, one willing to lay down His life for us and one who did. No one else can say that, but this Jesus, who reveals to us the Father, and oh what a good shepherd He is...

Consider the relationship between a shepherd and his flock. Who depends on who? What is the level of trust like in that bond? Do the sheep have to earn their shepherd's affection or protection?

_____

_____

_____

_____

---

[13] Romans 2:4

[16] Matthew 18:12-14

[17] John 10:14

Jesus says in **John 10:11** that He is the good shepherd which means we are His sheep. Think about your relationship with the Lord and compare it to how you described the relationship between a shepherd and his flock above. Is how you live your life reflective of that sort of relationship? How have you seen Him be a shepherd for you?

_____

_____

_____

Tuesday

I'm sure you can probably quote it, but open your Bible, turn to **Psalm 23**, and actually read it, soaking up each word today.

Take note of everything it says God, your shepherd, does. Write down every verb it says He does for you. Then, write down what He asks of you.

_____

_____

_____

Which of the words above do you need Him to be most right now in your current season? Why?

_____

_____

_____

Wednesday

Do you have anything so valuable to you, that if you lost it, you would stop at nothing to search for it until you found it?

_____

_____

_____

_____

In addition to what we looked at yesterday regarding the characteristics of God as a shepherd, let's look at the parable of the lost sheep in **Luke 15:1-7**. Write in your own words what Jesus is saying here.

_____

_____

_____

_____

What does this tell us about God's character?

_____

_____

Thursday

A good shepherd, a good Father, deserves regular expressions of gratitude for being who He is. Let's meditate on **Psalm 100** today.

In **Psalm 100:3**, who belongs to whom?

_____

_____

How are we to approach Him according to **verse 4**?

_____

_____

Thinking about your general approach to time with God, how do you tend to enter His gates? With what posture do you generally enter His courts? With praise and thanksgiving? With a laundry list of requests?

_____

_____

_____

Seriously evaluate the heart and motives behind your approach to your quiet times with the Lord today. Ask Him to change your mentality if it isn't one of humility, praise, and thanksgiving. This is where all prayer should begin. It doesn't mean He doesn't want to hear our requests, He clearly tells us to ask, seek, and knock in **Matthew 7:7**. He loves to hear what is on our hearts. But the posture of our hearts should always be one of thanksgiving.

Friday

It's so easy to believe the lie that we have to earn grace, that there are tasks we have to complete in order to receive acceptance into the Kingdom. It only makes sense, right? We're taught in this life that virtually nothing is free – most everything comes at a cost to us; we have to earn it.

What does **Ephesians 2:8-9** say about our salvation? Why is it this way?

_____

_____

As if that isn't a big enough deal already, according to **Romans 5:6-8**, what condition were man's hearts in when Jesus chose to sacrifice Himself? How does this passage make Christianity different from other religions?

_____

_____

_____

Our salvation does come at a cost – but not a cost to us – a cost that God chose to pay *even while we were still sinners*. Try to wrap your mind around the magnitude of that truth today.

Saturday Surrender

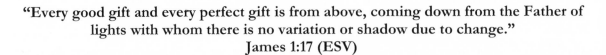

"Every good gift and every perfect gift is from above, coming down from the Father of lights with whom there is no variation or shadow due to change."
James 1:17 (ESV)

Our God is a good shepherd -- even when life isn't fair, when disaster strikes, when good things happen to bad people, and when bad things happen to good people. God is always good and is always working good.[18]

---

[18] Romans 8:28

So in these few moments this Saturday, open your heart to see the goodness of your heavenly Father, your Good Shepherd.

Maybe it's easy to acknowledge His goodness -- how He has protected you from harm, provided for you, guided your path even when you couldn't see Him leading, how He designed creation in so much detail from the smallest intricacies at the atomic level all the way to the grandeur of the galaxies...

Sometimes it's not as easy to recognize God's goodness. If you find yourself in a place or season where it may be a challenge for you to see how very good our God is, I encourage you to take this time today to surrender whatever it may be that's blocking your view... situations outside of your control, relational brokenness, health crises, financial setbacks... ask Him to open the eyes of your heart to be able to see His goodness in even the smallest gifts that have come your way recently. Remember every good gift is from the Lord. Write them down if you need to. If you ask, He will answer.

Sunday Sabbath

"He makes me lie down in green pastures; He leads me beside quiet waters. He restores my soul; He guides me in the paths of righteousness for His name's sake."
Psalm 23:2-3 (NIV)

Songs for Your Sabbath
Kari Jobe, *You are Good*
Peoples and Songs Ft. Josh Sherman, *Psalm 23 (I Am Not Alone)*

Yesterday, you surrendered things that may be blocking your view of God's goodness. And my prayer is you remembered some things He has done as well. Today, just sit in it, rest in it. Savor all the good you've experienced from Him.

Provision. Guidance. Creation. Love. Protection. Joy. Grace. Restoration. Salvation.

Anything good is a gift from your good shepherd -- including this Sabbath. So just like you do every Sabbath, steal away to enjoy your heavenly Father; guard this time for your heart to share with His, basking in the beauty of His perfect goodness.

Lord, it would be so easy to become overwhelmed with all the evil that is present in the world today. Thank You for being steadfast, true, and so very good in the midst of it all. Thank You, also, for choosing to lay down Your life for me when You didn't have to. I pray, Father, that You would make my heart more and more aware of Your goodness; of even the smallest ways in which You work out Your plan and purposes for my life. And as You do, I pray my heart would respond from a depth of gratitude because You are such a good, good shepherd...

Week 7

I AM the Resurrection and the Life

Monday

Read: John 11:17-44

Good Monday morning.

This next I AM statement of Jesus comes about in an interesting way. Jesus is approached and told that his friend, Lazarus, is dying. Yet, scripture tells us that He waits two more days before He goes. I could do a whole devotional on that alone… but we're going to focus on one thing today.

When Jesus arrives, He's first approached by Martha, Lazarus' sister. She's hurting and hostile.[19] She hurls accusations at Jesus as soon as she sees him. Jesus is patient and loving, yet leading her heart to a revelation He wants each of us to have about Him. "I am, right now, Resurrection and Life. The one who believes in me, even though he or she dies, will live."[20] Isn't that beautiful! Jesus endured death on the cross so that He could be resurrected from the dead so that we could have life forever! His resurrection serves as a reminder to you and I that this world is not our home, that we really are just sojourners and pilgrims travelling through. And because of His resurrection, you and I can experience resurrection in our lives both in living the John 10:10 abundant life here and the eternal life that awaits when this one is over.

Scripture says to be absent from the body is to be present with the Father.[21] This means that those who have a personal relationship with Jesus will never truly die. When this earthly body gives way, our spirit inside of us will immediately be present with Jesus. Then, when He comes back to gather us and bring us to heaven with Him, He will give us glorified bodies in which our

---

[19] John 11:25-26
[20] John 11:25
[21] 2 Corinthians 5:8

spirits will dwell. "It is the same way with the resurrection of the dead. Our earthly bodies are planted in the ground when we die, but they will be raised to live forever. Our bodies are buried in brokenness, but they will be raised in glory. They are buried in weakness, but they will be raised in strength. They are buried as natural human bodies, but they will be raised as spiritual bodies. For just as there are natural bodies, there are also spiritual bodies."[22] So, believers will never die. That is the beauty of resurrection.

So when He called Lazarus to come forth and Lazarus was raised from the dead, Jesus was giving them and us a picture of who He was and is and will be. Only God Himself, the Great I AM, could do such an amazing thing! But Jesus brings God to us in all of His resurrection power. So, in relationship with Jesus, you and I have the ability to have a resurrected life; that means that we don't ever have to taste death, spiritual death; we can live forever with our Father in the home that He's preparing for us. But it isn't just bodies He can resurrect, He can also resurrect dead marriages; He can resurrect dead hopes and dreams; He can resurrect dead finances and health. I'm not preaching a 'name it and claim it' thing here, I'm preaching that we have the resurrection and the life when we have Jesus. We do not have to live lives that are barely existing or trying to satisfy ourselves with a bread like we talked about in our first I AM statement that will never satisfy us. "I AM the resurrection and the life, anyone who believes in me will live even after dying. Everyone who lives in me and believes in me will never die…" We have the opportunity to know personally the resurrection and the life, friend, and His name is Jesus.

But I want to take it a step farther: we can also encounter that resurrection power in our lives today. Scripture tells us that the same power that raised Christ from the dead dwells in you and I[23] when we are in relationship with Him. So, I ask you, are you living a life that believes this truth and walks in it? Do you remind your own heart that resurrection life dwells in you? That you don't have to live a life barely surviving but you can live a life thriving in even the most challenging of seasons? Everything in Mary and Martha and Lazarus' world looked dead. But, oh friends, the Resurrection and the Life has come! Do not let anything remain dead when Jesus is here!

In what areas of your life do you need to experience Jesus' resurrection power? Your faith for something you've been believing for? Your health? Your finances? Your marriage? Your relationship with your children? Your relationship with your parents? Your job situation?

_____

_____

_____

_____

---

[22] I Corinthians 15:42-4
[23] Romans 8:11

What did Lazarus' resurrection do to the heart of his sisters? What did Lazarus' resurrection reveal about Jesus? What does His resurrection mean to you and your situations?

_____

_____

_____

Tuesday
꧁꧂

Read **Galatians 2:20** and reflect on what it means to be "crucified with Christ."

_____

_____

The beautiful thing about being crucified with Christ is that we also get to experience the fullness of His resurrection power. Our lives take on a new, deeper meaning – we're new creations, the Bible says in **2 Corinthians 5:17**. Think back to when you made the commitment to follow Jesus. What was your new life like? What changes happened in your heart? In your actions? In your approach to challenges? If you have never given Him your heart what are you afraid of? What life may you be missing?

_____

_____

_____

Wednesday
꧁꧂

Read 2 Corinthians 5:14-15 (MSG)

I just love The Message translation of this passage of scripture… what does it mean for His love to have the "first and last word in everything we do?"

_____

_____

How has Christ's resurrection power in your life allowed you to live a better life than you would on your own?

_____

_____

_____

As you go throughout the rest of your day and week I'd encourage you to put this verse to memory while being mindful of the magnitude of the resurrection power of Jesus' love – let that really sink in and impact the decisions you make in your interactions with others… with your spouse, your children, your coworkers, the cashier at the grocery store, the slow driver in front of you…

Thursday

You may already know John 11:35. It's quite often referenced as the shortest verse in the Bible. "Jesus wept." Today, though, go back and read the few verses leading up to it, **John 11:32-34**.

Based on that passage, why did Jesus weep?

_____

_____

Yesterday we talked about His deep love for us having the first and last words over everything we do. Even in our own sorrow and pain and seasons where life seems impossible, Jesus cares; He shares in our deepest places of pain. And it's all because He loves us that much. Know today that Jesus cares so deeply for even your smallest of details. When your heart hurts, so does His. Whatever may seem dead and beyond all hope of repair and restoration, our God is more than able to restore life to it.

Moving forward in the account of the resurrection of Lazarus, let's look at **John 11:38-44**. Remember, Martha was the one who initially accosted Jesus, blaming Him for why her brother was dead. Even despite her anger, though, she still confessed her belief in Him as the Messiah (v. 27).

When Jesus tells them to move the stone away from the grave, what does Martha say? (v. 39)

_____

_____

Martha knows who Jesus is. She is fully aware of the miracles He has performed. Yet when He asks to open Lazarus's tomb, she questions His decision. *Are you sure, Lord? It's nasty in there. I know better than you; you don't want to go in there.*

How many times do you and I do the same thing? We know that Jesus is the resurrection and the life. We know what He desires to do in and through us. All too often, though, we second guess Him. We think we know better. We question His motives. Take a few minutes to think about a time when you've done that recently. How did it turn out? What would have happened if you had trusted Him? What happened if you did?

_____

_____

_____

_____

_____

_____

Friday

The most beautiful part about this characteristic of Jesus is what it affords you in the life to come. Read **1 Corinthians 15:12-20**. What is the greatest gift about this I AM statement of Christ? What does the thought of your own resurrection bring to your mind?

_____

_____

_____

_____

Saturday Surrender

"And so, dear brothers and sisters, I plead with you to give your bodies to God because of all He has done for you. Let them be a living and holy sacrifice--the kind He will find acceptable. This is truly the way to worship Him."
Romans 12:1 (NLT)

Because of Christ's death and because of His resurrection we are able to truly live – not only in our present state but in eternity. Why wouldn't we, then, be willing to give every fiber of our beings, every ounce of our souls, to bring glory to Jesus who reveals Himself to us as "the resurrection and the life?"

Oh that we would so deeply internalize how beautiful of a truth that is. Our surrender is not a result of demand but a result of invitation and gratitude for the freedom that comes from trusting that God is who He says He is and knowing that full and abundant life cannot be experienced separate of Jesus.

May we choose today to stop our own efforts to resurrect and to submit to Jesus, THE resurrection; may we trust Him to move in and through us to bring life to otherwise barren places. And may we keep looking up and anticipating the ultimate resurrection to come.

Sunday Sabbath

"You make known to me the path of life; You will fill me with joy in Your presence, with eternal pleasures at Your right hand."
Psalm 16:11 (NIV)

Songs for Your Sabbath
Elevation Worship, *Do it Again Lord*
Chris Tomlin, *Resurrection Power*

It's that simple. God has shown us the path of life – and that path is through Jesus, the resurrection and the life. Jesus, who breathes life into marriages, bodies, dead dreams, dire financial situations, is the answer to whatever wilted and seemingly lifeless situation you may be facing right now.

So, just like each Sunday, carve at least a few minutes to steal away to your quiet spot to let that beautiful heart of yours sit in and reflect on the truths you walked through this past week. Find your way to His presence, to the safety of His mighty right hand…

Lord, what a comforting thing it is that You not only have the power to forgive my sins but that You have the power over life and death as well. Just like You raised Lazarus from the dead, just like You were raised to life Yourself, You have the power and authority to breathe new life into me, my hopes, my dreams and desires… I receive Your abundant life today; help me to walk as one grateful for and confident in Your resurrection power. And keep my heart perpetually longing and looking for the coming that will afford this body the ultimate resurrection.

Week 8

I AM the Way, the Truth, and the Life

Monday

Read: John 14:1-14

Good Monday morning.

One of my favorite theme park rides is Space Mountain at Disney World. I love the fact that you can't see where you're going (I don't like heights anyway, so it makes it easier!) and you just have to trust the track to get you back into the light.

Well, this week we're looking at one of those blind-trust moments for the disciples. They're breaking bread with Jesus for the very last time. Jesus tells them that this is the time they've been waiting for, that He is going to die and they're heartbroken, they don't want this to happen -- just like you and I wouldn't want to lose someone we love. In His attempt to comfort them He makes his next I AM statement. In fact, His statement comes as an answer to Thomas' humanness.

I love Thomas in this moment. He just puts to words what so many of us would say. Umm… Lord, I have no idea what You're talking about. This is way above my pay grade! I don't know how to get *to* You after this moment. I do not know the way. I can almost see a big old smile come across Jesus' face as He speaks to Thomas. "Oh my boy, I am the way; I am the access, I am the provision, I am the way to your eternal home. It's me. If you know me, you know the way."

Now it's important that we notice what Jesus wasn't saying here. He wasn't saying "I'm the way **to** truth and life," He was saying "I am **the** way. The only way you're going to get access to the Father, the only way you're going to get access to your eternal home is through Me." In other words, what Adam and Eve destroyed in Genesis 3, when they made the decision, the conscious choice, to depend on their own self sufficiency, to believe the lie of the enemy about God and eat that fruit, they were removed from having that one-on-one, face-to-face access with God. But when Jesus died, His death would bring access back to the Father. And knowing Jesus, having a personal relationship with Him, is the only way you and I get access to that home. We have to accept Jesus to have eternal life. Heaven comes in relationship with Jesus. It does not come separate of Him. I do not care what anybody else has told you, friend no one gets to the Father unless it is through Jesus.

He also said, "I am the truth." Jesus is truth. That means we, as believers, don't create our own truth. Often Christians are ridiculed as being haters or being people who are unkind because we believe Biblical truths. However, that is simply a smokescreen of the enemy to try to convince this generation that Christ followers are intolerant and hate-filled. We know that isn't true. But what is true is that when we walk in relationship with Jesus Christ, then our truth is the Word of God. It's our gauge, it's our compass for life. We don't get to make our own. Choosing Jesus chooses our truth. Remember, if we're the light of the world, then we're revealing the beauty and the love and the truth that Jesus is.

Finally, He says, "I am the life." I love this. First, He's life here on Earth because remember what He says in John 10:10 (NIV), *"The thief comes to steal, kill, and destroy but I have come that you might have life and have it to the full."* In the Greek "life" is the word *"dzo-ay"* which, according to Strong's Commentary, actually means, "life real and genuine, a life active and vigorous, devoted to God, blessed, in the portion even in this world of those who put their trust in Christ, but after the resurrection to be consummated by new accessions (among them a more perfect body), and to last forever."[24]

Then, there is life eternal. 1 Corinthians 15:45 (AMP) says, *"The first man became a living soul, an individual, the last became a life-giving spirit, restoring the dead to life."* Friend, this life is not the end. There is an eternity that awaits us and the state of that eternity lies in the condition of our hearts and what we have chosen to believe. And if we believe in Jesus, we have an eternal home prepared for us where we have direct access to the Father; where what was lost in Adam is restored in Christ. This passage of scripture in John 14 that describes our Jesus gives my heart so much comfort. There is a real thief that comes to steal, kill and destroy… but Jesus has come, The Life has come that we might have life and live it to the full.

So many people today believe the lie that there is no such thing as absolute truth; they believe truth is relative – that what we perceive as truth is unique to us and is therefore a definition of truth. Which means, based on that logic, that there can be as many definitions of truth as there are people. This leaves room for so many contradictions. Thankfully, as believers in Christ, we have one absolute Truth and one absolute Way to get to heaven. Write John 14:6 in the space below. Underline or highlight every time the word "the" appears. Thank the Lord today for this provision of only one, true, way to access His heart and the abundant life here on earth.

_____

_____

_____

---

[24] Strong's Number: G2222

Tuesday

I often have to remind myself that before Google Maps and Waze we used real live paper maps or called our friend on the phone who told us, "Then you take the third left past the purple painted house." But now, we use direction apps even around town; not because we don't know where we're going, but because they take traffic into account when telling us how to get somewhere and send us on the shortest route and if we need to be rerouted mid-trip it can handle that, too.

Quite often we want God to treat us like those navigation apps. We want Him to input a destination in us… our career path, who we're going to marry, where we're going to live, how we're going to serve the Kingdom… we want Him to clearly communicate our destinations so that we can then calculate the most efficient routes to get there.

That's basically what Thomas was asking in John 14 – tell us where you're going, Jesus, so *I* can figure out how to get there. But if I've learned anything in life, it's that it isn't about what I can do to get to Him. Often when I live that way my life can quickly become a performance, where I believe the lie that I can somehow make my way to heaven by what I do.

Read **Ephesians 2:1-9**. According to verse 5, what saves us?

_____

What about verse **8**, what does it say saves us?

_____

Nowhere in our journeys as believers does anything hinge on our performing, our getting things right, or our doing things well. It all hinges on Jesus. Larry Crabb writes, "You were saved by grace and you'll grow by grace." There is no responsibility on your shoulders to earn your place at the table of God.

According to **Romans 10:9-10**, what two things does it say will save us?

_____

_____

Jesus is enough. And having Jesus in you means you are enough.

So walk confident in that truth today, friend. Jesus already did everything that needed to be done for us to have access to the Father. His pleasure in you does not depend on your performance.

Wednesday

❧

Have you heard the saying, "There are three sides to every story: yours, mine, and the truth?" Praise the Lord that when it comes to the gospel, there's only one side. And it's the beautiful truth of God's love for us.

Read **John 8:31-32**. Knowing that Jesus is the way, the truth, and the life according to John 14, then what (or who, rather) is the truth being referred to here? And what does that truth do?

_____

Take a look a couple of verses ahead, at **verses 34-36**. What does Jesus say He sets us free from?

_____

Take some time today to ask the Lord to reveal anything in your heart you need to experience freedom from. Write down anything you hear Him speak.

_____
_____
_____
_____

He offers complete and total liberation from even the tightest of chains – what a beautiful thing it is to be set free, free indeed…

Thursday

❧

The third thing Jesus describes Himself as in John 14:6 is as *the life*. Those four little letters pack an incredibly huge meaning.

John 10:10 is such a powerful passage of scripture – I know I've had you read it before and I can promise you this won't be the last time I direct you to it. What type of life did Jesus come for us to have according to this verse?

_____

Read **Psalm 27:13.** What does this say about life here and now?

_____

_____

So here on earth we are promised abundant life, life to the full as followers of Jesus. What does **Romans 6:23** tell us about after our time here on earth?

_____

_____

Not only is Jesus the provider of a fulfilled life here in our present state, but, through Him, we also have access to eternal life with our heavenly Father! The life Jesus offers is more than survival; more than an apathetic, monotonous state of going through the motions. Jesus is the vibrant, vivacious, joyful, fully present and engaged life!

What does your life currently reflect? Monotony or excitement? Apathy and indifference or a healthy understanding of and engagement with your emotions? Dullness or vibrancy? Distraction or engagement? If negative, what is the lie you are believing about the abundant life God has given you?

_____

_____

_____

_____

Friday

There are a lot of things I utilize to live and enjoy this life God has given me here and now:

- Consistent time with Jesus
- Deep friendships
- Doing things I love that bring my heart to life
- Living present
- Bringing thoughts captive quickly that do not align with God's truth
- Waking up and immediately being mindful of what I'm thankful for
- Forgiving quickly
- Feeding my heart with good things, conversations, music, movies…

No one gets to choose for us, remember. We get to choose to believe and then live out the abundant life we were created for.

What things on this list might you need in your life? Are there some additional things you would want to add?

_____

_____

_____

_____

Saturday Surrender

"I have been crucified with Christ and I no longer live, but Christ lives in me. The life I now live in the body, I live by faith in the Son of God, who loved me and gave Himself for me."
Galatians 2:20 (NIV)

How often we make things so much more complicated than they have to be.

There is only one way to heaven. One truth to hold onto. One life worth living. Jesus.

Steal away today and ask your heavenly Father if there is anything in your heart you may need to surrender – any lies you may have believed about your access to His heart, any aspects of your life you aren't completely walking in by faith. Because, remember from the other day, once we surrender and are set free by Jesus, we are free *indeed…*

Sunday Sabbath

"The fear of the Lord leads to life, so that one may sleep satisfied, untouched by evil."
Proverbs 19:23 (NIV)

Songs for Your Sabbath
Pat Barrett, *The Way*
Zach Williams, *Chain Breaker*

Find your quiet place today, friend. Be refreshed by the presence of your God who loves you so much that He would not only give you direct access to His heart but would reveal to you exactly what that access looks like.

Lord, thank You for being true, for being the only truth. Thank you for clearly laying out for me how to get to You and what a privilege that access is. Thank You for being the way to full, abundant life. I ask that You show me anything that may be keeping me from truly experiencing all that You have for me. I want You and only You, Father. Empty me of myself and fill me with more of Your character, Your love, Your joy, Your peace, and Your wisdom.

Week 9

I AM the Vine

Monday

Read: John 15:1-17

Good Monday morning.

My parents have a beautiful Muscadine grape vine on the side of their home and one of my favorite things to do when they're in season is to go pick them right off of the vine. I mean, it's nice when my parents bring them to me but there is nothing like just standing there and pulling them right off that vine and eating them one after the other. Often, that experience reminds me of this powerful passage of scripture in John 15, our very last I AM statement. Jesus says, "I am the true grape vine and my Father is the gardener. He cuts off every branch of mine that doesn't produce fruit and He prunes the branches that do bear fruit so they will produce even more fruit. You've already been pruned and purified by the message I have given you. Remain in me and I will remain in you for a branch cannot produce fruit if it is severed from the vine and you cannot be fruitful unless you remain in me."[25]

We all know that if a limb was cut off of that vine, that limb would never produce another grape. We know that if we cut a branch off of the trunk that branch will never produce another leaf. Our lives are the same way; our lives will not produce what they were created for if we are not connected to the vine that is Jesus Christ. I'm not saying that we won't accomplish things as far as the world is concerned, but what I am saying is that what we're producing will not be what we were created for and it will not bear eternal, lasting fruit because He says, "apart from me you can do nothing." That means that what we produce has no real value in the eyes of eternity.

My mom worked with State Farm for right at 30 years. She didn't own the State Farm company. She didn't work at the headquarters. She simply went in faithfully day after day serving those that

---

25 John 15:1-4 (NLT)

sat in front of her desk or spoke to her over the phone and I am confident of this one thing: when eternity comes and she stands before her Father, person after person after person after person will come up and say it's because of you, Darlyn Goude, behind that desk at State Farm in Camden, South Carolina, that I know Jesus Christ. She knows the Vine and she stays attached to Him. And because of that, even what to some may seem like a simple task of just clocking in faithfully every day, she was producing fruit that remains. My parents will never be wealthy in what the world would consider wealth. But my parents are so wealthy because of the Vine they have attached themselves to and the fruit, the eternal fruit, that they have produced.

Friends, we may make a name for ourselves in this world. We may write books that stay on shelves long after we're gone or produce resources that people use, whatever it is that you may do, but this I do know: that nothing we do separate of being grafted into the Vine will remain. "I am the vine," Jesus says, "apart from me you can do nothing"...

What does it mean to you to "remain" in Jesus? How does, or should, that look like in your daily life?

_____

_____

_____

_____

_____

_____

Oftentimes we find ourselves as branches severed from the Vine that gives us life. We become parched, unable to bear good fruit – or, really, any fruit at all – and for some of us, we become barely able to survive. What situations, relationships, or experiences might you have let come between your heart and that of the true Vine?

_____

_____

_____

_____

_____

_____

_____

_____

Tuesday

Read **Isaiah 5:1-5**. List below all the good things the vineyard owner did in and for his vineyard (I counted at least four!).

_____

_____

_____

_____

Even though he took such intentional, detailed care of his vineyard, what does the end of **verse 2** say happened?

_____

_____

What does his response look like? **(Isaiah 5:3-6)**

_____

_____

He's disappointed. This vineyard represents Israel, God's chosen people (Isaiah 5:7). He did so much for them, for us. "What more could have been done for my vineyard than I have done for it?", He inquires in verse 4. But still they turned their back on Him. They separated themselves from the vine.

How can you apply this to your life? How many detailed ways has the Lord lavished His love and affection on you only for you to turn around and say or do something that isn't pleasing to Him or reflective of His love?

_____

_____

_____

_____

Read **Romans 1:18-32.** This passage makes it clear that from the beginning of time, the very supernatural aspects of nature, as well as their beauty, have afforded every human a witness to a divine Creator. A Creator many have chosen not to graft themselves into – Jesus Christ. List the byproducts of a heart and the bad fruit that results when we choose to offer our worship to something other than the Creator of heaven and earth.

_____

_____

_____

_____

_____

Think about all He has done for you and how often you may neglect to remember all those things. The sacrifice He made in Jesus. The abundant life He promises in relationship with Him. The detailed and extravagant love He lavishes upon you daily. Think about all the ways nature reflects Him. His love. His creativity. His beauty. His power. Who wouldn't want to be in personal relationship with this God who thought of everything?

May we choose today to be branches securely grafted in the vine that is Jesus – with direct access to the life and love of our heavenly Father.

Wednesday

Yesterday in Isaiah, we talked about bad fruit. Today let's talk about what good fruit looks like. Read **Galatians 5:22** and list what Paul outlines as the fruits of the Spirit.

_____

_____

_____

How do we cultivate these characteristics in our lives? Are they things we develop ourselves? Are they a byproduct of the Holy Spirit living in us… results of a surrendered heart to the will and authority of God? Pay another visit to **John 15:4-5**.

_____

_____

_____

Often we don't know something is there or we can't cultivate it until its use is required.

Which of the nine characteristics are being produced in you during your current season? Are you in a place where joy is hard to come by? Is self-control something you're needing to exercise a bit more than normal? Are you having a hard time being patient for something you feel like you should have had a long time ago?

_____

_____

_____

_____

_____

If you notice, these fruits just don't come naturally to us. It's so much easier to indulge, be impatient, throw pity parties, criticize, or be angry. But a heart filled with those types of reactions is a heart far from its Creator. Not that we don't have our moments… but if these are consistent patterns of behavior, there are definitely things we need to be paying attention to.

Remember, God is always working good in the circumstances of a believer – whether we see it or not – and staying rooted in Him, surrendering to Him, is the only way to see good fruit produced in our lives.

Thursday

-֍-

Let's dig a little deeper into what it means to "remain" in Christ. Read **John 15:9-10**. What does Jesus say to do in order to remain in His love?

_____

Now read verse 12. What is His command?

_____

How has Jesus shown His love for us?

_____

_____

_____

While it definitely isn't out of the question – many have done so – this doesn't mean we are to literally give our lives for someone. It does mean we're called to demonstrate our love by extending grace, sacrificing our own desires or comfort so that others may experience the transformational love of Jesus and recognize Him as their Lord and Savior so that then they can turn around and share that same love.

Looking at your interactions with others (your spouse, children, colleagues, the person who cut you off in traffic, the server who kept making mistakes…), how well have you fulfilled this command? Have your words been saturated with grace? Have you put others' needs above your own, in a healthy way, or have you fought to satisfy your wants first and foremost?

_____

_____

_____

_____

Friday

❦

Another place in scripture where we see fruits, or characteristics, of a believer who is in Christ outlined is in **2 Peter 1:3-9**. What seven things does Peter say to "make every effort to add to your faith?"

_____

_____

_____

_____

Belief is crucial to our faith journeys – so is action, exercising our faith. Now remember, we can't "work" our way to faith. But a deep faith can't help itself but work for the Lord. It's just a byproduct of a deep love relationship. In contrast, an attachment to the vine can't help but produce fruit. We should continually be seeing a growth in our personal character and in our personal disciplines.

What does **James 2:17** say happens to our faith if we don't back it up with action?

_____

Why? Because, again, a deep faith will inevitably produce good deeds. If it doesn't, it is an indicator that there isn't a genuine faith.

Take your own faith journey into account. Is more of it belief than action on your belief? Do you say "I believe God can provide for me and my family" or "I believe God can heal" or "I believe Jesus died for my sins," but then your actions reflect those of anxiety, stress, worry, fear, timidity, or shame? Can you give an example? Or an example of where your fruit is flourishing?

_____

_____

Be honest with yourself and with your Creator… and ask Him to begin to cultivate in you a heart that seeks to back up your faith with actions reflective of it.

Read **Revelation 22:11-15, Matthew 16:27, 1 Thessalonians 2:19-20,** and **Matthew 25:14-30.**

Have you ever considered eternal rewards? Every believer will one day stand before the Judgement seat of Christ, but because we have been covered by the blood of Christ, God no longer sees our sins. But He does see what we did with what He had given to us. There is also a judgement for those who refused to graft themselves in Jesus. Because sin has to be judged. And Jesus is the only thing that covers and pardons sin. What did these scriptures reveal to you both about rewards for believers and the judgement of unbelievers?

_____

_____

_____

_____

Saturday Surrender

"And He said to all, 'If anyone would come after me, let him deny himself and take up his cross daily and follow me. For whoever would save his life will lose it, but whoever loses his life for my sake will save it.'"
Luke 9:23-24 (ESV)

Consider for a minute what the reward in heaven will be like for my mom who sat faithfully at her State Farm desk and for Billy Graham as he arrived in heaven. I firmly believe our reward is based on our willingness to use what we had – whether large or small.

Hopefully, this week you've encountered the beauty of what it means and looks like to remain in Christ. Take some time today to really evaluate the fruit you see evident in your life. Use Galatians 5:22 as your gauge. Do you see evidence of love, joy, peace, patience, kindness, goodness, gentleness, faithfulness, and self-control or do you find yourself operating from places of anxiety and worry, fear, disappointment, anger and self-centeredness, or maybe shame?

Only a heart fully surrendered to Jesus, one securely attached to Him as the Vine, can truly produce good fruit. It doesn't wait for "big" opportunity. It simply serves and obeys in "any" opportunity. If you walk in relationship with Christ, ask Him today to reveal to you anything that may have severed you from Him or may have caused you to hide and surrender that. Walk in the freedom that comes by remaining, and resting, in the Lord.

Now, on this Saturday I want to speak to those of you who may not have a relationship with Jesus Christ. I never take for granted anytime I speak or write that those who are listening or reading have a personal relationship with Christ.

My prayer is that after these weeks of studying the I AM statements you feel like you know both the personhood of God and Jesus a little better now? The Great I AM is clearly more than enough for everything that we need and He made it all available to us in this indescribable gift called Jesus. He's provision. He's light for the world. He's the door which we walk through. He's the resurrection for the deadest places in our hearts and gives us access to eternity with Him from the mere fact that He is risen. He's the way to get to God. He's the truth in a world where few truths remain. And He is life. Abundant and full life available even here and now. If those are not truths to make your heart dance, then, friends, I do not know what else could do it!

My earliest memory is when my knees found a dirt floor as I knelt by a metal folding chair in the outskirts of Indiana. My best friend at the time, Dawn McPherson, knelt beside me in that open air, make-shift church as her mom prayed with us for Jesus to enter our hearts. I knew I wanted Jesus in my heart and I know that night He moved in on the inside of me. Even though sanctification of my heart has been a journey, my heart became His home on that Summer evening. This same Jesus has directed me in the great decisions of my life: moving to Nashville, the journey of learning how to write, getting my books published, birthing in me a desire to teach the Word of God, walking with me through the tragedy and loss of my first marriage and walking with me now as I continue to navigate huge steps of faith that we take as a ministry and as I lead our team, as well as in my life of wife and bonus-mom.

I do not know what I would do without Him. I don't know how people live separate of Jesus. I truly don't. I've said so many times that I would rather get to the end of my life having served Him and encounter the peace and joy and comfort that that brings and find out He's not real than to make it to the end of my life having not served and loved and enjoyed relationship with Him and find out that He is.

So I felt I would be doing a great disservice to your heart after these eight weeks of illuminating Jesus to you in this way if I didn't offer you the opportunity to surrender your heart to Him. My former pastor, Rice Broocks, the author of God's Not Dead, along with my precious friend and mentor, Pastor Dale Evrist, fashioned a new gospel creed, if you will, that is very powerful. It says:

"The gospel is the good news that God became man in Jesus Christ. Jesus lived the life we should have lived and died the death we should have died in our place. Three days later He rose from the dead proving that He is the Son of God and offering the gift of salvation and forgiveness of sins to everyone who repents and believes in Him."

By some counts there are over 300 prophecies in the Old Testament about the Messiah that would come. But, however many there are, Jesus fulfilled each and every one. Just for the sake of it, say He only fulfilled eight of the 300. Do you know what the probability would be if he had only fulfilled eight? It would be one out of 1×10.17 If you put all the zeros behind that "1," it's way too big a number for me to even begin to tell you... that's just fulfilling eight of them – and He fulfilled **all** of them.

And for the argument that He was just a "good teacher," CS Lewis says in one of my favorite books, Mere Christianity:

"I'm trying here to prevent anyone saying the really foolish thing that people often say about Him, 'I'm ready to accept Jesus as a great moral teacher but I don't accept His claim to be God.' That is the one thing we must not say. A man who was merely a man and said the sort of things Jesus said would not be a great moral teacher. He would either be a lunatic on the level with the man who says he is a poached egg or else he would be the devil of hell. You must make your choice. Either this man was the Son of God or else a madman or something worse. You can shut Him up for a fool, you can spit at Him and tell Him to kill Him as a demon, or you can fall at His feet and call Him Lord our God, but let us not come with any patronizing nonsense about His being a "great human teacher." He has not left that open to us and He did not intend to."[26]

Friends, we are invited into a personal relationship with Jesus Christ. We are invited into access from this realm of earth into a spirit realm to enjoy relationship with our Father. To be able to pray, "Your kingdom come, Your will be done…" and then watch as He does extraordinary things in our lives. Watch as He walks us through our trials with exceptional comfort and grace and faith; watch as He directs and leads us; watch as He redeems and restores our broken places; watch as He heals us in our spirit man and in our physical man; watch as He removes addictions and replaces them with His grace; and watch as He forgives sin and leads us into this beautiful, breathtaking adventure with Him.

I'm so grateful for the decision I made at four years old and all the subsequent decisions I've made since then to keep Jesus as Lord of my life. I want you to know that He meets our repentance with His saving grace. So I'm just going to offer you the opportunity today to pray this prayer. But I want you to pray it because you mean it. I want you to pray it because you're just ready to live a different kind of life. You may have prayed a prayer when you were little but you've seen no change in your life. I'm inviting you now to make a real declaration of faith so that the transforming power and work of Jesus Christ can come and dwell and reside and walk with you. If you want this, just pray this prayer…

Lord Jesus, I've encountered You in a way that I haven't in these last eight weeks. I see my need for You. I realize that it's my sin that is separating me from You, not Your grace. And so I ask You to forgive me. I ask You to wash me clean. I ask You to take out of me this heart of stone and put in me a heart of flesh. I surrender my life to You and give You full access into any area You desire. I want all that You have and all that You are. I believe You are Jesus Christ, the Son of the living God, and I want to do life with You. Thank You for saving me. Thank You for

---

[26] Lewis, C. S., *Mere Christianity*, London: Collins, 1952, pp. 54–56. (In all editions, this is Bk. II, Ch. 3, "The Shocking Alternative.")

washing me anew and thank You that You have gone to prepare a place where I will be able to dwell with You forever. I pray this in faith, believing; and I am confident that You have heard me and that I am a new creation in Jesus Christ.

Friends, if you've prayed that prayer, we have a resource to send you. We have direction for your next journey, your next steps in the Christian faith. So please contact us at reclaminghearts.org. And I want to tell you this – you have just brought your heart into relationship with the Great I Am! Welcome to the family.

Sunday Sabbath

"But the wisdom from above is first pure, then peaceable, gentle, reasonable, full of mercy and good fruits, unwavering, without hypocrisy. And the seed whose fruit is righteousness is sown in peace by those who make peace."
James 3:17-18 (ESV)

Songs for Your Sabbath
Michael W. Smith, *Above All*
David Phelps, *You are My All in All*

What sweet things peace is affiliated with… tranquility, rejuvenation, relaxation, freedom, Sabbaths…

May this Sabbath be a day of peacefully sowing seed that will produce righteousness. I promise you that guarding this time for your heart to rest in and enjoy your Creator is such good seed you're planting in the soil of your own heart that will produce good fruit multiple times over and will produce fruit that remains.

Don't neglect this invitation today, friend, to graft yourself even more tightly to the true Vine.

Lord, I know that apart from You I can do absolutely nothing; I can't see evidence of Your work in my life, I can't lead others to You, if I do not stay attached to you, the true Vine. I desire so deeply to fulfill Your command to love others as Jesus loves me. Let me not forget what that love looks like so that I am able to be a reflection of it to everyone I come in contact with – from those in my innermost circle to complete strangers. Knit my heart more tightly with Yours, Father. Help me not miss the opportunities that come my way for others to eat from my fruit. Help me not hold it selfishly, but instead, may I extend it sacrificially, knowing that it is only there because of You. Thank You for loving me enough to graft me in. May I continue to live a life of abiding and reflecting the gift that is You.

A Prayer Before We Move Forward

Do you feel like you know God and Jesus a little better now? The Great I AM is clearly more than enough for everything that we need and He made it all available to us in this indescribable gift called Jesus. He's provision. He's light for the world. He's the door which we walk through. He's the resurrection for the deadest places in our hearts and gives us access to eternity with Him from the mere fact that He is risen. He's the way to get to God. He's the truth in a world where few truths remain. And He is life. Abundant and full life — even available here and now. If those are not truths to make your heart dance on a Monday morning, then, friend, I do not know what else could do it!

My earliest memory is when my knees found a dirt floor on the outskirts of Indiana as I knelt by a metal folding chair. My best friend at the time, Dawn McPherson, knelt beside me in that open air make-shift church as her mom prayed with us for Jesus to live in our hearts. The knowledge that I wanted Jesus inside my heart that night was so real. And I am confident that is the night He made my heart His home even though the sanctification of my heart has been a journey. This same Jesus has directed me in one of the greatest decisions I ever made, which was moving to Nashville. He walked out with me the journey of learning how to write; He created opportunities for my novels to get published. He birthed in me a desire to teach the Word of God. He walked with me through the tragedy and loss of my first marriage. He walks with me now as I navigate huge steps of faith that we take as a ministry and I lead a staff as well as in my roles as wife, bonus-mom, daughter, aunt, sister, and friend.

I do not know what I would do without Him. I don't know how people live separate of Jesus. I truly don't. I've said so many times that I would rather get to the end of my life having served Him and encounter the peace and joy and comfort that that brings and find out He's not real than to make it to the end of my life having not served and loved and enjoyed relationship with Him and find out that He is.

So I felt I would be doing a great disservice to your heart after these eight weeks of illuminating Jesus to you in this way if I didn't offer you the opportunity to surrender your heart to Him. My former pastor, Rice Broocks, the author of *God's Not Dead*, along with my precious friend, Pastor Dale Evrist, fashioned a new gospel creed, if you will, that is very powerful. It says:

"The gospel is the good news that God became man in Jesus Christ. Jesus lived the life we should have lived and died the death we should have died in our place. Three days later He rose from the dead proving that He is the Son of God and offering the gift of salvation and forgiveness of sins to everyone who repents and believes in Him."

There are over 300 prophecies in the Old Testament about the Messiah that would come. Do you know that Jesus fulfilled all of them? But just for the sake of it, say He only fulfilled eight of the 300. Do you know what the probability would be if he had only fulfilled eight? It would be one out of $1 \times 10.^{17}$ If you put all the zeros behind that "1" it's way too big a number for me to even begin to tell you... that's just fulfilling *eight* of them — and He fulfilled *all* of them.

And for the argument that He was just a "good teacher," CS Lewis says in one of my favorite books, *Mere Christianity*,

"I'm trying here to prevent anyone saying the really foolish thing that people often say about Him, 'I'm ready to accept Jesus as a great moral teacher but I don't accept His claim to be God'. That is the one thing we must not say. A man who was merely a man and said the sort of things Jesus said would not be a great moral teacher. He would either be a lunatic on the level with the man who says he is a poached egg or else he would be the devil of hell. You must make your choice. Either this man was the Son of God or else a madman or something worse. You can shut Him up for a fool, you can spit at Him and tell Him to kill Him as a demon, or you can fall at His feet and call Him Lord our God, but let us not come with any patronizing nonsense about His being a "great human teacher". He has not left that open to us and He did not intend to."

Friends, we are invited into a personal relationship with Jesus Christ. We are invited into access from this realm of earth into a spirit realm to enjoy relationship with our Father. To be able to pray, "Your kingdom come, Your will be done…" and then watch as He does extraordinary things in our lives. Watch as He walks us through our trials with exceptional comfort and grace and faith; watch as He directs and leads us; watch as He redeems and restores our broken places; watch as He heals us in our spirit man and in our physical man; watch as He removes addictions and replaces them with His grace; and watch as He forgives sin and leads us into this beautiful, breathtaking adventure with Him.

I'm so grateful for the decision I made at four years old and all the subsequent decisions I've made since then to keep Jesus as Lord of my life. I want you to know that He meets our repentance with His saving grace. So I'm just going to offer you the opportunity today to pray this prayer. But I want you to pray it because you mean it. I want you to pray it because you're just ready to live a different kind of life. You may have prayed a prayer when you were little but you've seen no change in your life. I'm inviting you now to make a real declaration of faith so that the transforming power and work of Jesus Christ can come and dwell and reside and walk with you. Or maybe you've given your heart to Jesus, but you want this year to bring you more. More of His power! More of His Purpose! More of Him! If you want any or all of this, just pray this prayer…

Lord Jesus I've encountered You in a way that I haven't in these last eight weeks. I see my need for You in a whole new way. I realize that it's my sin that is separating me from You, not Your grace. And so I ask You to forgive me. I ask You to wash me clean. I ask You to take out of me this heart of stone and put in me a heart of flesh. I surrender my life to You and give You full access into any area You desire. I want all that You have and all that You are. I want this next year to unfold You to me in a way I've never encountered. I want you to dig up and plant a fresh crop to produce a magnificent harvest. I want my life, this life, this life where my heavenly spirit lives in this earthly world to have eternal impact. I don't want to get to the end of this life having missed the fact that You were available in every minute of it and I didn't access you. I believe you are Jesus Christ, the Son of the living God, and I want to do life with You. Thank you for saving me. Thank you for washing me anew and thank You that You have gone to prepare a place where I will be able to dwell with You forever. Thank you that this world is not my home and may I not live attached to it but to You working in it through me. I pray this in faith, believing; and I am confident that You have heard me and that I am a new creation in Jesus Christ.

Friends, if you've prayed that prayer we have a resource to send you. We have direction for your next journey, your next steps in the Christian faith. And I want to tell you this — you have just brought your heart into relationship with the Great I Am!

Welcome to the family.

Week 10

Guarding Your Heart

Monday

Read: Proverbs 4:1-23

Good Monday morning.

Imagine sitting in a lecture hall your freshman year of college. The professor takes his place behind the podium and says, "Okay class, *above anything else* we're going to do this semester, I want you to pay attention to…" Or imagine getting called into your boss's office. You sit down in front of him and he looks at you and he says, "Okay, *above anything else* we're going to do this whole year, this is what I want you to focus on…" Or you're standing at the altar with the person who's about to become your spouse and the minister leans in, looks you both in the eye, and says, "There's a rough world out there waiting to devour your marriage and so *above anything else* you do in this marriage, I want you to…"

You know, very often I block out extreme language. When my bonus kids were young they would come in the room and I'd hear, "You always…!" or "They never…!" It's always like this…!" It's basically like white noise in my head – I check out with extreme words. And yet there are moments in life where words are and should be arresting. This passage in Proverbs 4:23 that changed my life and is the core foundational verse for this ministry encompasses words such as that when it says clearly, "Guard your heart *above all else* for it affects *everything* you do."

Interesting isn't it? Of all the things the Lord could have told us to guard and protect, He tells us we are to guard and protect our hearts. That must mean that they are of the utmost value. It also must mean that if we are to guard them, then there's someone or something that can jeopardize them, can come against them, could wage war for them. John 10:10 says clearly we have a very real enemy who comes to steal and to kill and to destroy. It's like this progressive hiss, if you will; a hiss that began in the garden in Genesis chapter three when he approached Adam and Eve. He comes with this accusation towards God: "Did God really say…?" The enemy does much the same with our hearts today, trying to come at us with doubt and accusation against the God of our own stories.

Very often he is able to steal our hearts -- maybe through our self-sufficiency, maybe through our addictions, maybe through anger, or our fear, or our control. He's a master at thievery. Then the stealing can move to killing. The self-sufficiency can lead to exhaustion and depression. The addiction can lead to a life of shame. Fear can lead to an anxiety disorder. From the killing he moves towards his ultimate goal, the complete destruction of our faith story, our faith in our heavenly Father.

So what do we do? We have to realize our heart is a treasure. It's of indescribable value. Did you know that we can't even have relationship with Jesus Christ without our hearts? The Word says, "If you confess with your mouth that Jesus is Lord and believe in your heart that God raised Him from the dead, you will be saved."[27] So our heart has to be brought into the process, it's vital to the process of salvation. It's also vital to the process of growth in relationship. Scripture says, "Love the Lord your God with all of your heart and all of your soul and all of your mind and all of your strength."[28]

Your heart is invaluable. And on this Monday morning when you climb into that car or even when your feet hit the floor, it's going to be assaulted in every way imaginable... with doubt, with accusation, with anger, with things that don't go your way, with the commute to work and all the frustrating people, with the bombardment of advertisements that appeal to your lust and your carnal desires, with all of the things that pull and vie for your attention in order to steal something from your heart...

So, Denise, how do I guard this most valuable treasure? One of the greatest ways is by starting your morning by pouring the truth of God's Word into your very soul. You cannot combat a lie unless you know what is true. And the Word of God is true -- it's living and active and sharper than any double-edged sword.[29] If you don't have a desire to read the Bible, begin to ask God to give you a hunger for it. There are seasons where I have to pray this and I've been reading it diligently for decades.

Also, be in a good Bible-believing church with fellow believers so that you can grow in faith. From the very beginning we were created for relationship. It is why the enemy loves to keep us in isolation. That's why anytime we find ourselves moving towards isolation, or not wanting to tell someone what we are battling or wrestling with or going through, it is a clear indicator that we should. We need people that we do deep relationship with. Not surface conversation. Hell loves surface. Heaven always goes deep.

Spend time in prayer. Intentional time not just talking but listening as well. Read books that are edifying. Sit in worship music. And learn to give yourself space to rest and refresh and do things that bring your heart to life. Friends, I want you to know today that God has given us everything

---

[27] Romans 10:9 (NIV)

[28] Mark 12:30 (NIV)

[29] Hebrews 4:12

around us for our victory and for the guarding and protecting of our hearts. Let's use what He's given us because above anything else in this life, your heart is going to affect everything you do – that means every relationship you have, every emotion you experience and even the very ability to live the dreams in your heart -- so guard it for the priceless treasure that it is.

Dust off that dictionary on your bookshelf or pull up Google on your closest device. Look up the definition of "heart" and write the one below that describes what we've talked about.

_____

_____

In addition to that, Strong's commentary describes the heart in these other ways: the inner man, the mind, will, understanding; the inner part, or midst; the soul; knowledge, thinking, reflection, memory; inclination, resolution, determination (of will); conscience; heart (of moral character); seat of emotions and passions; seat of courage.

Taking all these descriptions into account, why, then, are our hearts of such great value? And in which one of these places is your heart often attacked?

_____

_____

_____

Remember these things as you go throughout your week…

Tuesday

Read **Ephesians 6:10-18**. What is the very last piece of the armor of God that Paul mentions here and what does it represent?

_____

_____

In battle, what is a sword's purpose?

_____

_____

Here, the sword is the only piece of the armor that can be used on the offensive. We need to go into some battles swinging – and the Word of God is the most powerful weapon we wield as believers. It is especially important to our fight of guarding our hearts.

Read **2 Timothy 3:16**. What are the ways scripture is used for the guarding of our hearts?

_____

_____

What are some specific scriptures that you could pray to help guard your heart? It is important to begin to look up scripture for yourself.

_____

_____

_____

_____

Wednesday
❧

Deep Christian community is another asset in our journey of guarding our hearts.

How would you describe your current community? Do you feel connected well to those around you? Are you actively involved in a local church, serving and/or plugged into a small group of some sort? Or do you not really have much communal support? Are you maybe a part of a church yet still feel isolated?

_____

_____

_____

_____

Read the following passages:

Proverbs 12:26
Proverbs 13:20
Proverbs 17:7
Proverbs 27:5-6, 17
Ecclesiastes 4:9-10

What do these verses communicate about deep friendships and community?

_____

_____

The early church in the book of Acts set the standard for rich, meaningful community. Read **Acts 2:42-47**. Describe what their fellowship was like.

_____

_____

_____

How is that similar to or different from what your community with other believers looks like?

_____

_____

_____

Does that make you want to do anything differently than you currently are? What are actions you may need to take to create community?

_____

_____

_____

Now, Read **Proverbs 18:1** in the English Standard Version. What does this reveal to you about isolation?

_____

_____

We were not created to do life alone. Battles are won by armies – not individuals. And armies are made of people who share deep connection, trust, and vulnerability. If you don't have those types of relationships in your life, I challenge and encourage you to ask the Lord to send you the right people to enter your circle. And if you find yourself desiring isolation you can rest assured you are in a prime position for an onslaught of the enemy. I heard Dr. Donald Lichi say once, "A man who doesn't have a friend will have a failure."

Thursday

Describe your prayer life. Nonexistent? Do you only pray when you need something? Is it a ritual or responsibility to check off a to-do list? Is it a part of your life, a practice woven into everything you do?

_____

_____

Read **James 5:16**. There's two-fold value of this verse when it comes to our hearts.

First, thinking about what we talked about yesterday, why would James ask us to confess our sins to each other like he did in the first part of the verse? What does it bring about?

_____

_____

It goes back to deepening those relationships, but do not discount the healing that it brings. *Hell loves surface; heaven always goes deep.* But let's take that a step farther. *Sin breeds in isolation, life flourishes in community.*

Secondly, according to **James 5:16**, what does a righteous person do that avails, that is powerful and effective?

_____

Why do you believe these verses are connected?

_____

_____

When sin is in us, it distances us from God. Like after he ate of the fruit God told him not to, Adam went and hid. Sin makes us desire to do that as well. That is why confessing it in relationship brings healing and effective prayer.

Prayer, talking to the Lord, listening for Him… are all ways to enjoy a love relationship with Him and to further guard our hearts.

Read **Exodus 29:38-46**. How did people talk to God in the Old Testament?

_____

_____

Read **Hebrews 4:14-16**. What did Jesus' death now afford us?

_____

_____

When you consider that for over four thousand years the only way to approach God was through a sacrifice and priests, and now with the death of Jesus, He has afforded us access to God anywhere at any time, this reality should make us so grateful for what Jesus did and what we now have.

Read **Hebrews 7:23-25**. What is Jesus' role for us now?

_____

Job, of all the people in the Bible, walked through the most pain. Sometimes I think his story is there just to let all of us know that there is always someone who has walked through more than us… namely, Job.

What did Job's heart desire most according to **Job 16:18-21**?

_____

_____

Isn't that something? His heart desired exactly what we now have. A friend that sticks closer than a brother[30] and Who ever lives to make intercession for us.

Jesus talks about prayer in the Sermon on the Mount in Matthew. What phrase does **Matthew 6:6** begin with?

_____

It's not an option not to pray, but it is an indescribable privilege. Jesus' death afforded us unfettered access to the very throne of God at anytime and anywhere. For us to not utilize such an invaluable tool in the guarding and protecting of our hearts would be foolish at best and pitiable at worst.

If you're serious about guarding your heart, then you have to be serious about cultivating a rich and healthy prayer life. The first step to doing that: prioritize prayer.

Friday

Thinking back on the tools and strategies we've discussed this week (feeding our souls scripture, surrounding ourselves with deep relationships, and prioritizing prayer), how might you have left your heart unguarded up until now?

_____

_____

_____

_____

_____

30 Proverbs 18:24

How do you think your guard being down might have affected different aspects of your life? Your relationships, health, finances, spiritual work, your dreams and vision…

_____

_____

_____

_____

The enemy wants nothing more than to steal from you and to destroy all those things. Fortunately, we serve a God who not only has already won the victory over the enemy of our hearts, but He has the ability to help us take back anything and everything we've allowed the thief to try and claim!

Thinking about guarding your heart from further schemes of his, though, what are some ways you sense God inviting you to guard it now?

_____

_____

_____

What are some changes you need to make in order for these things to happen?

_____

_____

_____

_____

Saturday Surrender

"Surrender to God! Resist the devil, and he will run from you."
James 4:7 (CEV)

Often, we begin our quoting of James 4:7 at "Resist the devil, and he will flee from you" – failing to realize there is a first part of that verse. It is in the surrender that we have the ability to resist at all. Isn't that so counterintuitive to our human reasoning? Resisting is a war word. Yet, we don't fight our earthly battles, we fight spiritual ones. And our victory comes in our surrender.

Hear me when I say that guarding your heart is not the same as building an impenetrable wall around it as if to never let anyone or anything in or out. We ultimately experience the best protection of our hearts when we surrender them to the Lord.
So as you're intentionally growing a deeper sense of community, pouring scripture into your soul,

and cultivating a prayer life full of listening as well as speaking, know that true surrender is what will keep your heart fully guarded, friend.

Sunday Sabbath

"Since, then, you have been raised with Christ, set your hearts on things above, where Christ is, seated at the right hand of God."
Colossians 3:1 (NIV)

Songs for Your Sabbath

Kari Jobe, *The More I Seek You*
Rita Springer, *Defender*

Guarding our hearts requires diligence, focus, and great intentionality. But we mustn't forget our heavenly Father's invitation to rest – not to lower our guard, but to settle into our surrender and savor His presence.

As you find your quiet place this Sabbath, close your eyes and become aware of your heart. Breathe slow, deep breaths. Know today that the God of heaven and earth cares so very much for the wellbeing of your heart.

Sit in that truth. And listen for whatever else He may be wanting to speak to you today.

Lord, I know there is an enemy of my heart. Thank You for showing me my heart's value and for equipping me with the necessary tools to be able to guard it. Father, I desire so much for my heart to beat in rhythm with Yours. Show me anything that may be in the way that I'm not currently aware of. Help me be ever vigilant on this journey You have placed me on. Increase my hunger for Your word, place me in deep covenant relationships, help me carve out time in each day for You and You alone, and help me surrender anything that needs to be. Thank You that Jesus came. Thank You for the access I have into the throne room of heaven. Thank You that Jesus sits there at Your right hand and intercedes for me. May I never forget the value of my heart or the privilege of Your presence.

Week 11

Reclaiming

Monday

Read : 1 Timothy 1:1-17
(International Standard Version)

Good Monday morning.

Are you familiar with the show Fixer Upper that was on HGTV? If you aren't, you need to go back and watch all the old episodes. It was truly one of our favorite shows on TV. I think I enjoyed it so much because Jo and Chip kind of reminded me of me and Philly (okay, more Philly like Chip). One of the things that I love that Joanna did, and you see designers do this a lot now, is take a piece of old wood that would probably be better fitted for the garbage dump and take it to someone who is a master carpenter. The carpenter will then take, what to the natural eye would seem completely used up and beyond all hope of functional use, and reclaim it and turn it into a piece of beautiful furniture like a coffee table or a dining room table. You stand amazed at this designer's ability to "see" what could be. What once was considered trash is now a piece that will be treasured by many for years.

I love the word "reclaimed." I mean, of course I love that word, it's the name of this ministry. Part of the reason is it's such a powerful word, even more than *repurposing* or *restoring* to me, because *reclaiming* has this sense of strength to it. It has the essence of doing something deeper, greater; it's taking something that the world has said has no value, is useless, is viable for nothing but the dump, and it says *oh no, no... I am reclaiming what the enemy has tried to destroy or define and I am saying let me show you what you are worth and what your value truly is*. That's what reclamation is. It takes us from something that looks as if it has no viability whatsoever and it reclaims it for the purposes it was created for.

The thing about God is He is always in the reclaiming business: societal, relational, and individual. Adam and Eve, with one choice, lost Eden. But God, through Jesus, has reclaimed us for a New Eden. He tells us this in such a beautiful way in Isaiah 43:1 (God's Word translation): *"the Lord created Jacob and formed Israel. Now this is what the Lord says, 'do not be afraid because I have reclaimed you. I have called you by name and you are mine.'"*

Friends, Jesus doesn't care where your life is right now. You may feel like you're on cloud nine or you may feel like you're on a waste pile in the slums of India. No matter where you are, He has called you. He has reclaimed you. He has called you by name. We don't have to neaten ourselves up -- He does the work, He's the master Carpenter; it's not up to us. The Lord God of Jacob, of the children of Israel, has reclaimed us and called us by name. He knows yours and He knows mine. May we not settle for the trash heap when He created us for the dining room. You're worth it to Him and you have been reclaimed.

Just like the piece of wood is almost unrecognizable after the master carpenter puts his touch on it, God does the same with us. Read **2 Corinthians 5:17**. What kind of creations are we when we're in Christ?

_____

We aren't "refurbished" or "updated." It says we are completely NEW! We don't always feel like new creations, though, do we? What may be in your way right now, keeping you from fully embracing that truth? A regret or a poor decision that keeps haunting you? An unhealthy relationship you seem stuck in? Maybe overwhelming pressure at work or from your family?

_____
_____
_____
_____

Whatever is in your way, let me encourage you today – as a daughter or son of God, you are in Christ, which means He has made you new; walk boldly in that truth today!

Tuesday

List below all the things you think of when you hear the word "reclaimed."

_____
_____
_____

Now look up "reclaim" in Webster's Dictionary and write out its definitions.

_____

_____

_____

Do you see "reclamation" differently now in any way?

_____

_____

Read **Revelation 21:1-8**. What does God say here that He's doing to "all things?"

_____

This passage in Revelation is about how the world will be "reclaimed" at the end of days after Jesus comes back with the new Jerusalem. What are some of the many ways this earth will be "reclaimed" with Jesus' return?

_____

_____

_____

I don't know about you, but it makes me incredibly excited and hopeful!

Wednesday

Read **John 10:3**. Here, Jesus is explaining how He is known to us as the Good Shepherd. With that in mind, who do the sheep represent?

_____

And how does He call them?

_____

So what does that mean about Jesus?

_____

Have you seen those parts in movies when a character will go to pray and they'll open with, "Hi, God, it's me again…?" Well according to what we read here in John 10, we don't have to introduce ourselves – He knows our names. It's so easy to accept that God cares about the big things… international affairs, social injustices, natural disasters, major crises… but, if your God knows your name, how much more, then, does He care about the seemingly small stuff?

What are some of the "smaller" things you might be holding back from bringing before the Lord?

_____

_____

_____

_____

Thursday

One of the things I love about God and Jesus is they are often "renaming" people. And in that renaming they are "reclaiming" their future by not allowing their past to define it. Abram is now Abraham. Sarai is now Sarah. Jacob is now Israel. Simon is now Peter. Saul is now Paul. So often in life we allow our circumstances to "rename" us – like Naomi.

Read **Ruth 1:20.** How did Ruth rename herself?

_____

But God says, "Oh no, I alone have the right to name you."

Read **Isaiah 45:9-10 (NLT)**. How do you understand the meaning of these verses? Have you ever said these things to God about things in your life?

_____

_____

_____

Have you allowed any circumstances in your life to rename you? Maybe something happened to you that was outside of your control. Or you made a decision, or a series of decisions, that led you to a place of pain and regret. Have you let your financial status define you?

_____

_____

_____

_____

Letting anything other than the Word of God name and define us is a sin. We have to call it what it is. And it is a sin. So what do we do when we need to deal with sin? We repent. It's not our right to tell the potter what to do with the clay.

Take a few minutes to ask the Lord to forgive you for allowing anything but His Word to name you. Once you do that, then ask Him what He would name you…

Friday

Are there any relationships or situations in your life right now that seem to lack any viability whatsoever, seem to have no hope or apparent value? How might God want to reclaim them? What may He be asking of you in light of them?

_____

_____

_____

_____

_____

_____

Read **Ruth 4:13-17**. How did God reclaim and restore for Naomi, who had at one time called herself "Mara" meaning "bitter?" What is said about who God is and what God did?

_____

_____

_____

_____

Take some time to ask God to reveal anything to you that you may need to do to move toward reclamation in those things you mentioned earlier and ask Him to do what only He can do…

Saturday Surrender

"I will tell of the decree: The Lord said to me, 'You are my Son; today I have begotten you.'" Psalm 2:7 (ESV)

We belong to God. He has called us. When we come, He reclaims us. And He has named us.

We've talked a lot this week about things that may need to be given back to Him in order to be reclaimed and made what He desires them to be. Reflect on those things specifically today in order for real reclamation to happen. Ask the Lord to show you what may need to be completely released to Him and what that release looks like… it may be a simple prayer; it may be a conversation with someone. Whatever it is, I'm confident He will surely show you…

Sunday Sabbath

"Moreover, I have given to you [Joseph] one portion [Shechem, one mountain slope] more than any of your brethren, which I took [reclaiming it] out of the hand of the Amorites with my sword and with my bow."
Genesis 48:22 (AMPC)

Songs for Your Sabbath
Tommy Walker, *He Know My Name*
Big Daddy Weave, *Redeemed*

Few people had more stolen from them than Joseph. Yet God did a powerful work of reclamation in his story. On this Sabbath, consider your own story. The places where things have been stolen and the God who has reclaimed, is reclaiming, and will reclaim. Rest, this Sabbath, in the simple, pure truth that you have been reclaimed by the redeeming power of the blood of Jesus Christ. Bask in the glory of the God who knows you by name – the name He has given you. Pause today and truly let yourself feel the waves of His love for you, friend.

Lord, I am so grateful that You know my name, that You care about even the smallest pieces of my story. Thank You for not only Your ability to reclaim things that seem fit for the trash heap, but for Your desire to do so. Father, let me not lose sight of my identity in You. You tell me I am called, I am chosen, I am loved by You. I wasn't made for the garbage dump. I was made for the dining room, to be seated with You in heavenly places. I surrender to Your reclamation work in my heart. Have Your way in every place, in my relationships, in my dreams, in my finances, and even in my body. Thank You that Your Holy Spirit lives in me and continues to reclaim all that enemy has stolen. Thank You that You get the last word over me every single time.

Week 12

In Need of a Resurrection

Monday

Read: John 20

Good Monday morning.

Have you ever truly considered the magnitude of what the resurrection actually did? This singular act is what makes Christianity different from every other religion in the world. Every other professed messiah lays dead somewhere. Ours? Not a chance. Right now He is alive and well and sitting at His Father's right hand making intercession for you and me. Our calendars are defined by this moment. Yes, the resurrection holds transformative impact. Yet, with the magnitude this one moment holds for history, its real impact is what it holds in our own hearts. That is the beauty found in today's passage. Three individual lives encounter the resurrection that is Jesus.

The first is Mary Magdalene. Mary is in the throes of grief. Her Savior, the one who saw her filled with seven devils and still found her worth salvaging, is gone from the very tomb she had just recently watched him be placed in. She's heartbroken. Afraid. Grief stricken. And where does Jesus turn up? Right in the middle of her pain. With just the mention of her name, in that way that only Jesus can do, He resurrects her hope and her faith while washing away her grief.

Then there is Peter. Mark records Jesus' words to Mary once she realizes who she is talking to, "Now, go and tell the disciples, including Peter, that Jesus is going ahead of you to Galilee." Where did Jesus last leave Peter? Denying Him. Three times, to be exact. This makes His specific inclusion of Peter's name a direct reflection of His desire to resurrect Peter from his shame.

Then there is Thomas. Doubting Thomas. "Won't believe it unless I see it" Thomas. And what does Jesus do? Shows right up in Thomas' doubt and lets him touch His hands and His side.

Can you see the beauty in these encounters? In the middle of this world-defining moment, Jesus cares just as much about resurrecting the individual hearts of those He so dearly loves. Resurrecting

Mary's grief. Resurrecting Peter's shame. Resurrecting Thomas' doubt.

And it is vital that we understand the significance of this in our own story. That no matter the exceptional needs of the times that we live in: the raging of the demonic forces ravaging the moral fiber of our nation, the mocking of the sanctity of life, the persecution of the world wide church, Jesus wants us to know that He sees every single one of those enormous battlegrounds. He is in the middle of the "big stuff." But He also cares about your battleground. The broken relationship with your child, your health crisis, the money you need for your mortgage, the doubts you're having, the grief you're feeling, the shame you're drowning in, the specific and detailed needs of your individual heart.

God may rule sovereignly over this universe, friends, but do not think for one moment that the significance of the resurrection of Jesus Christ is only about the defining moments of the universe. No, the most powerful truth about the resurrection is that it can define the world while still impacting your heart. Only our God could do that. Only the resurrected Christ can do that.

What is something in your life you feel needs to be resurrected in this season?

_____

_____

_____

Ask the Lord how you may need to partner with Him in that resurrection. Is it repentance? Surrender? Removing distractions? Greater faith? Letting go of shame? Choosing to live?

_____

_____

_____

_____

Now ask Him to give you the faith to be obedient to what He is asking.

Tuesday

Read the resurrection account in **Matthew 28**. What moments of that story stick out to you for your own story?

_____

_____

_____

What are some specific areas in your life you have seen God resurrect? Remembering previous ways God has shown up on your behalf and then thanking Him are powerful tools in increasing your faith for what He wants to do next.

_____
_____
_____
_____
_____
_____

Wednesday

~❈~

Today, look at the resurrection account in **Mark 16**.

What should resurrection power in our lives look like according to Jesus' charge to them?

_____
_____
_____

Does this operate in your life? How so?

_____
_____
_____
_____

Thursday

~❈~

Now take a look at the resurrection account in **Luke 24**. Luke provides more detail than the rest. What are some of the moments of this encounter that stick out to you the most?

_____
_____
_____
_____

What might God be personally speaking to you through them?

_____

_____

_____

_____

Friday

What does **Romans 8:11** mean to your own life?

_____

_____

_____

Who do you know that needs resurrection power in their life right now?

_____

_____

How might God be asking you to partner with them in seeing Him move?

_____

_____

_____

Saturday Surrender

"Now if we have died with Christ, we believe that we will also live with Him."
Romans 6:8 (ESV)

Have you ever wondered why Jesus asked the man by the Pool of Bethesda if he wanted to be made well? I mean, this man had sat by this pool for years hoping to be the one who could get in first when the water was stirred with healing. So, why in the world would Jesus ask such a question? Wasn't the man desperate for a resurrection for his body?

Sometimes we may think we are but we really aren't. For some of us those "dead places" in our lives have defined us and we don't even know what we'd do without them. If our marriage really were going to be resurrected would it require something of us that would be painful? Challenging? If our body were going to be healed would we have to eat differently? If our finances were going to be restored would we have to spend differently? Do we really want to be made well?

Today may really require a surrender you haven't thought of and honestly don't even want to do. But friend, remember, *nothing is ever lost in surrender.* The enemy may have you thinking that what you will give up will be too hard. But that is a lie. It may be hard, but what you will receive in resurrection will pale in comparison to what you surrender. And if Jesus is inviting you to surrender, you can rest assured He will be meeting you when you do…. with resurrection.

Sunday Sabbath

"For I know that my Redeemer lives, and at the last He will stand upon the earth. And after my skin has been thus destroyed, yet in my flesh I shall see God…"
Job 19:25,26 (ESV)

Songs for Your Sabbath
Kari Jobe, *Forever*
Elevation Worship, *Resurrecting*

Prayer
Father, You know exactly what needs resurrecting in my life. You also know if there is any place inside of me resisting what You may be asking of me. I ask that you give me a heart completely surrendered to what ever You desire to do. Then, I ask Father for You to do what only You can. I thank You for breathing life into every place that the enemy would try to convince me has died. You are The Resurrection and The Life! That is who You are.
And I thank You for resurrecting me in Jesus mighty name.

Week 13

Light and Momentary

Monday

Read: 2 Corinthians 4:17

Good Monday morning.

Isn't it amazing that a year can fly by and a moment can seem to last forever? I know in my years of being a bonus mom that some moments have felt like they've lasted forever and yet it feels like these years have just flown by; like, I blinked and the kids are graduated and in high school and college and driving cars. And if I feel this way, I can't imagine how their mother and father feel having raised them from the time they were babies. So it really is true, years pass so quickly but moments... well, some moments can feel like they last forever.

In that way that is so Jesus, the Jesus who knows how we feel, He addresses even this feeling for us. Yet, as is so Jesus He rarely addresses it like we would. "For our momentary, light distress [this passing trouble] is producing for us an eternal weight of glory [a fullness] beyond all measure [surpassing all comparisons, a transcendent splendor and an endless blessedness]!"[31] Now, when I read that passage of scripture, I'm thinking, "Um, Lord, I'm sorry but this affliction does not feel light nor does it feel momentary! I think you might want to rethink that one." You've probably thought the same thing.

Why? Because the pains of life can feel hard. They can be messy. They can last for years. Years. In light of this life, the pains and trials we walk through often feel anything but light and momentary. But the beauty of this verse is that this life is not our final life. If we are believers, this life is ultimately eternal. And when Jesus returns, and He will return, what awaits us is a state of perfection and peace and beauty and the presence of God that will last forever! I love how it is presented in 1 Thessalonians 4:17 (AMP). It says, *"Then we who are alive and remain [on the earth] will simultaneously*

---

[31] 2 Corinthians 4:17 (AMP)

be caught up (raptured) together with them [the resurrected ones] in the clouds to meet the Lord in the air, and so we will always be with the Lord!"

Can you sit in that for a minute? Can you let your mind just settle for a few moments on what eternity in that kind of Edenic state would be like? The thought that forever and ever and ever we will enjoy the fellowship of our Father, the love of our brother, Jesus, the beautiful presence of the Holy Spirit. We will finally not be rushed in our conversations. We can linger with family without watching the clock. We can see those our hearts have been separated from and have made these few years feel like centuries. Oh friends, Jesus was right! When we allow our hearts to truly meditate on eternity and the hope of it, then even the most painful things in this life feel survivable. When I know that, in view of eternity, they really are only a vapor.

With the knowledge that one day we'll be home in a place that has no pain and no end, this perspective can provide for us a reframing of the afflictions of this life. And not just a reframing, but hopefully they can even produce something eternal in us. These afflictions are making us greater representatives of the Father who waits for us in our eternal home in order to create a hunger in others to go.

Friends, this year is going to go by fast. We're going to blink and it's going to be gone. However, there will be moments inside of this year that are hard and challenging. But inside of those moments, I want us to remember that in light of the eternity of eternities that is even now being prepared for us, when the lion will lay down with the lamb and where we will be with our heavenly Father forever and all trouble and all affliction and all weeping from pain and all death will finally be gone forever... they really are light and momentary. I'm looking forward to that eternity and I pray I'll be spending it with you.

What might you be walking through right now that doesn't seem light and momentary?

_____

_____

_____

_____

Tuesday

In **Galatians 6:9,** what does it mean to you when we're promised that "at the proper time we will reap a harvest if we do not give up?"

_____

_____

But we do get tired and weary. Day in and day out of a seemingly endless challenging season can take a toll on us spiritually, mentally, emotionally, and even physically.

What happens to you, personally, when you're weary?

_____

_____

_____

What is the danger in continuing to press on with our own strength when times are challenging?

_____

_____

_____

_____

Wednesday

~❦~

According to **James 1:2-4**, what produces perseverance in us?

_____

And to what place does perseverance take us as believers?

_____

_____

_____

You wrote Monday about some things that may even be testing your faith right now.

What does or would or should "mature and complete, not lacking anything" look like in your daily life?

_____

_____

_____

_____

_____

What might the process of getting to that place look like? A conversation with and some questions for God? Some intentional, strategic decisions and changes?

_____

_____

_____

_____

_____

Thursday

Even though it might not feel like it at the time, suffering serves a purpose.

Read **Romans 5:3-5**. What purpose does suffering hold for us as believers in Jesus?

_____

_____

Our sufferings refine us. They grow aspects of our character. Take a minute to think about that. What or how does that speak to you?

_____

_____

_____

With respect to your story, how are things like perseverance, character, and hope needed in it?

_____

_____

_____

_____

And taking those three things into account, what is the Holy Spirit's role in our lives in regards to our growth and suffering?

_____

_____

_____

_____

Friday

There are times in the middle of life's storms when it's incredibly easy to feel like we are completely alone, like no one else has ever faced this. Not this.

Take a look at **Hebrews 4:15**, though. What does it mean?

_____

_____

_____

Just because Jesus never sinned doesn't mean He never had to deal with suffering and temptation. He walked through the worst possible suffering imaginable!

With this in mind, how might this truth affect the way you interact with Jesus?

_____

_____

_____

Does this comfort you in any way? How?

_____

_____

_____

Saturday Surrender

"I have told you these things, so that in Me you may have peace. In this world you will have trouble. But take heart! I have overcome the world."
John 16:33 (NIV)

Yes, we face big and scary things. But we serve a God immeasurably bigger than anything we walk through. And He has already won, already overcome, it all!

When the big and scary and messy things overwhelm us, we have confidence in the truth that in the grand scheme of eternity, they are light and momentary things. Only will our ultimate surrender take us to a place where we can truly understand this.

So take heart today, friend.

Release what you may be holding onto and let the overcoming God of your story do what He does best...

Sunday Sabbath

"For I consider that the sufferings of this present time are not worth comparing with the glory that is to be revealed to us."
Romans 8:18 (ESV)

Songs for Your Sabbath
Andrew Peterson, *Is He Worthy*
Mercy Me, *I Can Only Imagine*

As you steal away this Sabbath, take this time to focus on your heavenly Father's magnificent glory.

Our present sufferings are nothing compared to His glory, His goodness, His extravagant love, His majesty... all the characteristics of Him that those of us who are in relationship with Him will get to enjoy for eternity.

Maybe even list out as many characteristics of His that you can think of and, as you write them, thank Him for how He has shown Himself to be that for you in your story today.

Lord, thank You for choosing me to spend eternity with You. Thank You for showing me that because my heart belongs to You, anything I go through is an opportunity to grow in You – it isn't a punishment. Let the way I choose to handle suffering be an example of how You have called me to respond to it so that others might be drawn closer to You. And in those moments, Father, when the storms of life would try to overwhelm me, may I quickly remind my heart that there is an eternity awaiting me that will pale in comparison to these simple thorns of this life. That one day, all of this will be over and I will be home... with You, forever.

Week 14

The Detailed Love of God

Monday

Read: Psalm 37:23

Good Monday morning.

As Brad and Laura O'Shoney drove to Santa Rosa Beach for our inaugural Weekend Experience, they had been enjoying the prayer CD we had sent when they took a wrong turn. That wrong turn brought up the last 15 to 20 years of brokenness that was their story right into their car; the small action of the wrong turn created a huge reaction revealing the depth of the things that needed to be healed. As they pulled up to the host home to check in, Laura looked at Brad and told him, "Something's got to give…"

It's honestly a miracle they didn't just turn around and go home – because they talked about it. A lot.

But, instead, they walked up the stairs into the host home and were greeted by the entire team who was incredibly excited to meet the couple who had the best room in any of the houses. Brad and Laura really didn't care at that point, they were too angry to care; but when they got to the house where they were staying, there was a little placard on it with a name. Many of the homes in that resort area are named by the people who own them, and this home was one of the named ones. Wanna know what it was? *"Something's Got To Give."* Yep. And Brad and Laura knew at that exact moment, by the detailed love of God, that they were exactly where they needed to be for the healing of their hearts and the reclamation of this painful season of their story.

Psalm 37:23 says it this way in the New Living Translation, *"The Lord directs the steps of the Godly. He delights in every detail of their lives."*

Most of us know that God cares about the big pieces of our stories. If it's big, He's got it… the big financial crisis, the big sickness, the big marital crisis, the big political and social crisis… we believe

107

God can handle those, they're big things. But we're also dealing with the same Father in heaven who knows the number of hairs on our heads, who doesn't miss a fallen sparrow. When we learn, when we choose to believe, when we begin to see the love of God in the smallest details of our story, then our hearts begin to trust and love our Father in a deeper and richer way.

James 1:17 says, *"Every good and perfect gift comes from above."* Could it be coincidence? I don't think so. I believe God is intricately woven in every detailed piece of our story. I told one of my bonus daughters recently that I may get to heaven and God may look at me and He may say, "Baby girl, that was really sweet of you to give me the credit for all those seemingly detailed occurrences in your life... I didn't do a lot of them but that was really sweet of you to thank me." Or I could get to heaven and He could look at me and say, "Baby girl, thank you for seeing me in even the smallest of details because I was behind every one of them. And every time you noticed and thanked me, well, it made me want to do even more."

It also says this in Psalm 37:4, *"Take delight in the Lord and He will give you your heart's desires."* A heart that learns to see God in the detailed places of our story is a heart that delights in the Lord in a deeper and richer way which in turn allows God to put His desires in us. You trust God in a whole new way when you see and believe that He loves you in even the smallest places of your story.

So, I encourage you, friend, to look for God in your details. You don't have to scour Him out, you don't have to be fretful and frantic about trying to find Him. Just ask Him. Say, "God, the next time You love me in even the smallest place of my story, don't let me miss it, because I want to honor You and thank You, knowing that You delight in every detail of my life."

What is a moment or incident recently where something happened that was something you had been hoping for, praying for, or simply something that really meant a lot to you? When it happened, what were your thoughts about it?

_____
_____
_____
_____
_____
_____
_____
_____
_____
_____
_____
_____

Tuesday

Read **James 1:17** and copy it here.

_____

_____

_____

_____

Underline the words that would be considered "universal qualifiers," words that are extreme in nature and consist of restrictions to other options.

What does the reality of words like "every" and "no" in scriptures about the heart of God speak to you about your own story?

_____

_____

_____

This passage makes it clear that nothing good that happens in your life and no gift that comes into your life can come from ANYWHERE other than your heavenly Father. So if this is true, now think back to that experience you wrote about yesterday and reconsider what it really came to speak to your heart.

_____

_____

_____

_____

Wednesday

Are you familiar with what a love language is? If not, I highly recommend Gary Chapman's book, _The Five Love Languages_.

Your love language is how you best show and receive love. For instance, an encouraging note is nice, but it may not mean as much to you if your love language is physical touch or quality time and not words of affirmation. Knowing how those you care about most receive love best is a beautiful way to strengthen and deepen those relationships.

If you do know the love languages of people like your parents, your spouse, your friends, or your children, what are they?

_____

_____

_____

_____

_____

Read **Luke 11:5-13**. Would you intentionally give them bad things when they have asked for something and it is in your power to meet the need that they have?

_____

_____

Wouldn't your heavenly Father do the same for you? How does He talk your language of love?

_____

_____

_____

_____

Thursday

Our God is a God of intentionality, not a God of happenstance or luck. In fact, I dare say that when we get to heaven we will be shocked to realize all of the ways that God was so intricately involved in the smallest details of our story that we completely missed.

Read **John 10:17-18**. What did Jesus do with intentionality?

_____

_____

How does that impact you? How does that affect how you may view situations in your life? If this Jesus who could have chosen another way, still chose to die for you so that He wouldn't have to spend eternity without you and so you would never have to know eternal death and separation from Him?

_____

_____

_____

_____

How can believing, truly believing Romans 8:28 fundamentally change the way you view all the circumstances in your life?

_____

_____

_____

What would it look like for you to live with a heart that believes God loves you and is intentional about the smallest detail of your life?

_____

_____

_____

Friday

Read **1 Thessalonians 5:18**. What does it mean or look like to give thanks in *all* circumstances?

_____

_____

_____

According to **Psalm 103:1-5**, what does becoming a person who vocalizes gratitude for the benefits of God do in our lives?

_____

_____

_____

_____

With that in mind, what could it do in our lives when we begin to recognize His detailed love as gifts from Him?

_____

_____

_____

Read **Philippians 4:6-7**. What could happen if we do not live with hearts of thankfulness?

_____

_____

_____

I've learned that when I cease from thankfulness toward God for even the smallest things, that I begin to miss those things He is doing. Because as we know, the perspective we have about something determines how we actually see it. This means our perspective on God's movement in our life can determine how we feel about life, relationships, and even God Himself.

Saturday Surrender

"Through Him then let us continually offer up a sacrifice of praise to God, that is, the fruit of lips that acknowledge His name."
Hebrews 13:15 (ESV)

How easy it is to forget God is a God of the little things, too. He _delights_ in our details. He loves to love on us. But how often do we get so caught up in our chaos, in our schedules, in our stuff, to the point where we can't even see the ways in which He is trying to show His love to us?

Lay down the self-sufficiency today, friend. Remove the badge of busyness and release the tight grasp of control.

Ask the Lord to open the eyes of your heart so that you can begin to experience and be so keenly aware of Him in the smallest of the details...

Sunday Sabbath

"I keep my eyes always on the LORD. With Him at my right hand, I will not be shaken."
Psalm 16:8 (NIV)

Songs for Your Sabbath
Kari Jobe, *Mystery*
Phillips, Craig and Dean, *He'll Do Whatever It Takes*

Have you seen the Lord love you in your details any this week? Reflect on that this Sabbath as you find your way to your quiet place. Focus your mind and your heart on the God of your story who wants nothing but the best for you.

And if you haven't done so yet, ask Him to begin to help you see all the ways in which He expresses His love to you… through nature (the beach is where I sense a beautiful connection with my Father's heart), through your children or children in general, even through a certain smell that takes you back to one of your sweetest memories or times in life… He's speaking, He's wooing, quiet your soul today and listen…

Lord, that You would care about my details the way You do is so refreshing to my soul. May I not miss an act of Your sweet love, but may my heart always find itself in a posture of gratitude to You. And just as you are so very intentional with Your love towards me, I ask that You give me a heart that is mindful to, in turn, intentionally show how much I love and value those I am in relationship with as well.

Week 15

A Few More Thoughts On Those Details…

Monday

Read: 2 Kings 6:1-7

Good Monday morning.

I'm sure I've read this account in 2 Kings multiple times. But something about this time made it different. I saw inside of it this God who cares about the smallest details of our story. He cares about the things that matter to us that may not matter to another living, breathing soul.

Hearing stories of the detailed love of God and encountering it myself is just so encouraging to my heart… so I thought we could dig in deeper to this thought of the detailed love of God. Recently, I woke up early and was having some internal dialogue with my heavenly Father. There was a decision I needed to make regarding the ministry and I had some questions for Him. The ministry had taken some huge steps of faith out of what I truly felt was a heart of obedience and yet I hadn't quite seen the fruit of the faith yet. I was hanging in the balance of what I felt like the Lord had told me to do but not completely seeing the fruit of what He had asked. It is in that place you can find yourself almost double-minded, wondering if you've made the right decision or if you really did what He was asking of you. And as I was in that place, I asked the Lord to really confirm once again that I had heard Him -- because if He's asked me to do something, I'll be obedient.

Well, I had discovered this new thing called Periscope and that particular morning, after my conversation with the Lord, I looked down and it said "Beth Moore live on Periscope in just a moment." I thought, well, I do love Beth Moore so I'm going to see what she has to say. As she came on live she was walking in the woods during her own prayer time. She shared how the Lord had arrested her that morning and she felt she needed to share what He had spoken. Her words were an answer to the prayer I had just prayed. She said, *You've heard from the Lord, now stay the course; it's the season between the faith becoming sight.* I knew God had loved me in such a detailed way in what was a truly important question to the investment of the ministry and where we were in this season.

However, there are much smaller ways in which He loves us in our details. Once, near the end of the year, Philly and I were sitting on a really hard bench in a gymnasium all day long. I looked at him at one point and told him we needed to get a couple of those nice stadium seats that have the back & arm rests -- this old gray mare ain't what she used to be and sitting that long on those surfaces is a little harder on the body than it used to be in the past. So, this came out as a simple, nonchalant request in casual conversation.

A few weeks later we were at a Christmas dinner with one of my close friends and her husband. They had these two Christmas gift bags for us; they said they just had these things sitting in their garage and they felt like they needed to give them to us... and what do you think they were? Nothing other than two stadium seats with back & arm rests. But God showed off even more -- they were stadium seats with the logo of the school that most of our children went to.

Philly knew exactly what I was thinking. I had just mentioned these and here they were as a gift! Those seats had been in our friends' garage for years and right after the moment that I spoke the desire, they showed up in gift bags at Christmas! Let me read Psalms 37:23 to you again, "The Lord directs the steps of the godly. He delights in every detail of our lives… "

You may be thinking, *Denise are you serious? You're going to sit there and say that God cares about the fact that you wanted a stadium seat to sit on just to make you more comfortable when we live in a world that is filled with chaos?* Yeah, I guess I am. The God that I serve is the same God that spoke worlds into existence with nothing but a word. He is the one who places Kings and tears down Kings. Yes, I know He is capable and sovereign in the chaos that has become our world. But that is the same God who lets axe heads float to the surface and who sees you and me in the smallest detail of both need and desire and speaks to us in our languages of love.

Very often it is in those moments of chaos -- whether it's the huge season of chaos in my own personal story or it's the season of chaos or pain that we may see in the world today -- that going back to that small detailed, but intimate, way in which God loved me in my own story moves me from fear to faith. It's in the small yet profound act that I am able to know that if He can take care of that detail, then He can surely take care of what's going on in the larger story. In fact, if He can't take care of the smallest one then why in the world would we dare trust Him with the big stuff?! Friend, I've brought the idea of God's detailed love back up again this week because I pray it grows your faith and a desire to see and discover how God loves you in the details of your own story... because God does, He delights in every detail of your life...

We've talked about the detailed love of God before – since then, have you had any specific encounters of God loving you in your details? I'd so encourage you to journal them here today…

_____
_____
_____
_____
_____
_____
_____
_____
_____
_____
_____
_____

Tuesday

❧

Before we can truly begin to see God operating in our smallest details, we first have to believe that He even wants to love us in the small things in the first place. Is there any hesitation or reservation in your heart about God's desire – or even His ability – to do that for you? Why or why not?

_____
_____
_____
_____

Let's revisit **Psalm 37:23** in the New Living Translation:

> "The Lord directs the steps of the godly.
> He delights in every detail of their lives."

Look up the definition of "delight" and write it below.

_____
_____
_____
_____

And so if that's what delight is, then what isn't it?

_____

_____

_____

All those things that delight isn't, that's not how God responds to your details. So stand confident in that truth today!

Wednesday
~∰~

Take a look at **Exodus 28**. What is this passage of scripture describing?

_____

What stands out to you about it as a whole?

_____

_____

_____

Well, what are we described as in **Revelation 1:5-6**?

_____

So, if we're considered priests now and God cared as much as He did about the priest's outer garments, what does that speak to you about His heart towards the details of your story?

_____

_____

_____

_____

Thursday
~∰~

What does **1 Corinthians 3:16-17** compare us to?

_____

Take a look now at **Exodus 25-27**. What do you notice of the description of God's temple here?

_____

_____

_____

What does the Lord's attention to detail in the Old Testament say about His attention to detail regarding us, if we are now His temple?

_____

_____

_____

How does your heart respond to that truth?

_____

_____

Friend, you and your heart are far more valuable than any earthly, manmade thing or temple. And if the God of heaven and earth cared as much as He did about His earthly temple in the Old Testament, how much more, then, does He care about every single detail regarding you?

Friday

Oftentimes, God uses those detailed love moments to speak confirmation to us about something – like He did with me and the Beth Moore video I mentioned on Monday. When we're seeking that type of confirmation, it's so important to bring our questions about it before the Lord.

What questions are you currently seeking answers to? What confirmation may your heart need?

_____

_____

Read **Psalm 119:66** and write your own prayer below asking the Lord to confirm what you're seeking confirmation for or even for Him to redirect you.

_____

_____

Saturday Surrender

"Don't let your hearts be troubled. Trust in God, and trust also in Me."
John 14:1 (NLT)

We've seen this week exactly how important the details are to our God. They were of value to Him back when the Old Testament was written and because He is an unchanging God, they are still of value to Him today. The sooner we internalize that truth, the sooner we are able to start seeing Him at work in our lives.

So, take some time today to ask the Lord to show you anything in your way that would cause you to resist your belief that He loves you this way. You may already be there; if so, take this time to simply thank Him for His detailed love for you…

Sunday Sabbath

"If you decide for God, living a life of God-worship, it follows that you don't fuss about what's on the table at mealtimes or whether the clothes in your closet are in fashion. There is far more to your life than the food you put in your stomach, more to your outer appearance than the clothes you hang on your body. Look at the birds, free and unfettered, not tied down to a job description, careless in the care of God. And you count far more to Him than birds."
Matthew 6:25-26 (MSG)

Songs for Your Sabbath
Tommy Walker, *He Knows My Name*
Lauren Daigle, *Everything*

Oh, may your heart find solace this Sabbath in the sweet truth of how much your God values your details as well as the promise He makes to you to take care of every single one – even the ones you don't know you have.

Reflect on this past week, friend. Think back to the detailed ways you saw your Father loving you and just thank Him for them. Don't rush this time… you don't want to miss out on anything He has for your heart today…

Lord, even though there are times I may miss You, thank You for persistently pursuing me – down to my smallest details. Thank you for speaking to my heart in ways that only You can. Father, even in the chaos and turmoil, You are still so very present and active and I don't want to miss a single thing You're saying or doing. I'm humbled by the fact that You still choose to show Your love for me in spite of how often I ignore or even reject You. Thank You so, so very much…

Week 16

Restoration of Awe

Monday

Read: Psalm 33:6-9

Good Monday morning.

It's hard to describe how breathtaking it was, but Tennessee sunsets are often that way. As I rounded the corner to my street, the sky was completely overtaken with this brilliant pink hue and a sweeping of clouds that made me stop the car. Immediately, the passage of scripture that came to my mind was Isaiah 6:1 where it says, *"In the year that King Uzziah died, I saw the Lord. He was sitting on a lofty throne and the train of his robe filled the temple."* The sky that evening looked like the train of a robe; it stretched across the expanse of the horizon and arrested me. I remember speaking out loud, right there in my parked car, that if He has a robe, then I know that's exactly what the train of it looks like.

My heart was so full of awe and wonder in that moment -- just like Isaiah's was. Scripture says that after he experienced this profound encounter with the Lord, he was so struck by the majesty and the awesomeness of God that he immediately fell to his knees saying, "I am a man of unclean lips." This is what awe can do. When we truly allow our hearts to encounter the extraordinariness of our Father, it makes clear to us our lowliness. To Isaiah, God, in His sweet loving way, sent Seraphim down with coal and touched his lips and told him, "You are forgiven." Then the Lord gave a challenge to Isaiah; He asked, "Who will go for us?" And Isaiah said, "Here I am, send me." To us, God does the same. He comes in breathtaking sunsets and the charge of oceans. He collides with our hearts on the cliffs of the California coast line, or in the majesty of the Colorado mountains. And when we will look, when we will stop and take in the magnifcent displays of love, our hearts will be captured with awe and our lowliness revealed.

But yet, the enemy of our story does our hearts much the same way that he did Adam and Eve's hearts all the way back in Genesis 3. He often tries to take this extraordinary Creator of the universe and melt Him down and make Him so small that He's petty, trivial, and envious like us. The enemy looks at Adam and Eve and in his response when they tell him God said not to eat from the tree, the enemy of their soul and ours said "You will not surely die. For God knows that in the day you eat of it your eyes will be opened, and you will be like God, knowing good and evil."[32] In essence, he was saying, *God is just trying to hold out on you because He doesn't want you to be like Him.* And the enemy comes with accusation about God to our hearts just like he does theirs over and over again. He tries to take this extravagant God and make Him like us. But, friend, you and I both know that we need a God bigger than us. We need the God that the Psalmist writes about when he says, "The Lord merely spoke and the heavens were created. He breathed a word and all the stars were born. He assigned the sea its boundaries and locked the ocean in vast reservoirs. Let the whole world fear the Lord and let everyone stand in awe of Him for when He spoke the world began and it appeared at His command."[33]

That is our God. He's the God who paints skies just like the one I pulled over to the side of the road to savor. How heartbreaking it is when those things in life that should fill us with awe do not even catch our eye. That is a statement of our hearts. Brennan Manning says it in a way that is arresting. He says, "A Philistine will stand before a Claude Monet painting and pick his nose but a person filled with wonder will stand there fighting back tears." It's so true.

So I invite you this Monday morning, as you look into the face of this new week, to ask the Lord to renew your sense of awe. Awe is found in the smallest moments like a child's prayer before they go to bed. Awe can capture us on a bike ride in the middle of the Summer when the smell of Carolina Jessamine arrests our senses. Awe can capture us when we bite into the sweetness of a Summer fruit. And awe can consume our hearts with an overwhelming sense of the extraordinariness of our God when we see a sinner come home. The reason awe is so impactful, the reason awe is so needed in this culture that has taken the magnificence and beauty of who God is and has tried to make Him ordinary and trite is because when we truly encounter, like Isaiah did in the temple, the beauty of God and the wonder of who He is, we will readily answer "send me."

God, if that's who You are, if You can speak the world into existence with nothing but a word, send me; I can trust You with anything. I can trust You with the smallest detail of my story. Friends, our awe is vital to this journey. Ask the Lord to renew it, restore it, and reclaim it for your heart today.

Describe a recent time your breath was taken away by sheer awe and amazement of something. Is that something that happens to you often or can you hardly remember that last time you were moved like that?

_____

_____

[32] Genesis 3:4-5 (NASB)

[33] Psalm 33:6-9 (NLT)

Tuesday

Read **Exodus 14** and imagine yourself present, watching all of it happen. I'd actually highly recommend reading it in The Message translation if you have access to it.

Have you ever witnessed "the mighty hand of the Lord displayed" in your life?

_____

_____

_____

Why is their awe and wonder so important to the journey of the Israelites?

_____

_____

With that in mind, then, how is awe and wonder valuable to our own journeys?

_____

_____

_____

Wednesday

The enemy loves to make the extraordinary seem ordinary and the ordinary seem extraordinary. This is being done in culture more now than ever before. Culture is saying the things of this world are where our awe should lay and tries to convince us that the God of the universe is petty, like us -- that He really is trying to hold out on us so we can't enjoy life and that life is about what we "feel" not about the power of this God we serve.

In fact, recently, a very prominent former minister was interviewed by one of talk show's greats and said that "the church will continue to be even more irrelevant when it quotes letters from 2,000 years ago as their best defense..." Yet few things should inspire awe like the Word of God.

What do you think? Does God's Word inspire awe in you? If not or if so, why is that?

_____

_____

_____

Read **Matthew 5:18**. "The Law" here means the Word of God. What does this verse mean, then?

_____

_____

_____

This makes it clear that the Word of God is so powerful that heaven and earth would pass away before it could. Yet culture is trying to tell us that not only is it irrelevant but those who believe it will be as well.

What might you need to do in order to increase your sense of awe in the reading, studying and power of God's word?

_____

_____

_____

How do you see culture trying to diminish the power and glory of God? What about any of your closest relationships or even your very own heart, how might they?

_____

_____

_____

_____

Thursday

With so many lies and cultural norms steering us away from any sense of awe, it's an important practice to protect awe in our lives.

Read **Psalm 19:1**. What could this passage encourage us to do to protect awe?

_____

_____

So how do we protect awe in our own lives? One of the ways is to simply slow down. You know the old saying, "Stop and smell the roses?" We live with such high intensity that we don't know how to walk slowly, drive slowly, eat slowly, talk slowly, and, these days, even think slowly.

What are some practical ways you can begin to slow down?

_____

_____

_____

_____

Be mindful of that today, friend… you don't have to rush everything. Try taking a few things slower than you normally would – see what awe can be found in even something as simple as a relaxed pace…

Friday

Read **Psalm 145:1-4** in the MSG translation, again, and then grab yourself a colored pen or a highlighter.

Oh the power of recounting the things God has done. This is another way to protect our awe because it keeps the works of God in the forefront of our minds.

You know, one of the most powerful and awe-inspiring revelations of God is when God finally responds to Job in **Job 38-41**. Take a few minutes with that pen or highlighter you grabbed and underline/highlight anything you read there that you may have never thought of or that might fill your heart with awe.

Saturday Surrender

"Cease striving and know that I am God; I will be exalted among the nations, I will be exalted in the earth."
Psalm 46:10 (NASB)

We can't fully embrace a sense of awe and wonder if we allow ourselves to be constantly distracted. May we release anything standing in our way of fully experiencing the deepest feelings of awe we are capable of experiencing.

Ask the Lord today to reveal anything blocking your view of the sweet beauty He's placed around you and surrender to Him whatever that might be…

Sunday Sabbath

"The law of the LORD is perfect, refreshing the soul. The statutes of the LORD are trustworthy, making wise the simple."
Psalm 19:7 (NIV)

Songs for Your Sabbath
Jesus Culture, *In Awe of You*
Chris Tomlin, *Indescribable*

God's law, His Word, is perfect and refreshing to our souls… how beautiful is that?

You've covered a lot of scriptural ground this past week. As you take your time in your quiet place this Sabbath, look back at some of the passages that may have resonated a bit more with your spirit than others. Read them over again. Savor every word. Let them refresh your soul… and may a renewed sense of awe wash over your heart as you do…

Lord, I am so grateful that as a result of your detailed love for me You would purposely allow me opportunities to encounter Your love through such awesome and wonderful things. May my heart echo the prayer in Habakkuk 3:2 where it says, *"I stand in awe of your deeds, Lord. Repeat them in our day, in our time make them known."* You are the God of miracles. Keep my heart constantly mindful of Your mighty hand's work in absolutely everything, Father. May I not miss one opportunity to be awed by You.

Week 17

God of the Nations

Monday

❧

Read: Psalm 33:11-22

Good Monday morning.

Anytime I read in scripture about God being sovereign and in control of the Nations, it brings my heart great peace. And as we come out of this time of prayer for our nation together, I thought this passage might give your heart peace, too. It's found beginning in Psalm 33:11. We were actually there not too long ago talking about the awesomeness and awe of the Lord. This is the from the New Living Translation:

But the Lord's plans stand firm forever;
*   His intentions can never be shaken.*

Doesn't that give your heart peace? The revelation that everything in the Word will stand forever. We may not be able to count on the fact that a year from now the dollars in our wallet will have worth, but we can rest assured that not one dot, not one cross of a T will fall away in the Word of God, that every promise will come true. It continues:

What joy for the nation whose God is the Lord,
*   whose people He has chosen as His inheritance.*

Think about that. You and I were chosen as His inheritance. The God who created everything in the universe with His word, whose creation obeys His commands, who mountains bow down to, who owns it all, calls us His inheritance. Then, for the nations who call Him Lord, there is great joy -- thus the reason we should continually pray for the nation we live in, that it will make God its Lord. Not its wallet. Not its social justice. Not its tolerance. But God. His word. His Son. Because in that is great joy for the entire nation, whether everyone realizes where the blessings have come from or not.

Now, I'm an incredibly visual person and I just love the picture this next part paints -- I want you to picture this with me:

> The Lord looks down from heaven
>   *and sees the whole human race.*
> *From His throne He observes*
>   *all who live on the earth.*

Imagine those satellite visuals, if you will. You can start out on the street where you live, then zoom out and see your city; zoom further and see your state, then your nation, until you've zoomed out so far you can take in one side of the entire globe. Now, play that visual backwards. Start with the globe, then zoom into the nations, then zoom into your nation, your state, your city, your neighborhood, your home, your bedroom, your bathroom where you stand at the sink brushing your teeth to begin your day. That's how I see the Lord viewing us. And remember -- not one of us is lost on Him. Not the large pieces of our stories or the detailed pieces of our stories.

> *He made their hearts,*
>   *so He understands everything they do.*

The heart of you, yes, you, the one who stands by the sink and washes dishes, the one who makes school lunches, or drives carpools, or clocks in at the plant, or takes the money as the bank teller, or drives the truck, or sits in the corporate office… *your heart was made by Him.* And He understands it. Why? Because He made it. His hands fashioned it. The vessels that flow from it, He formed. The blood that pumps through it, He supplied. The thoughts that run through your mind, the wounds that pierce your soul, the doubts that arrive at nighttime, the joys that overwhelm you, the peace that can saturate you, He knows every piece of it and, more than that, He understands it. Jesus took on flesh so that He could. Isn't that a comfort? I cannot tell you how that knowledge comforts me.

> *The best-equipped army cannot save a king,*
>   *nor is great strength enough to save a warrior.*
> *Don't count on your warhorse to give you victory—*
>   *for all its strength, it cannot save you.*

It's interesting that this section comes now, after we have such a clear picture of the mightiness and, yet, the intimacy of our heavenly Father. This all-seeing, all-knowing God now wants us to realize how powerful He is. America has been touted for its military superiority for years, to the point that often we rest in that. However, according to this passage none of that can save us.

> *But the Lord watches over those who fear Him,*
>   *those who rely on His unfailing love.*
> *He rescues them from death*
>   *and keeps them alive in times of famine.*
> *We put our hope in the Lord.*

He is our help and our shield.
In Him our hearts rejoice,
  for we trust in His holy name.
Let your unfailing love surround us, Lord,
  for our hope is in you alone.

Friends, the only place we can afford to put our trust is in our all-powerful God! If we fear Him, if we rely on His unfailing love, if our hope is in Him alone, then we can trust that He can rescue us from death, that He can provide for us in times of famine, that He is our help and our shield. This, then, should produce an indescribable sense of gratitude and confidence that He is the only place we can put our trust.

I, like you, have been hurt or let down by virtually every relationship in my life. I, also, am confident that I have been the source of hurt or unmet expectations in the lives of others. That is why we can place our confidence in no other but God alone. He alone is where our hope and trust can not only find a resting place but a friend like no other. He is this for us as individuals and He is this for our nation as well.

Using the concordance in your Bible, find the word "nations" and look up scriptures that it references. List two that are specifically about nations being impacted by their serving the Lord.

_____
_____
_____
_____
_____
_____

Tuesday

We're fully aware of how our hearts toward the Lord affect our stories. Have you ever stopped to consider that even nations are impacted by their heart towards the Lord? How does that make you feel?

_____
_____
_____
_____
_____

The Bible also gives us specific insight regarding international relationships – with one nation in particular. Read **Genesis 12:1-3**. What nation is being referred to here?

_____

What is God saying about nations that honor this nation?

_____

_____

With that in mind, how would you pray for your nation's heart toward Israel?

_____

_____

_____

_____

Wednesday

Read **Daniel 2:21** and **Psalm 33:11**. What do these words mean for your own personal story?

_____

_____

And what do they mean for the world at large, especially in regards to kings and leaders?

_____

_____

On the flip side of that, though – what if there was no Lord over our life whose plans stood firm forever or who was sovereign over nations? What would that mean for us?

_____

_____

_____

Oh, what a true gift it is to our hearts to have the promise that our mighty God is in control of absolutely everything!

Thursday

Psalm 33:16-17 communicates to us how insufficient our self-sufficiency is.

When a lifeguard goes out to rescue someone who is drowning, do you know the first thing they say to the person they're trying to help? The lifeguard tells them not to fight, to simply lean back and let them do all the work. Why? Because, by continuing to flail and fight and save themselves, that can put both of them in great danger.

That's what self-sufficiency does. It is a drowning person continuing to flail in the arms of his rescuer.

What is our self-sufficiency viewed as according to **Job 36:9**?

_____

What might be some areas in your life where you tend to move toward self-sufficiency? Are there relationships you try to control? Situations that you choose to manage because "it will only be done right if I do it?" Maybe how you handle your finances shows more reliance on yourself than on God…

_____

_____

_____

_____

I've said it before and I'll say it again: nothing is ever lost in surrender… but, oh so much can be missed without it…

Friday

Look back at **Psalm 33:13-15**. Have you ever stopped to consider that God made your heart? Sit in that for a moment. What impact does this have on you?

_____

_____

Now consider that He understands you, the real you. He understands why you make the decisions that you make and believe the things that you do. How might understanding and truly internalizing this affect your thoughts toward God and even your perception of your own story?

_____

_____

_____

_____

Saturday Surrender

"No, for all the nations of the world are but a drop in the bucket. They are nothing more than dust on the scales. He picks up the whole earth as though it were a grain of sand."
Isaiah 40:15 (NLT)

Thinking about the current political, social, and economic climate of our nation is enough to really overwhelm us if we let it. Fortunately, we serve a God bigger than any national – or international – crisis. We are still called to lift up the heart of our nation and its leaders in prayer, ultimately surrendering and submitting it to the Lord, just as we do with our own hearts.

Sunday Sabbath

"Don't be afraid, for I am with you. Don't be discouraged, for I am your God. I will strengthen you and help you. I will hold you up with my victorious right hand."
Isaiah 41:10 (NLT)

Songs for Your Sabbath
Michael W. Smith, *Sovereign Over Us*
Israel Houghton, *We Speak to Nations*

What peace the truth and promise of God's sovereignty brings to our souls. As you settle into His presence in your quiet place this Sabbath, I encourage you to revisit verses 11-22 of Psalm 33; soak in the promises, truth, and encouragement that passage affords our hearts and the heart of our nation.

So pick back up a conversation you started with Him earlier in the week, start a new one, or just sit and enjoy the quiet with your heavenly Father today...

Lord, I know I am nothing without You nor can I accomplish anything without You. Thank You for the warnings, challenges, and encouragement You speak to my heart through Your Word. What a comfort to know that Your plans stand firm forever – for not only our individual stories, but for us as a nation. May the heart of our nation begin turning its gaze back to You, Father. Please reveal to me any areas in my life where I turn to self-sufficiency; my hope is in You and You alone, not my own strength and abilities.

Week 18

The Privilege and Power of Fasting

Monday

Read: Isaiah 58:6-11, Matthew 9:14-15

Good Monday morning.

When my dad cleaned out his library upon his retirement, he passed a lot of books down to my brothers and me. One I received was a book by Derek Prince, one of my favorite men of God, called *Shaping History Through Prayer and Fasting*. With this week including our National Day of Prayer, I found it fitting to share with you how this annual day originated -- I really didn't know until I read this for myself.

Originally called by President Lincoln, *A Day of Prayer, Humiliation and Fasting* began on April 30, 1863; the proclamation began this way:

"Whereas the Senate of the United States, devoutly recognizing the supreme authority and just government of almighty God, and all the affairs of men and of nations has by a resolution requested the president to designate and set apart a day for national prayer and humiliation. And whereas it is the duty of Nations, as well as men, to owe their dependence upon the overruling power of God to confess their sins and transgressions in humble sorrow, yet with a short hope that genuine repentance will lead to mercy and pardon and to recognize the sublime truth announced in the Holy scriptures and proven by all history that those nations only are blessed whose God is the Lord."[34]

I have taught now for over 20 years and I have taught often on the privilege and invitation of fasting. It's not necessarily something we'd really consider a privilege or an invitation, is it? But what I've discovered is that many people have never even heard a message on fasting. They've sat in church most of their lives and not one time have they been taught on the gift that this discipline affords. I describe it often as the most underutilized weapon in the arsenal of a Christian; it truly is that to me.

---

[34] Derek Prince, *Sharping History Through Prayer and Fasting* (Spire Books, 1973), 5,6

If you study scripture, you see that fasting was utilized over and over in the lives of God's children. Queen Esther, before she approaches the king for the salvation of Israel, commands a three day fast of the Jewish people so that she'll have favor when she approaches him. Daniel asks to fast when he doesn't want to partake of the Babylonian delicacies and his fast is a revelation to Babylon of His God. We see in one of my favorite stories, King Jehoshaphat, who is surrounded on every side by multiple armies, calls his people into a time of prayer and fasting. And do you know what? The other armies end up actually turning on each other -- he doesn't even have to fight the battle. He sends the praisers out ahead of his army and with prayer and fasting and praise he doesn't even have to lift a finger.

Each of these times of fasting are testaments to individuals and their impact on nations.

At the beginning of this year we talked about fasting in regards to our personal lives. But now, as we enter a season where we are praying for our nation, what might fasting and prayer do now, here, in a time like few we've ever seen?

Our nation needs an awakening, it truly does, just like this proclamation said over a hundred and fifty years ago. But a nation is made up of individual hearts, so could it be that our hearts need an awakening? I'm going to encourage you to get curious about what fasting could look like for you. Now, if you have medical conditions you need to talk to your doctor. But if not, why don't you ask the Lord? Maybe you could fast a meal, maybe you could fast a day, maybe you could fast your favorite drink or food for a season of time. Maybe you could find some friends and fast together for some things regarding our nation. "If my people, who are called by name, will humble themselves and pray and seek my face and turn from their wicked ways, then I will hear from heaven, will forgive their sin and I will heal their land."[35] Is this not a price worth paying for such a healing?

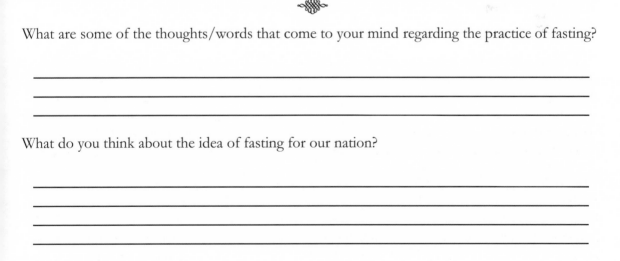

What are some of the thoughts/words that come to your mind regarding the practice of fasting?

_____

_____

_____

What do you think about the idea of fasting for our nation?

_____

_____

_____

_____

[35] 1 Chronicles 7:14 (NIV)

Tuesday

What do you see as the greatest need for our nation in this day and age?

_____

_____

_____

This culture we live in has moved so far from the truth. Very much like what **Jeremiah 2:11-13** speaks of. What are the sins identified here?

_____

_____

_____

How is our current generation like what Jeremiah is talking about?

_____

_____

_____

Wednesday

With regards to the relationship between prayer and fasting, Andrew Murray wrote, "Prayer needs fasting for its full growth. Prayer is the one hand with which we grasp the invisible. Fasting is the other hand, the one with which we let go of the visible."[36]

What does this mean to you?

_____

_____

_____

---

[36] ANDREW MURRAY (South African pastor and missionary, 1828-1916), WITH CHRIST IN THE SCHOOL OF PRAYER (Springdale, PA: Whitaker House, 1981), pp. 100-101.

Read **Isaiah 58:6**. What are the reasons behind the fast he describes?

_____

_____

_____

With those in mind, what are some of the "visible" things in our society today that fasting could allow you to release?

_____

_____

_____

What about some of the "invisible" things that prayer could allow you to grasp hold of?

_____

_____

_____

Thursday

Looking at the big picture, our nation's need for an awakening is an overwhelming idea – especially when you begin to think about what something that huge would need in order to happen in the first place.

Do you truly believe God can use one person to start something like that?

_____

_____

The Bible is full of accounts of God doing seemingly impossible, daunting things by using only one person to accomplish them. Take a few minutes to recall who some of those people were.

_____

_____

_____

_____

Remember, they were just regular people, too, like you and like me. They probably didn't believe they could be used for anything special, either, and look what the Lord did through them! Don't discount the value you add to impacting change.

Friday

The chaos, injustice, pain, and general evil overtaking our nation is ultimately a surface manifestation of something deeper. What does **Ephesians 6:12** say our battle is really against?

_____

_____

And how is the battle to really be won, based on what we read in **Zechariah 4:6**?

_____

How does your heart feel about that truth?

_____

_____

_____

_____

Saturday Surrender

He said: "Listen, King Jehoshaphat and all who live in Judah and Jerusalem! This is what the LORD says to you: 'Do not be afraid or discouraged because of this vast army. For the battle is not yours, but God's.'"
2 Chronicles 20:15 (NIV)

Ultimately, the battle really isn't ours; it's God's.

But that doesn't mean we don't have a role to play. Amazing things happen in the spiritual realm when we deny our flesh in the natural and choose to seek the Lord with intentional fervor. And so I urge you in this week of the National Day of Prayer to consider fasting something. History can attest – God does mighty things through that act of surrender.

Sunday Sabbath

"I appeal to you, brothers, by the name of our Lord Jesus Christ, that all of you agree, and that there be no divisions among you, but that you be united in the same mind and the same judgment."
1 Corinthians 1:10 (ESV)

Songs for Your Sabbath
Chris Tomlin, *God of this City*
Kari Jobe, *Heal our Land*

I'm not completely sure why exactly, but I always start any fasting season on a Monday (unless the Lord gives directives otherwise, of course). So as you quiet your soul this Sabbath, ask Him if there's any particular issue in our nation that He may be leading you to fast and pray for outside of this past week's National Day of Prayer.

Maybe there's someone or even a few other close friends He will lead you to include in this.

But be still. Be quiet. Breathe. And just listen…

Lord, what a true privilege it is to be able to access Your throne room directly through something as sacred as fasting. Oh what trying times our nation is in… I know You hear every prayer and petition we submit to You on behalf of our country. Father, I also know that all it takes is for one person to say "yes" to You to be the catalyst for an awakening. I say "yes" today. I am willing to do my part and anything You ask me to do to bring Your love and hope to the broken world in which we live.

Week 19

In Need of Restoration

Monday

Read: Psalm 23

Good Monday morning.

Stop for a minute this morning and consider this question, for your own heart. Where do I need restoration? For some of us it's in our minds – we battle fear, anxiety, depression, anger, feeling overwhelmed. For others we need restoration in our relationships – with our spouse or children or a friend. Still, for others maybe it's a financial restoration or a restoration of health. On this Monday morning, I want you to rest in this thought: God is in the restoration business.

For many of us we know the 23rd Psalm by heart, we learned it as little children, but I want you to read it in a very personal way today as we start this week off… this is from the *MSG* translation:

GOD, my shepherd!
   I don't need a thing.
You have bedded me down in lush meadows,
   you find me quiet pools to drink from.
True to your word,
   you let me catch my breath
   and send me in the right direction.
Even when the way goes through
   Death Valley,
I'm not afraid
   when you walk at my side.
Your trusty shepherd's crook
   makes me feel secure.
You serve me a six-course dinner
   right in front of my enemies.
You revive my drooping head;

my cup brims with blessing.
Your beauty and love chase after me
    every day of my life.
I'm back home in the house of GOD
    for the rest of my life.

Isn't that beautiful?

Did you notice what is absent from it? Our effort. Everything in this passage is about what God is doing and wants to do and will do for us if we abide in Him, as John says.[37] Another word for *abide* is actually found in the word restoration: *rest*. If we rest our hearts in confident trust of our Savior, then we are told that He will lead us, He will guide us, He will protect us.

We're told here that He's our Shepherd so that means He's before us. We're told that He's beside us. He's anointing or head with oil so He's over us. His goodness and mercy are pursuing us so He's behind us. He's even preparing a six-course meal for us in the presence of our enemies so He is both feeding us and justifying us. And then, as if that wasn't enough, we're told that in all of this He restores our souls – the only thing required of us is resting in confident trust that our God is able.

Friends, I have no idea what area of your life may need restoration today... your mind, your body, your heart, your emotions, your spirit man... but this one thing I do know is that John 15 tells us that apart from Him we can do nothing.[38] All the striving, all the flailing, all the working to try to make things work out in our lives is done in vain separate of Him. The only way things that get done last, truly last, is by resting in the arms of our faithful Shepherd, trusting Him. If we will rest in Him, if we will abide in Him, He will restore our souls and all the things that come along with it. Scripture says that God will perfect all that concerns you.[39] And I truly believe that this perfection He mentions, this restoration we need, is found in our *rest*. When we get "self" out of the way and instead surrender to Him, true rest comes.

One of your goals this week should be to prayerfully ask the Lord what needs to be restored for you. You may think you don't even have to ask. But I encourage you to, anyway. You might find what you need most you haven't even thought of.

As of right now, what are your immediate thoughts regarding what you need restored in your life?

_____

_____

_____

[37] John 15:4

[38] John 15:5

[39] Psalm 138:8

Now, ask the Lord what may be preventing restoration for you? Are you in the way? Are you trying to be God in a relationship? Are you holding on to unforgiveness that is preventing restoration from coming? All of these demonstrate a lack of trust in The God who made you, who leads you, and who feeds you. Write down what comes to mind.

_____
_____
_____
_____
_____

Tuesday

❦

As I mentioned yesterday, I believe there's a powerful reason why the word 'rest' is tucked inside 'restoration.'

Describe a time you can remember being incredibly well rested. How did you feel? What allowed you to be able to experience that type of rest? What were your interactions with others like?

_____
_____
_____
_____
_____

Real rest isn't just available in times that seem peaceful. In fact, one of the most beautiful gifts of having Jesus is that we can have rest even when the world has gone mad or our life is a mess. Read **Isaiah 26:3**. Who does God keep in perfect peace?

_____
_____

The ESV Bible says "those whose mind is stayed on you." What does your mind tend to stay on? Planning 'what's next'? Worrying about current situations or struggles? How does this affect your peace?

_____
_____
_____

Read **2 Corinthians 3:5**. Why would Paul say we need to bring "every thought captive?" What does that tell you about the power of your thoughts? How do you bring them under the "obedience of Christ?"

_____

_____

_____

_____

Read **Proverbs 23:7**. Write down the first part of the passage. What does that mean to you?

_____

_____

We are made up of three parts: spirit, soul, and body. When your spirit hit your body it made your soul. Inside your soul lives your mind, your emotions, and your will. This came to life for me while studying Neil Anderson's book, _Victory Over the Darkness_. What you believe in your soul, your body will live out. That is why what you allow to walk around in your mind, your body will ultimately live out.

When our mind believes we have no value, our body will try to find value somewhere else. When our mind believes we will never be good enough, our body will self-sabotage to prove this point. But when our mind believes, "I am the righteousness of God in Christ Jesus", our body lives and moves and speaks and views and listens to things that communicate this truth. Can you see this? We cannot afford to check our minds out and live by feelings and emotions. Because 1 Corinthians 2:16 says we have the mind of Christ! If we believe this and use this, everything about us will live and believe it as well.

I encourage you today to be intentional to steer your mind towards things of the Lord. His goodness. His love. His provision. His promises. His peace. When you do, I can assure you He will bring you to and keep you in His perfect, complete peace...

Wednesday

Let's stay in the same verse we were in yesterday, **Isaiah 26:3**. I want us to look at that last part.

According to this verse, why does God keep in perfect peace those whose minds are stayed on Him?

_____

_____

Just like most other things, it goes back to trust, surrender. Our ability to rest in God and His will hinges on our willingness to trust Him. A lack of willingness to trust and surrender will always prevent true and lasting rest and restoration. Any movement towards self is a movement away from surrender. Self-Sufficiency. Self-Preservation. Selfishness…

What may be hindering the restoration you need? Are you in the way, trying to juggle and handle everything on your own? Are you trying to be God in a relationship, constantly trying to play the role of 'savior' for someone else? Maybe you're even holding onto some unforgiveness?

_____

_____

_____

_____

_____

Any time we try to take and hold on to the reins in a situation and rely on self, we are demonstrating a lack of rest in God, which in turn suffocates any potential for real restoration to take place.

Thursday

~❧~

Are you familiar with Job's story? If you aren't, it's definitely worth sitting down and reading one afternoon. But let me highlight a few things here. First, Job's world was shattered by loss: loss of his cattle, loss of his servants and loss of his children. Second, even his wife told him to curse God and die. Then, his body was wrecked with sores and continual pain. Finally, his "friends" showed up to console him by informing him of all the sin that must be in his life for God to be punishing him this way. Can you imagine what Job wanted to do to his "friends?"

But I want to draw your attention to the end of his story today. The moment when restoration comes to him and his house. Read **Job 42:10-11**. What did Job do right before the Lord restored his fortunes?

_____

_____

I have learned in years of ministry that often unforgiveness holds people's destiny hostage more than anything else. Unforgiveness opens up a place of access for the enemy to steal or kill or destroy even more than was taken in the first place. What significance does his posture have for you today in your own story? Is there any place you need to pay attention to? Forgive? Surrender?

_____

_____

As you're seeking restoration for what you wrote down on Monday or even anything deeper the Lord may have revealed to you since then, consider following Job's lead in this manner as well; shift your attention outward, off of your own condition and desires. Pray for the restoration of someone else or seek to serve others. Mighty things are opened up in the spiritual realm when our inward focus becomes an outward one.

What could that look like for you? Praying for someone else? Beginning to serve – either those in your immediate circle or even your community or even someone who has hurt you?

_____

_____

Friday

As we talked about on Wednesday, operating from a place of "self" in any measure is completely against the way God intended for us to live. It is also such a set-up of the enemy trying to convince us that we have to have it all together before we can bring our needs to our heavenly Father. What a lie!

Read **2 Corinthians 12:9-10**. What does it mean when Jesus said His power "is made perfect in weakness?"

_____

_____

_____

So why would Paul gladly boast about his weakness, then?

_____

_____

_____

The idea of parading, boasting about your weaknesses – how does that make you feel?

_____

_____

It just isn't in our nature to want to focus on our weaknesses. We want to be strong and have it all together – or at least be perceived that way.

But we have a valuable lesson here from Paul. If our heart's desire is to point to Jesus, and if His power is more clearly revealed in our weakness, then we should celebrate where we are weak because that allows His strength and power to be revealed.

What might it look like for you to 'boast' about your weakness?

_____

_____

Saturday Surrender

❧

"Come to Me, all who are weary and heavily burdened [by religious rituals that provide no peace], and I will give you rest [refreshing your souls with salvation]. Take My yoke upon you and learn from Me [following Me as My disciple], for I am gentle and humble in heart, and you will find rest (renewal, blessed quiet) for your souls."
Matthew 11:28-29 (AMP)

Our limited perspective equates surrender with bondage and a loss of freedom. But our heavenly Father just doesn't operate within our parameters. Surrender to Him means freedom – including freedom to rest our souls even in the middle of the worst storms, because that's when restoration is needed most.

So ask Him today to reveal anything you may still be holding onto, preventing you from experiencing the restoration He wants to bring into your story…

Sunday Sabbath

❧

"In His kindness God called you to share in His eternal glory by means of Christ Jesus. So after you have suffered a little while, He will restore, support, and strengthen you, and He will place you on a firm foundation."
1 Peter 5:10 (NLT)

Songs for Your Sabbath
Vertical Worship, *Restore My Soul*
People & Sons (Josh Sherman), *Psalm 23 (I Am Not Alone)*

Like I've mentioned before, God is in the restoring business. It's His job. Not yours. Not mine. And we can't encounter His restorative power until we trust, surrender, and rest in His perfect will.

Accept His invitation to still your soul and rest in His presence, His arms today.

Get quiet.

Get curious.

Let your heavenly Father, Himself, work on your behalf this Sabbath...

Lord, I'm sorry for trying to do and fix things on my own, for resorting to self-sufficiency instead of resting and trusting in You. May my mind always find its way to You and Your perfect ways so that I can fully know Your life-giving rest despite what season I find myself in. Help me be more aware of my thoughts, as well, learning the power and responsibility of bringing my thoughts captive. I want my life to live out the truth of who I am in You. Because in truth comes restoration as well. Only You can restore what has been lost, or broken, or stolen. Thank You that Your word says You can and my faith believes You will.

Week 20

Reaching the Next Generation

Monday

Read: Psalm 78:1-4

Good Monday morning.

When we received our first application for the Next Experience, our ministry for 11th & 12th grade students, I didn't expect what I would read. The words jumped off the page with desperation and deep need. Her thoughts of suicide were expressed candidly. We did all the necessary things that you do in a situation like that and as we navigated the challenging waters, it led her right into this ministry we began. Today she is a thriving young woman, mindful and honest of all God has done in her life.

The first few months as she would come to my home and engage the other girls, everything about her – her smile, her words, her heart – everything was on guard. She did not let you in nor did she open up. We had tried everything we knew until one night, after sharing a meal at a Mexican restaurant, she and one of the other teens saw a hot dog in the middle of the parking lot. Yes, you read that right, a hot dog. And for some reason it got them tickled. I mean slap-silly. That laughter busted a dam inside of her. From that moment on she was engaged, open, and present.

By the time her Senior year rolled around and she became the mentor to a rising Junior, she was often the first one to laugh, ask a question during our study time, or offer to pray. The transformation in her took my breath away. At our very first fundraiser who gave their testimony? She did...

When I was reading Jim Collins' book, *Great By Choice*, the sequel of *Good to Great*, a few years before the launch of The Next Experience, I read a statement that challenged me. He said we should always be reaching the generation coming after us. It made me stop and consider if I was I fulfilling this commission not only in my personal life but if we were doing it as a ministry as well. It didn't interest me. At all. At that time, all of my bonus-kids were teenagers and the thought of more made me want to break out in hives. But, I began perusing some statistics and found that according to Rainer Research, 70% of youth that attend church today that are active in their youth group, by the age of 22, will have left the church; Barna Research estimates that 80% of those raised in the church will be disengaged by the age of 29. Those were realities I could not ignore. Thus, the Next Experience began.

Truth be told, this is a calling and a responsibility to each of us. Scripture says in Psalm 78, starting in verse one, *"Oh, my people listen to my instructions. Open your ears to what I'm saying for I will speak to you in a parable. I'll teach you hidden lessons from our past, stories we have heard and known, stories our ancestors handed down to us. We will not hide these truths from our children. We will tell the next generation about the glorious deeds of the Lord. About His power and His mighty wonders."*[40] If you and I are in relationship with Jesus Christ, boy, we've got a lot of stories that we can share with our children, with the kids in our neighborhood, with the kids that carpool in our car, with the youth group at church, or with the community we build for ourselves.

Friend, you have no idea the impact your life and your stories and what God has done for you can do to the generation coming behind you.
Are teenagers scary?
Yes! Often.
Are they fascinating?
They are a test group in the unbelievable.
Are they a mine worth mining?
They are a wealth of gold.
Our children are facing things you and I would have never dreamed of facing and they desperately need the truths that we know. They are attending schools from elementary to universities that have demonic agendas to strip them of all the belief of Christ they possess. This is not happenstance, this is intentional agenda. We have to be just as vigilant and intentional with the hearts of our youth. You may be in a season where you're doing your best to feed into your own little ones; that is the greatest job. You may feel like your mission field right now is your home. That's okay, too -- it is our greatest mission field. But some of you may simply have time to serve, to mentor, to give to a young person or a pack of them! They need you. Because you have deep riches and a deep well of which to offer this next generation. Without a Godly foundation of for our future what will the righteous do?

Who would you consider the next generation behind you? How is their life different from what yours was?

_____

_____

_____

_____

_____

40 Psalm 78:1-4 (NLT)

149

Tuesday

Read **Judges 2:6-10**. What are ways we can make sure the next generation remembers the works of the Lord?

_____

_____

_____

Thinking about how you defined the next generation after you yesterday, who are some specific people in that age group that you have contact with?

_____

_____

_____

How could you increase your impact in their lives?

_____

_____

_____

What are ways you could impact the children in your own home in a deeper way?
Kids in your neighborhood or your children's peer group?
The younger generation at work?
Young people or college age people at your church?
Younger moms?
Younger fathers?
Young entrepreneurs?

_____

_____

_____

_____

We all have people we can influence -- and we have so many tools with which to use. By the time you read this, Snapchat may be the oldest thing ever. But for now, it is a way I can communicate and stay relevant with each one of my bonus kids as well as my nieces and nephews. It is so worth finding ways that speak the language of the generation behind us.

Wednesday

1 & 2 Timothy are letters written to Timothy from Paul.

Take some time today to overview both of these letters. What is Paul passing onto Timothy?

_____
_____
_____
_____
_____

What are some specific things, giftings, or resources you have that need to be passed on to others?

_____
_____
_____
_____

Thursday

Read **1 Samuel 3:1-10**. What did Eli teach Samuel in this moment?

_____
_____
_____

How can you and I teach the next generation to hear the voice of the Lord?

_____
_____
_____

Friday

What do you feel might be obstacles for you when it comes to pouring into the next generation? Lack of time or opportunities? Fear?

_____

_____

_____

_____

Read **Acts 16:1-3**. Where did Paul meet Timothy?

_____

_____

Don't feel like you have to "make" something happen in this area. I have always served where I was planted. Yes, we created the Next Experience, but that was in regards to a ministry. The discipleship group that I lead one Saturday a month is simply made up of women who have come into my life who simply asked to be mentored through the years. I led Sunday School because I go to church. Years ago, I taught girls in my neighborhood because that's where I was. I didn't feel like I had to go create some big thing. I just served where I was planted.

Paul found Timothy just doing what Timothy was called to do — and that's where you'll find opportunities to reach those coming up behind you.

Saturday Surrender

"But be doers of the word, and not hearers only, deceiving yourselves."
James 1:22 (ESV)

As followers of Jesus, we can't pick and choose which parts of the Bible we want to believe and obey. It's all or nothing. And we are given a commission to teach, to disciple, the generations after us.

You reflected yesterday on obstacles that might be in the way of fulfilling that commission. I encourage you today to dig into what those things are and why they're there. Have you let your obstacles become excuses? Be honest with yourself and with the Lord.

Sunday Sabbath

"As each has received a gift, use it to serve one another, as good stewards of God's varied grace:"
1 Peter 4:10 (ESV)

Songs for Your Sabbath
Cynthia Clawson, Gaither Videos, *Tell Me the Story of Jesus*
4Him, *Future Generations*

Seeing and seizing opportunities we are given to pour into the next generation requires a certain level of awareness that comes with being fully present where we are. How easy it is to become preoccupied with our stuff, our struggles, our needs and our plans to the point that we fail to see sweet moments to love on, to teach, and to pour into a younger heart that may need wisdom and insight that we can offer.

So my prayer for you this Sabbath, as you settle into your quiet place, is that you would ask the Lord to help you to stay your mind, to remove the distraction of the ever-growing to-do list, and to just be... be aware of the details... be attentive to those around you... to be in the moment...

Lord, the responsibility of training up the next generation is a huge task that You have trusted me with in my sphere of influence. Thank You for all You have taught and are teaching me so that I can pour into those hearts You have entrusted me with. Father, let me see clearly the opportunities to love, encourage, and challenge the next generation. Remove from me the fear of making something happen. But instead, may I be sensitive to my environment and the opportunities that exist right where I'm planted. May I move in step with You and may You use the truth inside of me to make sure this generation does not fall away from the truth that is You.

Week 21

The Reward of Honor

Monday

Read: Matthew 10:40-42, 1 Corinthians 6:19-20

Good Monday morning.

When my Pastor steps onto the platform on a Sunday morning and invites us into one of his stories he then follows that with an opening of His Bible to read the passage for his sermon. When he finishes he says, "This is God's word, for God's people. Hear it and live." He reminds us that this moment is about something bigger than him. That for the next few moments he is going to share with us what has been shared with him in the private of his study, in the intimacy of his prayer time, in the stillness of his most quite moments. He is going to speak to us from the heart of our heavenly Father. In those moments on a Sunday morning he is God's representative to our hearts. Let me say it another way, he is God's mouthpiece. God's prophet. God's righteous man. And how our hearts receive him matters. And it matters because we are told that in the way we receive our Pastor when he delivers God word, is in essence how we are receiving Jesus.

I don't always remember the holiness, privilege, or responsibility in this truth. You know what Sunday mornings are like. For whatever reason the preparation for church reveals our need for it greater than anything else. For some we've herded kiddos out the door as if we were preparing to run with the bulls in Barcelona. We've endured arguments, lost shoes, forgotten keys, or spilled coffee. By the time we actually find a parking place the first verse and chorus of *Oh Happy Day* have already been sung and we're grateful we didn't have to fake it. We're frazzled, out of breath and needing a few moments of time out ourselves. We are the Joneses. Don't try to keep up with us, or you'll be late everywhere you go.

But as we lean our heart into worship, after we move our heart towards prayer, we settle in for the sermon, and it is in this moment that we are not always aware of the responsibility to honor the servant before us. Honor him with our attention. Honor him with our timeliness. Honor him with our listening and obedient heart. Not because it is Pastor Mike, but because Jesus uses Pastor Mike. He appointed him to lead us and feed us. And in being moved by the beauty of Jesus, I am moved to honor my pastor and his sacrifice of not just a week of preparation, but a lifestyle of preparation.

That is what prophets and righteous men do, they live entire lives that honor God. Not moments. But real heart sacrifices. And in our love for the sacrifice Jesus made for us, we honor theirs.

The scripture then goes a step farther. "Whoever gives one of these little ones a cup of cold water… " So now we move from pulpit to pew. From principle to preschooler. This, for me, makes the message very clear. It is not about what someone can do for me, but it is about what Jesus already did. We give because we have received the greatest Gift. We give honor to teachers and policemen, our president or our pastor, the widow and the orphan, the employee and the employer, the friend and stranger, because we know the Giver of all life. Honor isn't about what we can get. In fact, teach a class of preschoolers and it won't take you long to realize this principle. Or better yet, a class of teenagers… but God sees. He sees the honor we give. As we honor them with our speech. Honor them with our obedience to what is being taught. Honor them with wages that respect their lifestyles of righteousness and self-less offering. Honor them blessing them in any way the Lord may lead all because God has blessed us in ways we never deserved.

❧

Why do you think honor matters to God?

_____

_____

The first time honor is ever mentioned it is found in **Exodus 20:12 (Read). Ephesians 6:2,3.** What does it say will be your reward for doing this? This is the only commandment with a promise.

_____

_____

What does honoring your father and mother look like to you? How can you still be honoring even if they don't honor you or even with healthy boundaries?

_____

_____

_____

_____

Read **Hebrews 13:4**.

155

Why is honoring our spouse and our marriage covenant so important? What are ways we dishonor it? What is lost with dishonor?

_____

_____

_____

_____

_____

Tuesday

Read **Colossians 4:1.**

If you are an employer or have people below you how do you treat them? Why does being an honoring employer matter? How does your Heavenly Master treat you?

_____

_____

_____

_____

_____

Read **Colossians 3:22-25.**

How do you honor your employer with your work? How should your work be done? How can you do this even in an environment where you aren't valued as an employee?

_____

_____

Read **Proverbs 3:9-10, Psalm 50:10.**

How do you honor God with your resources? What does it say about our heart when we don't? What is the gift when we do?

_____

_____

_____

Wednesday

Read **Romans 13:1-7.**

Governing authorities are a gift to a nation. Just imagine what a world would be like without them. How do you honor those in authority in government? Police Officers, IRS, etc. What has been your attitude toward governing authorities? How is that a reflection of your heart?

_____

_____

_____

_____

What happens when governing authorities are not honored? How would that affect daily life?

_____

_____

_____

_____

Read **2 Timothy 2:1-2.**

Why is honoring the offices of Kings and World Leaders important? How can we do this even if we don't agree with the way they govern? How does it affect the world and even our own lives when we do what God asks us to do in this passage?

_____

_____

_____

_____

_____

_____

_____

_____

Thursday

꧁

Read **1 Timothy 5:17, Hebrews 3:17, 1 Corinthians 9:11**.

Why does God want those who deliver the message of His Gospel honored?

_____

_____

How is the occupation of Minister of the Gospel different from other occupations?

_____

_____

What are some specific ways you could honor your pastor or a ministry leader this week?

_____

_____

_____

Friday

꧁

Read **Revelation 5:13**.

Why is God worthy of honor?

_____

Read **Romans 12:1, 1 Corinthians 6:19**.

How is the way you live your life an opportunity to honor God? What are ways you would live that would be dishonoring?

_____

_____

_____

Read **John 12:26**. What does this passage say to your heart?

_____

_____

Saturday Surrender

**Whoever pursues righteousness and love
finds life, prosperity and honor.
Proverbs 21:21 (NIV)**

If honor is found in righteousness that means it is ultimately found in surrender. Often times honoring can only be done when we surrender our pride, our way, our get even attitudes, or even our prejudices and past hurts. Honor cannot exist with clenched fists. It can only live and thrive and dwell in open hands. And only when our hands are open can God get honor back to us.

Maybe you need to surrender the past hurts of your parents or the pain in your marriage.

Maybe you need to surrender how you wish your church or your office should run.

Maybe you need to surrender your resources knowing they have simply been given to you to steward.

Maybe you need to surrender how you wish government ran and begin to pray that it would run according to God's design and purpose. The same God who sets up kings and tears down kings. Ultimately leaders rule at His divine placement often through the prayers of God's people.

Sunday Sabbath

**"For the LORD God is a sun and shield;
the LORD bestows favor and honor.
No good thing does He withhold
from those who walk uprightly."
Psalm 84:11**

Songs for Your Sabbath
Elevation Worship, _For the Honor_
Hillsong Worship, _I Give you my Heart_

John Eldredge wrote a book called *Free to Live, The Utter Relief of Holiness*. Holiness is rest. Honor is holy. So in honor we find rest for our souls. When we live lives of dishonor our hearts stay bristled and in motion. But when we honor, we can be at peace regardless of how the other person may move or act in our lives. What a relief holiness is… it isn't a punishment. It is freedom.

Lord, thank You for all the countless ways you have honored me. The mere fact that you gave me life because you desired me is honor of the highest kind. I am humbled by it, even though there are times I have failed to offer it in return. I repent of that today, Father. Thank you for this reminder that honor matters. That without it in my own life, it prevents you from being able to get it to me. You can't get anything into clenched fists. Not because You don't want to. But because we aren't allowing you to. Help me honor even those who don't deserve honor in my life. I didn't deserve it in yours and yet you gave it to me through Jesus. May I live this life unto You and You alone. Thank you for the privilege and freedom to live an honoring life.

Week 22

Finding God in the Desert

Monday

Read: Hosea 2:14-16

Good Monday morning.

Who reads Hosea at their wedding? Hosea, the book of the man whose wife, Gomer, leaves him over and over again to run into the arms of other men. And time and time again he goes after her to bring her home. God tells him that this is an example of what He has done for His bride… Israel and, well, for us.

Ken Edwards is a ministry partner to me now and an executive coach for Philly, but he also counseled both Philly and I after our divorces. He didn't introduce us, but walked with us through those painful seasons individually, then counseled us prior to marriage and we were honored to have him officiate our wedding. In the brokenness that is our story, it seemed a gift that he read this passage.

Hosea 2:14-15 (NLT) says, *"But then I will win her back once again. I will lead her into the desert and speak tenderly to her there. I will return her vineyards to her and transform the valley of trouble into a gateway of hope. She will give herself to me there as she did long ago when she was young, when I freed her from her captivity in Egypt…"* He's talking about His children in Israel but I want you to hear this for your own story. "'When that day comes,' says the Lord, 'you will call me 'my husband' instead of 'my master.'"[41]

Sometimes God will lead us and allow us at times to go into the desert seasons of life. He does it because it is in those moments when our hearts are often most desperate to hear Him. When life around us is at its most barren, it leaves us with the unavoidable question: Are we going to press in or give up? Yet, it is in this place most barren where the kindness of God is so real, "there I'll

---

[41] Hosea 2:16 (NLT)

speak tenderly to her."[42] Isn't that beautiful? He doesn't berate us. He doesn't scold us. He doesn't press into the wound. No, He speaks in that tender way that only our heavenly Father can do. I can honestly say, I have never in a moment of pain or in a desert place in my life ever had God speak anything but kindness to me. He may speak words of correction, but even His correction is given encompassed by His mercy and wrapped in His kindness. His goal in those desert places is to push us so He can then woo us.

Inside the desert, God speaks tenderly to us and, then, He transforms our valley of trouble into a gateway of hope.[43] God has done this in Philly's story and in mine, too. And in those darkest of the dark seasons He has given us a hope that He is doing something holy in them. It also fundamentally changed the way we saw Him and felt about Him. Our desert places moved Him from master to husband.

Friend, if you're in a desert season, I shared all of that to say this to you: God desires to speak kindly to you. He desires to transform your valley of trouble into a gateway of hope. Listen for His voice. Know that you can trust Him and realize that what you're desperate for in that desert place is not another relationship, it's not another trip to the mall, it's not another piece of chocolate cake, it's not even another conversation with a friend to relieve your trouble. What you are so desperate for is the Living Water who says if you drink of Me you will never thirst again. He takes our trouble and He transforms it; where we had just been servants, we are now brides. "I led her into the desert and I spoke tenderly to her there"... My prayer is that you hear the tender words of your loving Father to your heart this week... because, oh, how as a bride He loves you...

When is the last time you found yourself in a desert place? Are you in one currently? What did/does it look like?

_____

_____

_____

Deserts hold within them the ability to have us blaming God and getting angry, or running to God. In your last desert moment, if you ran to Him what did you hear Him speak? If you blamed Him what do you believe He wanted to speak?

_____

_____

_____

_____

---

[42] Hosea 2:14 (NLT)
[43] Hosea 2:15 (NLT)

Tuesday

Read **Exodus 14:13-31**.

What has God just done for the Israelites in this passage of scripture?

_____

_____

What are some moments in your life when God has parted waters – when it seemed like there was no hope for freedom, for escape, and He performed the miraculous?

_____

_____

_____

Take some time to let that "Red Sea experience" settle in your heart and mind today.

Wednesday

Let's continue reading in the Israelites' story…

Read Exodus 15:23-25 (AMP). What did the people do?

_____

_____

What did Moses do?

_____

_____

We just read yesterday that these people had just seen an extravagant miracle done with water, no less. Why do you think they so quickly moved towards grumbling and complaining? How quickly from your last red sea parting experience to your desert experience were you able to forget the parted red sea?

_____

_____

_____

Why do you believe the people and Moses had different responses to the same conditions?

_____

_____

Whose response created impact?

_____

How could your response be affecting your desert experience?

_____

_____

_____

Thursday

David spent quite some time in the literal desert when he was on the run from King Saul.

Read Psalm 63:1-8, which he wrote during that season. What are some of the verbs he uses to describe his response to God even in the desert?

_____

_____

_____

_____

Think back to yesterday and the responses of the Israelites to being in the desert.
How does your response compare? Do you relate more to the Israelites or to David?

_____

_____

_____

Friday

Read **Jeremiah 17:5-6**.

What type of person is being described here?

_____

_____

Write down all the truths found in this passage.

_____

_____

_____

_____

_____

Where does this person dwell?

_____

_____

Now read **Jeremiah 17:7-8**. What type of person is being described here?

_____

_____

Write down all the truths found in this passage.

_____

_____

_____

_____

_____

What is the effect on this person's life, even in the desert and drought?

_____

_____

_____

Saturday Surrender

"Blessed is the man
who walks not in the counsel of the wicked,
nor stands in the way of sinners,
nor sits in the seat of scoffers;
but his delight is in the law of the LORD,
and on His law he meditates day and night.
He is like a tree
planted by streams of water
that yields its fruit in its season,
and its leaf does not wither.
In all that he does, he prospers."
Psalm 1:1-3 (ESV)

What are some things that need to start today to move you from dwelling in parched places to one who lives by the stream, to make you a bride instead of a slave?

Could it be God allowed the desert place so you'd see the new places of depth your roots need to travel? Ask Him to give you wisdom on how to press into Him in a greater way in this season to make that happen.

As He increases in our lives, we decrease. He loves us enough to bring us to desert places so He can speak lovingly to us. Even His correction is loving because it is protection from more difficult things.

Maybe you need to spend more time with Him, making it a priority in your life. Ask Him to increase your hunger for this and your hunger for His word.

Maybe you need to become a member of a body of believers. We were not created for isolation. The enemy thrives in isolation. We were created for community.

Maybe you need to surrender something you're holding onto. Ask Him what it is, He loves you enough to reveal it.

Sunday Sabbath

"For I will pour water on the thirsty land, and streams on the dry ground; I will pour my Spirit upon your offspring, and my blessing on your descendants."
Isaiah 44:3 (ESV)

Songs for Your Sabbath
Nicole C. Mullen & Kathie Lee Gifford, *The God Who Sees*
Hillsong United, *Desert Song*

Friend, one of the beautiful things about seasons is that, by definition, they change. So even in the seemingly perpetual desert, there is always hope for the next season. Hold onto that promise today. Rest in that truth this Sabbath. Nestle into your quiet place and let your mind settle on the free-flowing love of God that satisfies and brings to life even the most parched places of your soul… you may feel like you're wandering in the desert but you're being led to a place of deeper relationship with your heavenly Father.

Lord, thank You for seasons of dry desert places. It's in those times that Your power is on full display and I'm more aware of my need for and dependence on You. Continue to remove my sinful nature out of me and replace it with more of Your qualities; I want to be a reflection of You to everyone I meet. I trust that You have a good and perfect plan for leading me into the desert and am even more grateful for the thirst-quenching power of Your Word and Your Spirit because of it. Father, where desperation is lacking, make me desperate.
Where thirst is needed, make me thirsty.
Where surrender is needed, I surrender.
May You become my husband in every way.
Thank you for how kindly You have spoken. May I remember Your words when I am in the desert and when the desert season is over, in Your name I pray.

Week 23

Peculiar Is a Good Thing

Monday

Read: 1 Peter 2:9-10

Good Monday morning.

A couple years ago, I was standing in the kitchen and Philly was on the other side of the counter. I was sharing something with him, something I felt the Lord had been speaking to me, when I stopped mid-stream and asked, "Babe, do you think I'm weird?" He paused… too long. I fidgeted. Eventually he said, "I wouldn't say you're weird... I'd say you're extreme." Knowing he had been deeply wounded by spiritual jargon through the years, and my perpetual talk about Jesus, there were times I wondered what I sounded like on his ears. But these words, that I was "extreme," I actually appreciated. Because I'd just read in the MSG translation of 2 Corinthians 5:13-14 *"If I acted crazy, I did it for God. If I acted overly serious, I did it for you. God's love has moved me to extremes. His love has the first and last word over everything I do."* When I read that scripture the first time, it freed me from what other people think about me; it is now one of my favorites because it so identifies my heart. It's why I share so often with you about the detailed love of God – because it is that very love that moves us to become people of extremes. This God of our details. This God who gave us Jesus. This God who knows us and sees us and cares about us. It is this God and His unrelenting love that will move a heart who sees and believes to extremes.

1 Peter 2:9-10 (MSG) says this about us, *"But you were the ones chosen by God. Chosen for the high calling of priestly work, chosen to be a holy people, God's instruments to do His work and speak out for Him to tell others of the night and day difference He made for you. From nothing to something, from rejected to accepted."* The translation that many of us are familiar with says, "You're a holy priesthood, a royal nation, a peculiar people." As a child of God this is what He has called us to be. Why? So that we can be instruments of His Word and speak out for Him, "to tell others of the night and day difference" He's made in our lives.

When we go into the strip clubs with our ministry, Love Nashville, and we walk in those dark, dark places -- the darkest places that our city holds -- and we encounter the brokenness of their lives, they need something different than their own story. They need something different than the husband who encouraged them to work there. They need something different than the money they are so desperate for because they believe that's the answer to their questions. The men who sit in that place need something different than the lie that this is what is going to finally make them feel like a man, that this is going to answer the question of their hearts, *Am I man enough?* These people need to know their value. They need to know that they were bought with a price so high that it affords them, if they are willing to receive it, the opportunity to trade the pit for the palace!

This world also needs people that are peculiar. It needs people who are peculiar enough that they would leave their families for an evening to walk into the very pit of hell and declare Jesus is real and loves them with His whole heart. This world needs people peculiar enough to talk differently, to believe with unquenchable faith, and to live the abundant life they were created for, free of sin and shame and addictions and strongholds that hold us captive to lies.

This culture needs hearts and lives that are moved to be extreme, to be radical proclaimers of the good news of Jesus Christ. You and I won't be able to help but become extreme when we truly grasp the extreme lengths Christ went to reach us. You and I will become extreme when we sit in the reality of the depths of the darkness that we were slaves to and the freedom we now experience. When you know a God whose love has the first word over your story and the last word over your story, then you are crazy enough to believe Him and to announce to others that they can, too. You want to walk different. Be different. Love different. Speak different. Live different.

Recently at the dinner table we were going around telling each other what their most used word was. My youngest bonus daughter looked at me and shouted out, "Yours is Jesus!" We all immediately busted out laughing because it was so true. But to be honest, I have to say, of all the things she knows about me I'm so grateful that she knows this.

If I acted crazy I did it for God. If I acted overly serious I did it for you. God's love has moved me to extremes... let's be peculiar. We live in a world that's desperate for peculiar people.

What are the areas in your life where you live in extreme ways? Extreme habits? Extreme words? Extreme thoughts?

_____

_____

_____

If you have trouble answering that, think of the last three friends you hung out with -- what did you talk about? Think of the last three websites you visited, what were they? Think of the last three things you spent money on, what were they?

_____

_____

_____

169

Tuesday

Read **Deuteronomy 7:6**. Who is being talked about here?

_____

God made the nation Israel. It is the only nation of all nations that He Himself made.

He started it with Abraham when He made a covenant with Abraham and said that his descendants would be more than the sands of the seas and more than the stars in the sky. He solidified it when he changed Abraham's grandson's name from Jacob to Israel. Jacob would then go on to have 12 sons that would become the 12 tribes that would make up the Israel we know today.

These people are God's chosen nation.

However, they have rejected Him even to this day. So, God allowed the message of Jesus to be taken to the Gentiles. Gentiles are any of us who were not born Jews. And because of their rejection we have been able to receive the good news that is Jesus!

Read **Ephesians 1:4-6**. What does this passage tell you about God choosing you?

_____

_____

_____

Wednesday

Look up online a few commentaries and read their notes on **1 Peter 2:9**. Bible Study Tools online has multiple commentaries you can reference or you can read from the commentary notes in a Study Bible itself.

Write down your understanding from these commentaries of what a "chosen generation," "holy priesthood," "royal nation," and a "peculiar people" are according to this passage.

_____

_____

_____

How does your heart respond to that idea? Do you feel like a part of what's being described or do you feel like maybe it's something you're not included in?

_____

_____

_____

As a child of God and joint heir to the throne with Jesus, that is your identity! Ask the Lord for increased awareness of and confidence in that truth if it's something you may be struggling to really see yourself as a part of.

Thursday

❦

Look up the definition of the word "peculiar" and write it below.

_____

_____

_____

Why do you think people see Christians as peculiar?

_____

_____

_____

Read **2 Timothy 3:1-9**. This is a litany of what the world will look like in the last days which I do believe we are living in. How do you look and live differently from the world? How do you live like the world?

_____

_____

_____

Why do you think it is important for the world's sake that we live as peculiar people?

_____

_____

_____

_____

Spend some time in quiet prayer this morning and ask the Lord to reveal to you one or two ways that He is asking you to live peculiarly in this season. What did you hear?

_____

_____

_____

_____

Friday

What are some things that might keep us from living as peculiar people?

_____

_____

_____

Read **Matthew 5:10-12**. What are times you have felt any of those things (persecution, being mocked, lied about, etc.) in your own life?

_____

_____

_____

_____

What are ways believers are persecuted now?

_____

_____

_____

How does this passage in Matthew 10 encourage us even in the midst of persecution? What do we have to look forward to?

_____

_____

_____

_____

Saturday Surrender

"So humble yourselves under the mighty power of God, and at the right time He will lift you up in honor. Give all your worries and cares to God, for He cares about you.
Stay alert! Watch out for your great enemy, the devil. He prowls around like a roaring lion, looking for someone to devour. Stand firm against him, and be strong in your faith. Remember that your family of believers all over the world is going through the same kind of suffering you are.
In His kindness God called you to share in His eternal glory by means of Christ Jesus. So after you have suffered a little while, He will restore, support, and strengthen you, and He will place you on a firm foundation."
1 Peter 5:6-10 (NLT)

The Greek roots of the word "enthusiasm" are *en* which means "in" and *theos* meaning "God." So that tells me that the only way to be truly enthusiastic, passionate, *extreme*, is to be *in God*.

Who wouldn't want to have a true enthusiasm about life and all the goodness God offers?

I encourage you today, friend, to do a sincere heart check regarding your level of enthusiasm towards things of God – scripture reading, prayer, corporate worship and things that are holy in nature… and if the idea of those things doesn't stir up excitement in your heart, get curious with Him about what might be hindering you, what you might need to surrender in order to move your heart to a place of enthusiasm for all things of God.

Sunday Sabbath

"Finally, all of you should be of one mind. Sympathize with each other. Love each other as brothers and sisters. Be tenderhearted, and keep a humble attitude."
1 Peter 3:8 (NLT)

Songs for Your Sabbath
Selah, *All of Me*
Phillips, Craig & Dean, *Crucified with Christ*

As followers of Jesus Christ, with the Holy Spirit dwelling in us, we are called to live by a different standard than the culture in which we live.

As you're in your quiet place this Sabbath, thank the Lord for His holy, set apart, standard of living and for His invitation to be peculiar, to be different…

Lord, You have taken me from a place of death and brought me to a place of life; from darkness to the light; from despair and bondage to hope and freedom. And for that I am so very grateful. May my heart's response to Your love for me always be one of extreme enthusiasm and joy. Let me walk boldly in my calling to be part of Your peculiar people so that Your kingdom would be made known here on Earth.

Week 24

When God Pricks Our Pride

Monday

Read: 2 Kings 5:3-15

Good Monday morning.

Recently, I was reading a story in the book of 2 Kings about a man named Naaman, you might know it. I've read it many times, but during this particular reading the Lord revealed a different aspect of the story and tugged at my own heart in a personal way regarding it. It was in the area of pride. I felt the Lord ask me, "Where has pride caused you to miss something that I want to do for you?"

Naaman was the leader of the armies of the king of Judah. He also had leprosy. Leprosy during this time caused one to be completely removed from their home and even their city; then they were sequestered outside of the city walls and quarantined from the rest of society. So, obviously, Naaman's condition had just recently developed or it was a mild case because he was living and working inside of the kingdom. In his household was a slave girl who had deep compassion for him and said in 2 Kings 5:3 (NIV), *"If only my master would see the prophet who is in Samaria! He would cure him of his leprosy."* So Naaman, upon this most precious request of his slave girl, asks permission of the king to go to the prophet, Elisha, and permission is granted.

Yet Naaman was angry when the prophet didn't come out to see him. He was also angry that the prophet didn't do it the way he wanted him to. Oh, the arrogance of a man in a desperate place. It was this same pride and offended spirit that almost caused him to miss his healing. You would think his desperation would cause him to run to the Jordan. It makes me curious about just how desperate he truly was.

As I read the story, it caused me to ask myself, and I challenge you to ask yourself as well, is there an area in my life that needs to be healed? A relationship? My mind? My body? My emotions? Yet, healing isn't happening. So why? Could it be that what God desires of me is something I don't want to do, like forgive, or surrender, or use self-control? Could it be He is inviting me to healing via a route I do not want to take, thus the very thing I need is the thing that I lack?

Wow! How many times have I done this? Lived this way? Walked around in my pompous anger while healing was extended? Friends, I encourage you today, this week, to be willing to let go of whatever you need to let go of; to forgive if you need to forgive; to move if you need to move; to act in obedience if you need to act in obedience, knowing that He is inviting you into healing. Healing may not come the way you think, look the way you hope, or happen in the timeframe you desire. But what I can promise you is if He's asking you to do something, He's going to honor your obedience in it. And, oh, the healing that will bring!

Go wash, Naaman, seven times in the Jordan River and you'll be healed...

May we not let our pride cause us to miss what God is inviting us to. So, go wash, friend, in whatever river He said, do whatever He asked. I know I am. I'm paying attention to that command. Lord, I will do whatever You ask me to do for healing to occur.

What areas in your life might pride be a hindrance? Your finances? Your relationship with your spouse, another family member, or a friend? Your physical body?

_____

_____

_____

Tuesday

Read **Isaiah 14:12-17**. Who is this passage talking about?

_____

What was his sin that had him cast down from heaven?

_____

Satan's pride got in the way of his fulfillment of his purpose.

What would you say is the opposite of pride?

_____

What does **Proverbs 11:2** say its opposite is?

_____

And what comes with humility, according to that verse?

_____

What are the specific areas in your life you need wisdom right now?

_____
_____
_____

Wednesday

꧁꧂

Read **Proverbs 21:24**. What is the name of one who acts with arrogant pride?

_____

Look up the word _scoffer_ and write its definition below.

_____
_____

What areas in your life in this season do you feel you are moving in pride? If you do not readily know, ask the Lord to reveal them to you and sit quietly in His presence. Write down what you hear. If you do not hear anything immediately, He will speak so you can come back and write it later.

_____
_____

What do you feel your pride may be causing you to miss in this season?

_____
_____
_____

Thursday

꧞

Read **James 4:1-10**. Why do we not receive according to this passage?

_____

_____

Why does God call them adulterous?

_____

_____

What are the two things we must first do before the enemy flees?

_____

Have you ever considered that the word "submit" is first in this passage of scripture? Where might you need to submit to God?

_____

_____

_____

Why does God oppose the proud?

_____

_____

How may you need to draw near to God in this season? How may you need to humble yourself in this season?

_____

_____

_____

Friday

✺

Read **Genesis 3:1-7**. What does Satan appeal to in the heart of Eve? What does it lead to?

_____

_____

_____

Read **Proverbs 16:18**. How does this confirm Genesis 3?

_____

_____

_____

Saturday Surrender

✺

"You must have the same attitude that Christ Jesus had.
Though He was God,
He did not think of equality with God
as something to cling to.
Instead, He gave up His divine privileges;
He took the humble position of a slave
and was born as a human being.
When He appeared in human form,
He humbled himself in obedience to God
and died a criminal's death on a cross.
Therefore, God elevated Him to the place of highest honor
and gave Him the name above all other names,
that at the name of Jesus every knee should bow,
in heaven and on earth and under the earth,
and every tongue declare that Jesus Christ is Lord,
to the glory of God the Father.
Philippians 2:5-11 (NLT)

I always say that, as the Son of God, if Jesus did something, how much more, then, do we need to do it? Jesus set the ultimate example for humility; His last act before the cross was washing the feet of His disciples. Then, He chose obedience to His Father even though He knew how great the cost would be. Jesus put aside His own personal desires and placed our wellbeing ahead of His own in the greatest act of humility by surrendering to death for you and me.

Ask God today if there is anything in you that you need to lay aside in order to humble yourself and place someone else's needs above your own.

Maybe you even already know what needs to be done.

Know that your trust and obedience in that act will be honored!

Sunday Sabbath

**"The arrogant cannot stand
in your presence.
You hate all who do wrong…"
Psalm 5:5 (NIV)**

Songs for Your Sabbath
Steffany Frizzell Gretzinger, *Letting Go*
Chris Tomlin, *We Fall Down*

You've done a lot of digging and surrendering this past week, friend. As you're in your quiet place this Sabbath, invite the Lord to reveal anything else to you that He may want to speak into.

Get quiet.

Ask him to open your heart – you don't want to miss a single thing He has for you…

Father, I am so very grateful for Your extravagant grace even when You press into the places in my heart that can be the most uncomfortable. Father, I ask that You reveal any pattern of pride-driven decisions and as You do, purge them from me. Redirect the motives and intentions of my heart. I know You desire nothing but healing and wholeness for me and so I am willing and ready to do whatever You ask.

Week 25

What is Lost in Unforgiveness

Monday

Read: Matthew 18:21-35

Good Monday morning.

I don't know any of us who haven't had the great privilege of learning how to forgive; Jesus knew it would be such a part of our story that He pretty much told Peter not to worry about counting because forgiveness in the life of a believer must be a lifestyle.[44] Why? Because God knows much is lost in unforgiveness. He also knows the price He gave and the price Jesus paid to ensure our own. So forgiveness, to God, is ultimately a statement of you and I understanding how much we have been forgiven of. This is why it matters to Him that we resist the desire to count… after all, if He counted, we'd be in a mess of trouble.

Yet some still choose not to forgive. One of the most sobering stories in scripture in regards to holding on to unforgiveness is found in 2 Samuel 6. Michal, the daughter of King Saul, was given in marriage to David. Saul hated David. In fact, the primary reason he agreed to let Michal marry David was because Saul wanted to use Michal as a way to trap David. What Saul never counted on… how much Michal loved David and how much David loved her. So, in one of Saul's jealous fits of rage, he shipped Michal off to another man in order to hurt David and there she lived for ten years with another man. Finally, after Saul's death, David got her back.

But, oh, all the pain Michal's story held… the father who should have protected her used her like a pawn and she was ripped from the arms of the man that she loved. Then she was sent to live with another man and remained there for ten years before David got her back. However, we can tell how deeply this other man loved her because of his reaction when she is taken. You wonder

---

44 Matthew 18:22

if or when her voice ever mattered. Granted, this would make for a great novel. But it wasn't a novel. It was her heartbreaking story.

However, once she was returned to David, she did not release the pain. Instead, she had become bitter and hard and angry. This was all revealed one day as she was looking out the window watching as David came up a procession in the streets. He was bringing the Ark of the Covenant, the place where the presence of God dwelt during this time, back into Jerusalem. The city God originally intended it to be. Bringing the ark back to Jerusalem was David's greatest heart's desire. Something you would think, as his wife, she would know. The joy of this moment had him dancing and worshiping and praising the Lord in front of the Ark its entire journey through the streets of the city, all of which she observed from her upstairs window. When the procession was done, he went upstairs to see Michal, I'm sure to celebrate this moment with her, the woman that he loves. Unfortunately, she didn't share one iota of his joy. Instead, she informed him in a bitter tone of the fool he had made of himself out there, dancing around. But David, this man after God's own heart, would not be mocked even by his wife in regards to his love for the Lord and His presence. So he responded saying, basically, "If you think that's something, you haven't seen anything." Scripture says that from that moment on in her life she was barren. She produced nothing. No seed, no life, came from her womb.

Who of us with any compassion couldn't look at her situation and understand why she would be angry. Shouldn't she be?
Isn't she a victim?
Of course she is.
Who wouldn't be angry?
No normal person, that's for sure.
Her life was so unfair!
It was inconceivably unfair…

Her hurt is beyond justifiable. But in each of our stories, no matter what we've been through, there comes a moment where we have to make the decision that we are no longer going to let the enemy steal through a door of unforgiveness we leave open. Because walking in unforgiveness, choosing to hold onto our offense, ultimately leads to bitterness. The actual Hebrew word for bitterness means *rebellion*. So that means we are making a choice to rebel against what God is inviting us into and asking us to do; we're rebelling against the heart of our Father.

He tells us over and over that we are called to forgive. In fact, when the disciples asked Him, "Lord, how are we to pray?" Matthew 6:12 says, *"Forgive us our debts as we forgive our debtors."* The Amplified Bible says, "Letting go of both the wrong and the resentment." So it means we're not just saying "I forgive you," it means we're even letting go of the resentment that we feel.

Now, I want to tell you something: this kind of forgiveness cannot come separate of a relationship with Jesus Christ. We just don't have it in us. We're not capable of this kind of forgiveness separate of receiving Jesus into our hearts and making Him Lord of our lives – that's the only way this kind of forgiveness can come. But, friends, we cannot afford to live in bitterness. Why? Because it is a destroyer. It destroys families. It destroys relationships. It destroys marriages. It destroys futures. It destroys vision. It destroys the birthing of new things.

Both Joyce Meyer and Beth Moore, who are powerful ministers of the Gospel, were both sexually abused as young children. Joyce Meyer tells the story that she was sexually abused by her own father and Beth Moore shares that she suffered severe sexual abuse as a child. Yet both have walked in powerful forgiveness. This forgiveness allowed Joyce Meyer the privilege of not only leading her father to the Lord, but to baptize him and care for both he and her mother before they died. You want to talk about forgiveness? Now, think about the impact these two women alone have had on the body of Christ in the last few decades. Would either of them have had this kind of impact had they chosen to stay in their unforgiveness? I do not believe they would have and, oh my, what the Body of Christ would have missed.

Friends, once again, there is nothing in this life worth missing because we hold to our offense. Not only do we need to forgive, but we need to forgive quickly. If we don't, it can become a foothold for the enemy which can deepen and deepen and deepen…

God is a just God. He will right every wrong. But our greatest prayer should be, "Lord, may we all know and encounter the grace that You give that perpetually covers even a multitude of our own sin."

Do you look at your life and feel like you're just kind of living in a parched, dry land; that things are not coming to life, but instead, it feels like things are dying? Do you have relationships that are failing? Do you have business ventures that you put your hand to but they never come to fruition? Do you find that you aren't living with joy and peace? Could it be a by-product of unforgiveness? Once you list the things you are having trouble seeing coming to fruition, it is the question you should ask.

_____
_____
_____
_____
_____

Tuesday

How would you describe or define *bitterness*?

_____
_____

Anytime we choose bitterness, we are moving towards self instead of moving towards God.

Read **1 Samuel 15:23**. How does the Bible view unforgiveness?

_____

_____

_____

I've learned personally that whenever I find myself struggling to forgive, I have to remind myself of three things: first, I have to remember how much I've been forgiven; second, hurt people hurt people; and, third, I must pray for them and I must do it quickly. I say, "Lord, whatever it is that's going on in their heart and life, You know. You know what they need. Your kingdom come, Your will be done in their life. Let them see Your love for them. Remove whatever that hurt is and let them be willing to let it go so that You can move in their lives." What might you need to remember right now about your own forgiveness?

_____

_____

_____

What prayer might you need to pray for someone who has offended you?

_____

_____

_____

Wednesday

Jesus modeled and taught us how to pray in **Matthew 6:9-15** (Read in the ESV & AMP).

What does He say there about forgiveness?

_____

_____

What does that mean?

_____

_____

_____

Our forgiveness of others is not independent of God's forgiveness of us. It's our sin when we choose to harbor unforgiveness. Sit in that for a few minutes today. It may be a tough pill to swallow, but it's a truth we truly need to internalize. My friend and mentor Dr. Albert Lemmons, suggests that "our unforgiveness hinders God from getting His blessings and best to us." What a sad way that would be to live.

Read **Romans 12:19**. What does this speak to you about your Father?

_____

_____

_____

_____

Thursday

According to **Ephesians 6:12**, who is your real battle against?

_____

What energy are you wasting fighting individuals?

_____

_____

_____

I have learned, like Dave Ramsey says about debt, "Until you get angry at what debt is stealing from you then you won't do anything about it." The same is true about anything in our life that is robbing from us.

Unforgiveness is a thief. It robs relationships, joy, vision, and can make you barren. I daresay that the act that led to offense we choose to hold onto costs much less than what holding onto unforgiveness is costing. Because holding onto unforgiveness, just like it did in the life of Michal, makes our lives barren, producing nothing of value. Could anything be more heartbreaking than knowing we had the ability through a choice to stop the devourer in our own stories and still choose unforgiveness?

Oh, friend, God wants you free! Yes, you may have to forgive over and over and over. Often God will allow relationships in our lives that perpetually cause us to have to wrestle with forgiveness until we get to the place where we refuse to allow the enemy to steal anything else than what has already been stolen.

Read **John 10:10**. What does it say about Satan? What has he stolen, killed, or destroyed through unforgiveness?

_____

_____

_____

Are you angry at what has been stolen?

_____

Friday

Read **Hebrews 12:14-15**. Who does it say is being defiled?

_____

Have you ever considered that your unforgiveness could be infecting and affecting someone else? Who may be affected right now by your choice of unforgiveness?

_____

_____

_____

Read **Philippians 4:13**. How can true forgiveness occur?

_____

_____

Read **Matthew 6:14-15**. What is one of the best ways to help your heart to forgive?

_____

_____

_____

Talk about it. Don't hide it. Expose it. Invite someone you trust into that space of unforgiveness to help heal the wound that is there and move forward.

Saturday Surrender

"Let all bitterness and wrath and anger and clamor and slander be put away from you, along with all malice."
Ephesians 4:31 (ESV)

Do you remember when your mom or dad would say, "You need to get happy and get happy now?" This to me is Paul's version. It's time to put it away. Put it away now. It isn't a three-step program. It comes with each moment the offense arrives. We take it. We feel it. Then we surrender it. "Father, this is yours. I don't want it. I don't want anything else stealing from my life. Here, I'm putting it away."

So, that thing, that person, that situation, that offense you've taken to Jesus over and over and over... keep taking it, keep laying it down, keep putting it away where it belongs...

Sunday Sabbath

"Hatred stirs up strife, but love covers all offenses."
Proverbs 10:12 (ESV)

Songs for Your Sabbath
TobyMac, *Forgiveness*
Tenth Avenue North, *Losing*

The greatest response to offense: love.

In the ultimate act of love, God sacrificed His Son in order to bridge the gap between His heart and ours. He wanted to afford us the opportunity to be in right standing with Him.

Choosing love isn't our natural, go-to response when we feel wronged. We feel justified in our resentment, anger, and bitterness. But, oh, what a healing work acts of love can do...

So, today, in your quiet place, really let your heart soak in the magnitude of God's act of love toward you; let that understanding move you to a place of love so deep – even towards those who you feel justified in your bitterness against.

Remember, even God was justified in His wrath towards mankind; yet He still chose, in love, to offer a way back to His heart even though we didn't deserve it and some have even yet to ask for it.

Father, thank You for the extravagant love You so willingly lavish on me. Help me recognize the lie of the enemy that holding onto any unforgiveness is justified. I want to be an example of You to everyone I know and come in contact with. Please reveal to me any places of harbored unforgiveness, bitterness, or resentment I may still have in my heart; let me always be mindful to surrender those to You. I don't want anything else to be stolen. I don't want anything to cause me to miss Your plan for my life or cause my life to be barren. I want to be fruitful in all You've called me to do. Thank You that You came to forgive and from my forgiveness may I freely give it to others – those who will ask for it and those who never will.

Week 26

A New Look at Valentine's Day

Monday

Read: 1 Corinthians 13

Good Monday morning.

It's not hard to quickly notice when Valentine's season has arrived. Before Christmas decorations are even removed from the store the hearts are hanging everywhere! It is interesting however, how Valentine's day can conjure up quite a bit of anxiety and a reminder of wavering hopes and unfulfilled dreams for many. For a woman, she wants her own personal Hallmark movie, the chocolate, the kisses, and the happy ending. For a man, he is bombarded with unrealistic expectations and endless marketing schemes. So, just a little pressure on a holiday marketed for fairy tales while crashing into reality. But it makes me curious – does it have to be that way?

I remember one time, Philly and I were watching one of our favorite shows at the time, The Biggest Loser. I think one of the reasons we loved it so much was because it really was the Reclaiming Your Heart message. You watched these people who were shut down under the symptom of food addiction, which is really just a heart issue because any symptom is ultimately an indicator of a deeper heart issue. The trainers knew this, too, and spent the entire season helping each contestant get to the root of their individual issue, and since as in the natural goes the spiritual, they ultimately always got to a heart issue and when the contestant could have their personal revelation they would experience a breakthrough in weight loss.

One of the aspects in the show was the "temptation challenge." One particular episode fell around Valentine's Day, so the temptation was a room filled with any kind of chocolate you could imagine: chocolate kisses, chocolate mouse, chocolate cheesecake, a chocolate fountain... you get the picture. The contestants had to come into the room for about three or four minutes and try to avoid, to resist, the temptation of eating *any* of the chocolate. One of the girls who made it through the challenge without eating anything said as she was leaving the room, "I hate Valentine's Day anyway! February 15th is my favorite day of the year!"

Something about those words really stuck with me because I remember in my first marriage, Valentine's Day was often met with a lot of pain and disappointment, some warranted by my own expectations. So, my very first Valentine's Day after my divorce, I began to ask the Lord to reframe this day for me so that it was no longer identified by pain or self. What I felt like the Lord invited me to do was to get out of the "I need" or "give me" or "I expect" mentality and instead, give. He was asking me to love on and give to people whom I loved and to take the focus off of me. I got really excited about this. I went and bought all these cute cards for my friends and family and I wrote Valentine love notes to them. I told them how much I loved them, how grateful I was for them, and that Valentine's Day should be a day to remind people how much they are loved. The way the Lord reframed this for me brought a deep enjoyment to a holiday that, as a single person, might have instead moved me towards self-pity. But I went even farther and grabbed two of my friends and went to one of our favorite restaurants where we ate way too much and had a big ol' honkin' dessert; more friends ended up coming into the restaurant so we sat with them for quite a while... we celebrated every moment of that season.

The Lord just redeemed all of this ridiculous, cultural expectation and showed me the beauty of giving love away while celebrating the love you have. But shouldn't God be able to redeem this holiday and simply make it one of love? Because isn't that the very essence of who He is? "This is how much God loved the world: He gave his son. He gave His son because of love. He gave His one and only son and this is why: so that no one would need be destroyed by believing in Him. Anyone can have a whole and lasting life."[45] Then in 1 Corinthians 13 we can read how His message of love goes farther still. If you've never read it in The Message translation I'd encourage you to do so. The every day language makes it even more challenging, yet beautiful, I believe.

Friends, God has called us to live with a whole heart and live an abundant life. One of those ways is by giving love away. So for your next Valentine's Day, what if you got curious about ways to give love away, to not be worried about some marked day meeting some movie-type expectation that no one can ever live up to? What if you were to take all the expectation out of it and you just gave love away? I've done that for Philly multiple times... where I planned our dinner, booked our show and even called him and told him what I wanted for a gift! He had no pressure whatsoever! And do you know what? I loved him in that gift and my heart was free in giving it. My expectation isn't on Philly. My expectation is on my heavenly Father.

We can give love in each beautiful Valentine's season because God gave us love in such an extravagant measure when He gave us His one and only Son. No one has ever loved like that.

In the weeks leading up to Valentine's Day, how does your heart typically respond to this season?

---

[45] John 3:16 (MSG)

Excitement and joy? Indifference? Fear? Anxiety? Self-pity? Pain and anger?

_____

_____

_____

What might be the reason for the way you feel about it? Good or bad prior experiences – or a lack thereof? Society's definition of the season?

_____

_____

_____

Tuesday

~~❈~~

Maybe your perspective of Valentine's Day has affected your expectations. What expectations have you placed on yourself or others regarding this season? Do you expect perfection? Grand gestures? Are your expectations focused on self and what you want – or even feel you deserve?

_____

_____

_____

_____

Read **1 Corinthians 16:14**. In what way are we to do everything?

_____

_____

Does holding onto high or unrealistic expectations for ourselves or others reflect a posture of love?

_____

_____

What might it look like to begin releasing those expectations? A frank conversation with someone or with the Lord? A reframing of what love looks like?

_____

_____

_____

_____

Maybe even showering those in your close circles with love that week is something you could do to begin releasing those expectations. Who might those people be and what might it look like to love them well during that season?

_____

_____

_____

_____

Wednesday

Learning to love deeply, unconditionally, is truly about letting go of our expectations of others. Wow, what a hard way to live... but it is where real living is found.

Read **Psalm 62:5**. Where does David's hope, or expectation, come from?

_____

What does it mean to you to live and love with your expectation on the Lord?

_____

_____

_____

And, so if you were to come to a place where you live and love with your expectation on the Lord, what would that do for your heart?

_____

_____

_____

What would that do for your relationships and interactions with others?

_____

_____

_____

Thursday

It's not always easy to show love. Sometimes there are seasons where it's harder to express love – in general or even to a particular person.

Who may be someone right now that is difficult for you to love?

_____

Let's rewind and look back at the reason behind our calling to love; what does **1 John 4:19** say that reason is?

_____

If we realize the magnitude and expanse and purity of God's love for us, then that puts things into perspective – especially when it comes to loving others when they are simply hard to love.

Taking it a step farther, consider your relationship with that person you mentioned earlier. If you were to look at it in light of putting your expectation on the Lord instead of them, how would that impact how you love him or her? Would it affect your interactions with and heart towards them?

_____

_____

_____

_____

Friday

Look back at the passage from **1 Corinthians 13** in the text from Monday. I just love how it's worded in the MSG translation. Pay attention to all the things Paul says about love there.

Of those things, which are the easiest, most natural, for you?

_____

_____

_____

Which ones might be the most difficult for you to embrace and practice?

_____

_____

_____

Are there any specific situations you've had where you think God might be "inviting" you to grow in one of these areas? Remember, God doesn't bring things to our attention until it is time for us to deal with them, knowing He has everything we need to do so.

_____

_____

_____

_____

Spend some time today and sincerely ask the Lord to show you what any underlying heart issues might be that may be keeping you from being able to operate from a place of pure love.

Saturday Surrender

"If you keep my commandments, you will abide in my love, just as I have kept my Father's commandments and abide in His love."
John 15:10 (ESV)

This Saturday, may your heart seek continued surrender of any expectations you may have that are not of and from the Lord. By doing so, He is able to reframe any wrong or misguided perceptions about Valentine's Day or any other holiday, and love in general, and enable you to place your expectation on Him.

Get curious with God today and ask Him to show you anything you may not have noticed yet or to keep growing in you a heart of surrendered expectation.

Sunday Sabbath

"And above all these put on love, which binds everything together in perfect harmony."
Colossians 3:14 (ESV)

Songs for Your Sabbath
Mercy Me, *The Love of God*
Kari Jobe, *You are Good*

You asked the Lord quite a few questions this week. Maybe you've gotten clear directions and answers. Maybe you need to spend some more time seeking the answers you need.

Either way, take the time today to pause and enjoy His presence. Rest your mind. Focus for a while on His love, on why He loves you… just you. Think about the fact that He created you because of that love alone. Then focus on how He demonstrated His love for you – in the giving of Jesus. Finally, thank Him for the model He is in regards to love.

Lord, the love You choose to lavish on me is beautiful and truly humbling. I want my expectations to only come from You – not what I think they should be or what I'm told they should be. But just on You. Help me to release expectations where they need to be released and trust that You are more than enough for all I need. Help me, as well, to see others through Your eyes and let me love the way You love: sacrificially, selflessly, with no expectations or strings attached. Make me an example of Your love to all those you privilege me to do life with. May they see the Giver of Love in all that I do.

Week 27

Let's Talk About Marriage

Monday

Read: Ephesians 5:21-33

Good Monday morning.

Have you ever thought of the significance of why God places the first two people He creates in a marriage relationship? It is because the marriage relationship is supposed to be a direct reflection of Jesus and His bride. One would have to live in an underground bunker with no access to outside life to miss the assault on marriage today. Why? Think about it, think about all that is lost when two parents are not in the home. It causes more children to grow up in poverty cycles.[46] Children of divorce are more susceptible to depression, acting out, and suffering problems academically and much of this can last them into adulthood.[47] But ultimately divorce paints a dire and often petty picture of Jesus and His church. In fact, if you wanted to trace the beginning of the decline of the nation of America you could point back to the moment that "irreconcilable differences" was given as an option for divorce. From that moment assaults on marriage, redefinition of marriage, and even gender in general has not only been given room to be introduced, but to flourish. If so much is lost when marriages fail, why wouldn't the enemy of our hearts attack marriage mercilessly and relentlessly?

Satan's original assault happened to God's first couple. In Genesis 3:1 Satan sets God up with false accusation to Eve. "Did God actually say you shall not eat of any tree in the garden?" He was saying to her, *"Did God really say…? Can you really trust this God…? Is He really faithful…? Is He just setting you up because He doesn't want you to really be happy?"* He hisses doubt about God into the heart of Eve. And if we are honest, he does the same thing to our hearts millenniums later.

---

[46] https://www.brookings.edu/opinions/how-marriage-and-divorce-impact-economic-opportunity/

[47] http://vc.bridgew.edu/cgi/viewcontent.cgi?article=1056&context=honors_proj

Eve believed this lie. Scripture says, "She took of its fruit and she ate. She also gave some to her husband who was with her and he ate." Every time I read that last sentence my curiosity heightens. *Where was the conversation? Where was Adam's caution? Alert?* Why didn't *he* snatch it from her hand? Why didn't *he* recognize the lie? In light of what we read in our scripture reading, God affords us a clear hierarchy, if you will: Christ, then man, then woman.

In fact, before God ever made Eve He told Adam that he was supposed to both tend and keep the garden He was placing him in; he was the caretaker of the garden. So, when Eve arrived, God had given Adam a special assignment, to be the tender of the literal garden and the tender of the garden of his wife's heart as well. Not to be her lord or master or ruler. But to be her protector, her shepherd, her leader, her tender. This was not a role of power but a role of privilege.

Then God gave woman her assignment. She was meant to be man's helpmate. Not his leader or controller, but his partner, his helper, his co-laborer. Yet, inside of Genesis 3, Satan twists masterfully because Adam is not living out his role in this scripture. It is evident by both of their actions that neither is operating in their God design.

This entire abandoning of God's design leads to "The Fall." With the fall comes the consequences that sin brings – because sin *always* has consequences. God reveals them first on Satan. Then on the woman He says, "I will surely multiply your pain in childbearing; in pain you should bring forth children. Your desire shall be for your husband and he shall rule over you." That actually means that *you will have a desire to take authority over your husband and he will have a desire to rule over you.* Thus, the power struggle began.

We see that so often... how roles in marriages get so twisted by the scheming hand of the enemy. Women try to control and manipulate. Men try to dictate or even abdicate. And in this distorted way of living, marriages crumble beneath the sin of our story. However, Christ came to redeem everything that the fall brought. That means you and I are equipped with the grace and with the power, if we'll utilize it, to not walk in these ways. We have to walk in an intentionality of spirit. Change does not happen by wishing. Change in a marriage occurs by owning our sin and surrendering to the heart of our Father. Change in a marriage occurs by making sure God is our God and our spouse isn't. Change in marriage occurs by releasing offenses quickly and believing the best in our spouse while being faithful to the privileged position we've been given before God and in the other's heart. But rest assured, our flesh will battle our spirit and what we feed will win.

God gave us specific roles inside of marriage but it isn't about one being better than the other. We're both created in His image but, at the same time, our parts to play are each unique. Not subordinate or dominated or one is less than the other, but uniquely ours. A man was not created to do or be what a woman was. Nor a woman a man. A husband is to love his wife as Christ loved the church and gave himself up for it.[48] And a wife is to submit out of reverence to Christ.[49] So

---

[48] Ephesians 5:25
[49] Ephesians 5:22

anytime a man abdicates his role as head of the home whether by fear or apathy, he is setting his home up for failure. Anytime a woman tries to take control and lead the home, she is setting her marriage up for failure. Anytime a man tries to lead by fear and intimidation or in abuse -- be it verbal or physical – he has set his marriage up for failure. Anytime a woman walks in fear and intimidated submission she has set her marriage up for failure.

This is my word to you this week. If you're married, ask the Lord, "Lord, am I walking in the rightful order, the rightful place, in which You have called me in this marriage covenant that You have so graciously given me? And if I'm not, Father, I'm asking You to reveal it to me and then give me the wisdom and the strength and the courage to be the person -- either the tender or the helpmate -- You called me to be." If you are single don't toss this aside, but hide it in your heart and ask God to make you into the person He desires you to be in order to be the best spouse you can be down the road. Friends, I'm confident that if we ask for bread He will not give us a stone[50]; He will answer our prayers. And our marriages will be all the better for having prayed them.

Read **Genesis 1:27**. In what ways is your spouse made in God's image that is different from how you are made? How do those character traits partner with you in doing life? For my single friends, think about this in the context of your potential spouse.

_____

_____

_____

_____

_____

Tuesday

Take a look at **1 Corinthians 13:4-7**. Do you love this way? Which aspects do you struggle with the most?

_____

_____

_____

_____

---

[50] Matthew 7:9

What steps do you need to take in order to bring your heart back to this kind of love?

_____
_____
_____
_____

Wednesday

Why are the things mentioned in **Ecclesiastes 4:9-12** important in a marriage?

_____
_____
_____
_____

Are they evident in your marriage? If you're not married, how would you want these things to be a part of your future marriage?

_____
_____
_____
_____

What does this passage reveal about the power of the marriage union?

_____
_____
_____

What are ways submission to your spouse needs to grow in your marriage? Or how would you cultivate that in a future marriage?

_____
_____
_____
_____

Thursday

Read **Ephesians 5:21-33**.

If you're a husband – how are you portraying this call to love your wife? If you aren't portraying this, what is preventing you and what needs to happen for you to do it?

If you're a wife – are you living this kind of love out in your marriage? If you aren't, what is preventing you and what needs to happen for you to do it?

_____

_____

_____

_____

_____

It is important to realize that these passages are not based on the others' actions. They are based on our surrender and submission to Jesus Christ. One of the greatest lies of the enemy is to convince us that our response is based on how another person is acting. Recently I heard a husband defend his anger because of how his wife was acting. Now, I am not saying that there aren't situations where we need to respond in a certain way based on an action. But, instead, I am talking about excusing our sin because of how someone else is acting. Those are two very different things.

According to **1 Peter 3:7**, what can be hindered for a husband if he does not treat his wife as he should?

_____

Friday

Read **Genesis 2:24**.

This passage, I believe, can have theological backing to make this statement true for both men and women. Jesus even quoted this very same passage in the New Testament.

Having a parent's involvement to the level where their desires can usurp the spouse's decision-making or voice or having a parent that is overly critical of a spouse, can cause indescribable damage to a marriage.

Are there ways your relationship with your parents could be causing friction in your marriage (or could end up having those effects on a future marriage)? Are there healthy boundaries you need to begin to put in place to stop these patterns of behavior? (Some great resources on the topic are: Melody Beattie's, *The New Codependency,* Henry Cloud's, *Boundaries,* as well as his, *The Mother Factor.*)

_____
_____
_____
_____
_____
_____

Saturday Surrender

"He must become greater; I must become less."
John 3:30 (NIV)

At our Weekend Experiences for Married Couples we encourage them to spend the weekend focusing on their own hearts. Why? Because no marriage can move past one of the partner's chosen spot of stagnation.

Are you that heart? Are you that weaker link? If so, we encourage you to seek out the help you need. Get honest with someone. We highly encourage counseling, as well, because God has gifted counselors with unique discernment, wisdom, and gifting in these areas.

If you are not married, begin asking the Lord to prepare you to become the best spouse you can be. Dig into inner places of healing that are needed *now* so you are not having to dig into those places during your marriage.

God created marriage. He looked at man and said it wasn't good that he was alone. So, then, wouldn't God have a plan to make marriage successful? I believe He does. And I believe that plan is you and I being willing to be the people He intends us to be, love the way He intends us to love, forgive when we need to forgive, believe the best, and serve with all of our hearts.

Sunday Sabbath

"Dear friends, let us continue to love one another, for love comes from God. Anyone who loves is a child of God and knows God."
1 John 4:7 (NLT)

Songs for Your Sabbath
Casting Crowns, *Broken Together*
Matthew West, *When I Say I Do*
Stephen Curtis Chapman, *I Will Be Here*

The health of any relationship always boils down to how deeply we understand the love of our heavenly Father for us. We can't truly love our spouse, or anyone well if we aren't operating from a heart that receives the pure and extravagant love of God.

So, on this Sabbath, re-center yourself in the presence and love of your Creator. Ask Him to envelop you in His arms and give you a deep understanding of the magnitude of His love for you.

Father, thank You for the beauty that is the marriage union. I want to be a spouse who is reflective of Your deep love; I surrender my fears, insecurities, dreams, and plans to You. You have given me a specific role as a boundary of love and protection; help me walk confidently in that role, fulfilling the purpose You have set before me. Let me serve well, forgive often, and believe the best. Help me to resist accusation and speak life. Help me to never be the weaker link. May I love sacrificially because of how You have sacrificially loved me. May a heritage of divorce never be the heritage I leave for my children. Where divorce has come, redeem what the enemy stole. Make me an instrument of reconciliation and may my marriage be a representation of You on this earth.

Week 28

The Power of Our Thoughts

Monday

Read: Philippians 4:4-9

Good Monday morning.

Our minds… it's where the battle between what God has asked us to do and being obedient to it happens. Where the battle between what God says about us and what we will choose to believe about ourselves will be waged. Where the battle of what God says in His word and what our circumstances scream in our today will be fought. The greatest battlefield, as Joyce Meyer says, has been and always will be our minds.

Just like you and I have the ability to choose to speak life or death over people and situations in our own lives, we also have the ability to choose where we will let our minds stay. Not that we can choose all the thoughts that flood through them on any given day, but we do have the ability to choose what we will allow our minds to dwell on or put into them.

Verse eight in the section you read today is so beautiful. Even reading the descriptive words makes your heart feel peaceful. The Message Translation says it this way, "Summing it all up, friends, I'd say you'll do best by filling your minds and meditating on things true, noble, reputable, authentic, compelling, gracious, the best not the worst… " This reminds me of 1 Corinthians 13 where it says that, "love believes the best." That's because when Jesus resides in us, love believes the best[51] so it makes perfect sense that true love, God's love in us, thinks the best as well. After all, the things that become beliefs ultimately are the places we choose to allow our thoughts to dwell. So, if our thoughts perpetually turn to believing the worst in others or perpetually placing our own judgements on them and their actions and we let our mind stay there, it should be no surprise that believing the worst can become our truth whether it is true or not.

---

[51] 1 Corinthians 13:7 (MSG)

I know a young woman who is a master at a lie becoming truth for her. I've watched this pattern over and over in her life. Something happens. She lets her thoughts and not reality define it, and her thoughts almost always choose the worst belief whether it was reality or not. Because of this she has missed out on many valuable relationships and lives with an exceptionally critical spirit.

Culture is not our friend here either. The media is negative. Television is demeaning, violent, and often perverted. Social media can be brutal or self-absorbing. And in no time our own mouths can start exporting what our minds have imported. Our words can become critical. Our attitude angry. Our thoughts or actions unholy. This is no surprise if what is going in isn't pure or praiseworthy.

So *we* have to be gatekeepers of our minds. No one else will do this for us. And it's important to understand that we were not created to absorb or consume all of the things this culture has tried to tell us are okay or all of the lies the enemy of our soul throws at our hearts to try to steal from us, kill us, and destroy us. We weren't created for that. Philippians 4:8 tells us what we were created for; listen to these words again,

"Whatever is true…" Don't you love truth? The Word says that truth sets us free. And it is true. The truth of God's Word sets our hearts free.

"Whatever is honorable…" Isn't your heart just captured when people are honored or things that deserve honor are given honor?

"Whatever is right…" What about when things that are right and just should happen, do happen?

"Whatever is pure… whatever is lovely… whatever is admirable… whatever is excellent… whatever is worthy of praise… think on these things."

Did you know that the Apostle Paul wrote this passage of scripture from a jail cell? There is no telling all the thoughts that ran through his mind that he could have settled on at any given moment -- the hopelessness, the despair, feeling forsaken or rejected. But he didn't. Not only did he not focus on them, but he instead chooses to speak life to the Church, to people who are free. So if Paul can live this way and make these choices in the middle of a jail cell, then surely you and I, in the freedom we have through Jesus Christ, can make the choice to not let thoughts of negativity, despair, rejection, and hopelessness settle into our minds and hearts.

Our mind is such a powerful piece of our story. The Word says we're to love the Lord our God with all of our heart and all of our soul and all of our mind. Friends, we have a choice this week. Just like we do with our words, we have a choice of what we're going to do with our minds. Where will we let it abide? May we choose to settle our minds on God's best because He gave us His best. We have a choice. May we choose well.

What are the greatest weapons the enemy sends against your mind? Fear? Doubt? Anger? Rejection? Hopelessness?

_____

_____

What do you do when they come?

_____

_____

_____

Spend some time finding three to five verses related to the specific area Satan attacks your mind, whether it's fear, doubt, anger, temptation, criticalness, shame, etc. List them below.

_____

_____

_____

_____

_____

Now, focus this week on memorizing at least two of them. Whenever Satan comes at you in this area, begin to speak these scriptures you have memorized. The Word of God is one of your most powerful weapons.

Tuesday

What does **2 Corinthians 10:5** call those things that wage war against our minds?

_____

What is their goal?

_____

_____

Their goal is to wage war against the truth of who God is and what He desires to be to you and me.

So how do we, then, have to battle these thoughts?

_____

_____

_____

And how do we take them captive? What does that look like?

_____

_____

_____

_____

Wednesday

❧

Read **Matthew 4:1-11**. What did Jesus combat the enemy with?

_____

_____

Write down the three scriptures He used.

_____

_____

_____

_____

According to **2 Timothy 1:7**, what kind of mind has God called you to have?

_____

What does it mean to have a "sound mind"? Strong's Concordance (available online) is a great resource.

_____

_____

_____

Thursday

❊

Read **Proverbs 3:5**. How does leaning to your own understanding get you in trouble? (Remember what we've studied regarding Isaiah 55)

_____

_____

_____

_____

Discipline and self-control require intentional focus and have to be practiced. What are ways these can be practiced in regards to your mind? Philippians 4:8 is a helpful place to start.

_____

_____

_____

_____

Friday

❊

Read **Romans 12:2 (AMP)**. What is the "world?"

_____

How and why do we renew our mind according to this passage?

_____

_____

_____

This world lives contrary to the Word of God. So it is vital that the Word of God is put into us so it can come out of us. That is what is meant in this passage when it says, "renew your mind."

That word "renew" in the Greek means "renovate." That is what the Word of God does. It renovates our minds, transforming them from the world's perspective to an eternal perspective. Remember, you are a spirit man living in a natural world. And because of that, it should affect how we perceive situations and how we choose to respond to them.

What situations in your life do you need to let God renovate your perspective and thoughts through His Word?

_____

_____

_____

_____

How can you begin that process?

_____

_____

_____

Saturday Surrender

"Those who belong to Christ Jesus have nailed the passions and desires of their sinful nature to His cross and crucified them there."
Galatians 5:24 (NLT)

You might have heard it said that "temptation isn't sin until it is conceived."

Temptation, in its practical sense, is just temptation (unless it is being intentionally engaged). But it becomes sin when we don't make it go. When it arrives in our mind and we allow it to stay. When we let the lustful picture and thought turn over and over. When we let the anger stir and stir or the criticism and judgement spin and spin. That is when it can become conceived. And when something is conceived it can then give birth to sinful behavior in our lives. That is why we have to take *every* thought captive. This is simply part of the warfare we face as believers and followers of Jesus.

How do we do that? By not allowing it to linger. By not allowing it to move to our conversations. By not allowing it to take up root in our heart. By speaking to it as soon as it comes into our minds. By simply saying, "Father, I reject that thought. That isn't truth. And it isn't from you." We are then submitting the thought to the Lordship and truth of Jesus Christ. Because it isn't His thought and it isn't from Him. And remember – James 4:7 says that when we "submit to God, resist the devil, he *will* flee!"

Sunday Sabbath

"…let us draw near with a true heart in full assurance of faith, with our hearts sprinkled clean from an evil conscience and our bodies washed with pure water. Let us hold fast the confession of our hope without wavering, for He who promised is faithful."
Hebrews 10:22-23 (ESV)

Songs for Your Sabbath
Truth, *The Mind of Christ*
Chris Tomlin, *Whatever is True*

The only way to have access to something is to be close to it. We can't combat the lies if we aren't near Truth. Let your mind draw near to the Truth this Sabbath.

Rest in the truths of the scriptures you began memorizing this past Monday. Press into His presence. And may your proximity to the throne bring an equipping of your heart and mind unlike any you've ever experienced. Then spend some intentional time today reflecting on things that fulfill Philippians 4:8.

Lord, I recognize that a war is being waged for power over my thoughts. Forgive me for allowing negative, hurtful, unholy thoughts to linger. Forgive me for times I've placed things in my heart that had no value. Thank You for providing me with the tools – the weapons – to be equipped for daily battle. Help me keep my mind focused on things above and to promptly take any thoughts captive that are not of You or honoring to You. Help me to enjoy the beauty of the invitation to think on beautiful things. Knowing You know how to guard and protect me because my heart is so exceptionally valuable to You.

Week 29

His Thoughts Are Not Our Thoughts

Monday

Read: Isaiah 55:6-9

Good Monday morning.

Have you ever picked up your Bible only to read a passage you've read many times and have aspects of it illuminated to you that you've never seen before? That is such a statement to me of Hebrews 4:12 that "the Word is living and active…" because it is always speaking to us something new and something real. Recently this happened to me in Isaiah 55.

It starts in Isaiah 55:6: "Seek the Lord while He may be found, call upon Him while He is near." Have you ever stopped to truly consider that there is a season where God is found and there is a time when He is near but, taking it a step farther, there will come a day where He may no longer be found and a season where He will no longer be available to call upon? It's not that He wants any to be lost. In fact, He delays His return; as 2 Peter 3:9 records in the Amplified Bible, "The Lord does not delay [as though He were unable to act] and is not slow about His promise, as some count slowness, but is [extraordinarily] patient toward you, not wishing for any to perish but for all to come to repentance." Any time that the Lord allows Himself to be found is because He doesn't want anyone to perish. But there is a moment when Jesus will return and when that happens, the season of finding Him, calling upon Him, and coming to salvation will be ended.

Now look back at verses 7-9. Haven't you read verse nine many times? For some of us we can even quote the truth that God's thoughts aren't our thoughts nor His ways our ways. But there is a sobering truth I discovered in verse seven; Gods calls "our ways" and "our thoughts," "wicked" and "unrighteous."

Wow. Isn't that sobering?

I had never truly mediated on that before. But when we do, it forces us to consider how many times in our fear or disappointment or anger or shame we have moved to trying to figure out or orchestrate life according to our way and our thoughts. This maneuvering to self opens wide the door to the lie of the enemy that, somehow, these little finite minds of ours can or need to put reason or understanding around all of the ways and power and purposes of an infinite and all-powerful God.

What an arrogant posture of our hearts. What a wicked lie. So, what's the remedy? Recognition and then repentance.

Recognition that, there is no way a created being can ever comprehend the mind of its Creator. Yet, oh my how often have we tried. So we need to own that. Then repent of it. Repentance immediately yields the compassionate heart of our oh so compassionate Father. And He immediately forgives. When you and I try to put the God of the universe into this little box between our ears, we are creating a God that is far less than we need. I've said it many times, I need a God bigger than me; I need a God whose mind is not limited to my simple, human capacity.

Friend, I want to encourage you today. We have a God who has a far greater capacity for bigger and higher thoughts than we could ever think or imagine. That is such wonderful news! So do not get discouraged in your life or in your faith journey when things aren't happening the way you think they should be. But instead, be grateful that your Father in heaven has thoughts that aren't your thoughts, ways that aren't your ways, that are past finding out. We have a Father bigger than you, and bigger than me, and for that we should be utterly grateful.

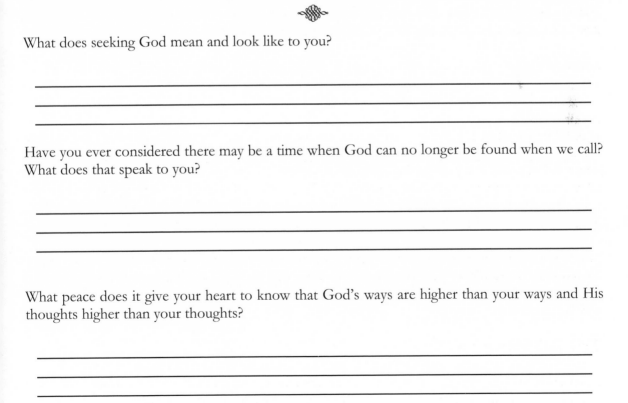

What does seeking God mean and look like to you?

_____
_____
_____

Have you ever considered there may be a time when God can no longer be found when we call? What does that speak to you?

_____
_____
_____

What peace does it give your heart to know that God's ways are higher than your ways and His thoughts higher than your thoughts?

_____
_____
_____

What are some areas in your life that you need His higher ways and His higher thoughts, a God bigger than you?

_____

_____

_____

Tuesday

Recently I was in my prayer time and was praying for a specific friend. As I was praying for her, the thought came to my heart that I should invite her to do a one-on-one Bible study with me; however, I wrestled with this thought out of fear that she might reject it or feel obligated to accept it. So, I simply asked the Lord, "Father, if this is really You, please confirm it to me in a way that I will know for sure You are asking me to do this." A simple but honest prayer. I sat down and began my daily Bible reading in Acts 8 where an Ethiopian eunuch is reading a scroll from the prophet, Isaiah. Philip, one of the new disciples, is prompted by the Holy Spirit to go to the carriage that the eunuch is riding and ask Him if he understands what he is reading. The eunuch responds, "How could I understand unless someone guides me correctly?" I immediately knew this was the Lord confirming to me through His Word that I was to contact my friend, that she needed a guide to help her understand. I was shocked when she responded with both willingness and gratitude that I had even asked. She even said, "I have always wanted to do something like this. But I didn't even know where to start in the Bible." That melted me.

What might have happened if I had paid more attention to my thoughts and resisted the promptings and direction of the Holy Spirit?

_____

_____

_____

Is there something in your life you feel God has spoken that you have resisted? If so, what?

_____

_____

_____

Read **Psalm 91:15** and **Proverbs 8:17**. What are the promises for those who call on the Lord and those who seek Him?

_____

_____

Take a look at **Psalm 119:105**. What are some ways the Lord speaks to us?

_____

_____

_____

Wednesday

In Genesis 15 God makes it clear to Abram that he has a son that will be his heir and that his descendants will outnumber the stars of the heavens and the sands of the sea.

Read **Genesis 16:1-4**. What did Sarai do in response to God's promise to Abram?

_____

_____

What were the consequences of moving towards her thoughts and her ways? Read **Genesis 16:4-6**.

_____

_____

What, in this season, are some areas in your life that you do not understand or are not working out according to your picture?

_____

_____

_____

Today, some almost six thousand years after this decision by Sarai to move toward her own thoughts, this world still deals with the consequences of this decision. The Palestinian nation are descendants of Hagar's son, Ishmael. Israel is a descendant of Sarai's son Isaac. The two still cannot live in peace to this day.

Why don't you spend some time here asking the Lord to reveal any areas in your life where you have moved toward your thoughts and your ways. Write them down here and then ask Him to forgive you.

_____

_____

Thursday

What is your normal response when you find yourself stressed and burdened with anxious thoughts?

_____

_____

_____

What does **Philippians 4:6** say to do when you begin to worry or become anxious?

_____

_____

What does **verse 7** say happens as a result?

_____

_____

What are some areas in your life where you are struggling feeling peace? What does this passage reveal to you?

_____

_____

Be mindful of that today and moving forward. Swimming in our own thoughts, worries, and fears will get us nowhere fast. Relying on the Lord gives us supernatural peace and clarity.

Friday

The stories of Job and Joseph and Daniel in the Old Testament are three powerful stories of God allowing circumstances to work out in ways we never would in order to accomplish things we would never dream. In the book of Daniel, a young Jewish boy is taken as a slave to the nation of Babylon. And, here, this young man of excellent character is tested and tried. **Read Daniel 1 & 6.**

What was the culture's way and what was Daniel's way?

_____

_____

What was Daniel's crime against the government?

_____

How was he punished?

_____

What was the result of God's powerful deliverance of Daniel?

_____

_____

If Daniel had tried to figure it out and not trusted God, what might have been the outcome? What does this speak to you of the situations of your own life?

_____

_____

_____

_____

Read Romans 9:20. How often have your actions or thoughts made this kind of statement to the God who made you? What might He be trying to accomplish in your life through a Daniel moment?

_____

_____

_____

_____

Saturday Surrender

"O Lord, I know that the path of [life of] a man is not in himself;
It is not within [the limited ability of] man [even one at his best] to choose and direct his steps [in life]."
Jeremiah 10:23 (AMP)

What a gift we have in a God who is bigger than us, bigger than any of our circumstances, past choices or any of our stuff. And because He is bigger than and in control of it all, there is no reason for us to fret or worry about the outcome.

If you are His, then He is working for you.

The only thing you need to do is surrender your thoughts, your plans, your desired outcomes to Him. We are so limited… in our strength, our sight, our abilities… but our God is so very limitless in what He is able and willing to do on our behalf.

So with those things you may have written down on Monday or anything new that has come to mind or happened since then, take some time today to really release your thoughts about them and ask God to let you see those people or situations through His eyes, trusting that His thoughts are incredibly higher and better than yours.

Sunday Sabbath

"Then Jesus said, "Come to me, all of you who are weary and carry heavy burdens, and I will give you rest. Take my yoke upon you. Let me teach you, because I am humble and gentle at heart, and you will find rest for your souls. For my yoke is easy to bear, and the burden I give you is light."
Matthew 11:28-30 (NLT)

Songs for Your Sabbath
Chris Tomlin, *Our God is Greater*
Tenth Avenue North, *Control*

Just like surrendering is a practice, truly resting our minds, bodies, and souls is, too. As you settle into your quiet place this Sabbath, as you slow down to be fully present with your heavenly Father, think about His goodness; think about His deep, limitless love for you and how in His great love, He has plans far beyond the plans you have for yourself. His promises are true, friend, and because our God is so very big, He is more than capable of fulfilling His word to us. Rest in that beautiful, reassuring truth today…

Lord, I am grateful that You are so much bigger than anything I'm currently up against. I'm so glad that even though I may not see or understand why things are the way they are, I can trust that as I seek Your heart You are faithful to work everything for my good. When I find myself becoming anxious and worried, may I point my heart back to You and the promises in Your Word. Help me recognize any place in my heart in this season where I move towards my ways or my thoughts. Help me to surrender those to You, knowing that I need a God bigger than me. And that You alone are that God.

Week 30

God Can't Help Himself

Monday

Read: Isaiah 55:10-11

Good Monday morning.

One of the things that I love about the Word of God is the power that it holds. John said in his first chapter, "In the beginning was the Word, and the Word was with God, and the Word was God."[52] "And the Word was made flesh and dwelt among us..."[53] This Word became flesh in Jesus and so the Word of God holds inside of it all the power of Jesus, Himself. He was the Word in the beginning. And if you remember, how was everything in the entire first chapter of Genesis created? By the Word of God. This Jesus, present at the very beginning, was the creative force of Creation, itself. It is this same Jesus that is the Creative force behind the Word of God in our lives because He is God's Word made flesh. My prayer today, and this week, is that you will see the power of the Word in a whole new way.

So last week we talked about Isaiah 55:6-9. Now I want us to walk through verses 10 and 11. We all know what the rain and snow do. We've seen it. We've seen the rain come down and we've seen the snow come down. What we haven't seen is it go back up without watering the earth. Separate of a miracle, when rain and snow fall they cannot help themselves. They have to water the earth.

In God's responses to Job in Job 38-41, He poses the question to Job in 38:28, *"Has the rain a father, or who has begotten the drops of dew?"* [54]These were rhetorical questions, of course. God was

---

[52] John 1:1 (KJV)

[53] John 1:14 (ESV)

[54] Job 38:28 (ESV)

making it clear to Job, who had spent much time questioning God, that Job had no idea the power of the God he was questioning: yes, this God, the Father of the rain, and the One whom Himself begot the drops of dew. So why wouldn't this heavenly Father who created both the rain and dew make sure they accomplished their purposes? And this passage states that they clearly do. Do you know why? Because they can't help themselves. They are doing what rain and dew were created to do.

He uses this analogy to make it clear to us that His Word does the same thing. It can't help itself either! Isn't that the most wonderful news you've ever heard?! The Word of God has to do what it says it is going to do. Just like rain and snow have to water the earth, the promises in the Word of God can each and every time be prayed in faith and with thanksgiving because this passage tells us they have to return a harvest. They cannot return empty but they have to accomplish that which God purposed and succeed in the things which He sent them to do! Remembering though, that God's promises are for God's people. His promises are for His children. If we are not in relationship with God through the receiving of Jesus Christ, then we forfeit the benefit of the promises. Just another reminder why relationship with Jesus is such an extravagant gift not to be missed!

The power of God's promises is one reason why I have made praying scripture a fundamental part of my prayer time. I pray scripture over my bonus children. Isaiah 54:13 says, *"All your children will be taught by the LORD, and great will be their peace."*[55] That is the promise of God. When I pray over Philly, I pray that "The heart of man plans his way, but the LORD establishes his steps."[56] When a painful situation walks into my life, I thank the Lord for Romans 8:28 and its truth, that "in all things God works for the good of those who love Him, who have been called according to His purpose"[57] I tell God, "Lord, I don't know how it's going to turn out. I don't know how You're going to do it. But what I do know is that You're working for our good so I don't have to worry. I don't have to be afraid or fret; I have confidence that Your word will not return void and it will accomplish that which You purpose and it will succeed in the thing for which it was sent."

Isaiah 55:10-11, to me, is one of the sweetest and most powerful passages regarding the power of the gift found in God's Word. And if that doesn't light up your Monday morning and put a kick in your step for this week, I don't know what to tell you…

So I just want to encourage you, friend; grab hold of that truth. Get yourself in the Word. Find promises to pray over your situations and then the next time you see that rainfall water the earth, I want you look up to heavens and I want you to say to the Lord, "That is *exactly* what Your promises are doing in my situation… they simply can't help themselves."

---

[55] Isaiah 54:13 (NIV)

[56] Proverbs 16:9 (ESV)

[57] Romans 8:28 (NIV)

Read **Job 38:16-38**. What do reading these scriptures speak to you about your God?

_____

_____

_____

How does that encourage you where you are in your current season?

_____

_____

_____

Tuesday

Read **Romans 8:28-30**. Who does God work good for?

_____

_____

What is the ultimate good to be worked out in our life according to verse 29?

_____

_____

Yes, us becoming more and more like Jesus is the ultimate goal of every situation we face – as well as us having a greater understanding of Jesus and His role in our life. When we are in relationship with Him it gives Him the access to work good for us even in the situations that make no sense or are painful.

What does the beauty of that passage do for you in the situations that you are facing now in your own life?

_____

_____

_____

_____

Wednesday

The Bible is full of promises for God's children that relate to every aspect of our life. What is an area in your life right now that you are struggling with? Trust? Fear? Shame? Love? Grace?

_____

_____

Do a word search in the concordance of your Bible for that specific area and look up some passages of scripture. Write down the passages that are promises from God for His children.

_____

_____

_____

_____

_____

_____

_____

_____

Now begin to pray those out loud asking God to give you the faith to fully take Him at His word. Begin to make praying these passages a weekly practice until they get into your spirit. Then, you will find as you begin to struggle in this area you can immediately bring to mind these passages in order to win the battle for your mind.

Thursday

Read **2 Corinthians 10:3**. Why would we not war in our flesh?

_____

_____

_____

It is because we are spiritual beings living in a physical world. Yet the enemy of our soul has been a master at trying to get us to believe we are physical beings living in a spiritual world. But that is a lie. That is why physical weapons will not win the battles that we face. Yelling at others, holding onto our unforgiveness in order to make someone pay, getting even, fighting our battles ourselves… none of those things work when you are a spiritual being. Oh, they may work in the short-run, but eventually we will end up like Sarah and Hagar like we talked about last week.

Continue on to **2 Corinthians 10:4-6**. Where does the enemy attack us the most according to verse 5?

_____
_____
_____

He attacks our minds. So we have to stop the thought that is contrary to the Word of God as soon as it arrives. How would you do this?

_____
_____
_____
_____

For me, it is often at night that the enemy tries to fill my mind with fear of all the "what ifs." Greatest in that battle are the "what ifs" of my future with my bonus-kids. In those moments, because of my years of praying scripture over them, I am able to recall to mind immediately the truth to the lie that will tell me, "You are going to have a broken relationship with your bonus-children down the road and with your grandchildren." I say, "No, that is not true, because scripture tells me…", and I state out loud one of the many passages of scripture I have professed over them throughout the years. Do you know what I have just done? I have taken a thought captive and brought it under the obedience of Christ.

So, what is a practical application of what this would look like in your daily life?

_____
_____
_____
_____
_____
_____

Friday

Read **Ephesians 6:10-17**. List below all the components of the Armor of God.

_____

_____

_____

_____

_____

_____

Of the six pieces of this armor, only **one** is a weapon of offense. Which one is it?

_____

And what does that piece represent?

_____

So what does this tell us about the role of God's Word in our lives?

_____

_____

_____

_____

Saturday Surrender

"Yes, I am the vine; you are the branches. Those who remain in me, and I in them, will produce much fruit. For apart from me you can do nothing."
John 15:5 (NLT)

How do we guard our hearts and stay rooted in Christ? A huge way is by saturating ourselves with the rich promises God's Word holds.

You've spent a lot of time this past week diving into some of those promises for your own story. In order to get and maintain a solid grasp on them, though, we have to first let go of any lingering doubts or fears that may be in the way of full, open-hearted trust of His Word.

So seek the Lord today; ask Him some questions about your heart and be brutally honest with yourself and with Him. Because only then, in true, regular surrender is He able to work in your story the way He so desires.

Sunday Sabbath

"But to all who believed Him and accepted Him, He gave the right to become children of God."
John 1:12 (NLT)

Songs for Your Sabbath
Vertical Worship, *This We Know*
The Belonging Co. (feat. Natalie Grant), *Isn't He (This Jesus)*

What a promise. What pure, beautiful truth we have readily available to us, friend. I encourage you this Sabbath, for just a few minutes, to remove yourself from the chaos and the demands and just be…

Be quiet.

Be still.

Be present.

Be attentive to anything the Lord may have for you. I encourage you to revisit the promises you discovered this past week and simply thank Him for giving them to you as well as for the fact that His Word just can't help itself…

Lord, thank You for the comforting truth that the promises in Your Word have to and will accomplish what You sent them to do. Thank You for sending Jesus, Your Word in flesh, to fulfill the law, to make a way for me to be able to enjoy eternity with You. And, Father, as I pour Your Word into my heart, speak to me, reveal more of Your heart to me. May I use that word to bring the lies of the enemy captive. May I declare it with faith and with a heart of thanksgiving. May I hide it in the arsenal of my heart to pull out against the fears that would try to wage war against me. Thank You for the armor You have given me and the promises You have promised me. I rest in them and You…

Week 31

Power of Our Words

Monday

Read: Proverbs 18:21

Good Monday morning.

Have you ever stopped to consider the impact of your words? Every now and then we can actually see their impact. Recently, Philly and I were in the car and I said something and immediately I saw the little twitch in his jaw start and his grip on the steering wheel tighten. I realized I had really struck a chord in his heart with my words. Then there are other times that I can speak words of affirmation to him and see him come to life -- his smile gets bigger and his chest puffs out a little bit more. I'm sure you've witnessed this same thing, whether when speaking to your child or a friend, a coworker or your spouse.

Proverbs 18:21(AMP) says, *"Death and life are in the power of the tongue and they who indulge it shall eat the fruit of it, for death or for life."* Our words have the ability to create life or death. Think about it: God *spoke* everything but man into existence. Genesis 1 is the recounting of the power of His words. Now consider that we were made in His image. So that makes Proverbs 18:21 even more powerful, revealing that our words too, have the power to create. In the book of James, our tongue is compared to the rudder of a ship making the revelation of this truth deeper still as we realize this little instrument, as tiny as a rudder is to a ship, can move our entire being as well as the hearts and lives of others with nothing but a word.[58]

A few years ago, Philly and I were in a season in our lives that was very challenging. If we had done nothing but look at it from a natural perspective, we could easily have spoken words of hopelessness to it. But God has given us a Book of promises; that's why I'm such a firm believer in praying scripture. Because as we've already studied, scripture "cannot help itself" in the life of a believer. It has to accomplish *all* that it was set forth to do and succeed in *all* it has promised. So instead of Philly and me choosing to see our situation in the brokenness that it was in the natural, we looked

---

[58] James 3:4-5

at it through eyes of faith, doing what the Bible talks about, calling those things that are not as though they are.[59] We then spoke to them based on what God's promises say. We didn't speak death over our circumstances even though a lot of people may have looked at them and said, "This is the most hopeless situation I've ever seen." But, friends, we don't serve an impotent God. We serve a Father who keeps His word, who nothing is impossible with and we hold onto His promises. Then, when we speak His truth into our situations and hold Him to His promises we create an atmosphere where He meets our faith.

It's also important to know that "...whatever is in your heart determines what you say" (Matthew 12:34 NLT); another translation says, "Out of the abundance of the heart the mouth speaks." This is another reason why it is so important that we pour the Word into us so that in the situations of our lives it is the Word coming out of us, but also that we guard our hearts from all of the offerings this world desires to deposit inside of them. I've learned to pay attention to seasons when it seems that critical words are flying out of my mouth or words of despondency or self-pity or victimization. This is always a clear indicator that there's something going on in my heart that I need to pay attention to. So, I recalibrate. I create and then guard space where I have intentional time with the Lord in order to make sure His Word is getting into my soul. When He is what is in me, then He is what comes out of me.

Friends, pay attention to the words that come from your mouth, because they both reveal what is going on inside of you and life and death dwell there and those who love it *will* eat its fruit.

Think back over your past 24 hours and the types of interactions you had with others – your family, coworkers, friends, the people waiting in line with you at the grocery store – and describe what those were like. Life-giving? Or were they not as positive as they could have been? How could you have spoken differently?

_____
_____
_____
_____
_____
_____
_____
_____
_____
_____

---

[59] Romans 4:17

Tuesday

If life and death are in your tongue, what are statements you have been speaking over the situations you are currently walking through?

_____
_____
_____
_____

What does it reveal about the state of your heart?

_____
_____
_____

Read **Proverbs 18:1-19:13**.

Underline all the phrases that have to do with words or our mouth. Then, take each one of those passages and write it down along with what it speaks to you or what God may be speaking to you.

_____
_____
_____
_____
_____
_____
_____
_____
_____
_____
_____
_____
_____

Are you surprised at how many times the tongue or words or our mouth are mentioned? That's just what one chapter and a half has to say about the topic. If you want to dig in deeper, I'd encourage you to take the time to do this with the entire book of Proverbs.

Wednesday

If you were to ask your three closest friends what your words do to them, what do you think their responses would be?

_____

_____

_____

Take a look at these three verses:

Proverbs 10:19
Proverbs 17:27
Proverbs 21:23

What do these passages reveal to you about our words and lack thereof?

_____

_____

_____

Now read **Proverbs 12:18**. What are you to others? What do you desire to be?

_____

_____

_____

Few things are as painful as those who speak without thinking. I have a friend who has taught me the value of being a "prayerful listener." A prayerful listener isn't someone who finishes your sentences because they can't wait for the words to get out of your mouth. They also aren't the one that jumps in with an answer before you've even finished. They aren't the one who always has to turn things back around and make it about them. No, they are the one who listens, prays, and then speaks if needed. They are also the one to know when no words are needed at all. Just prayer.
May you and I both be people who desire to bring healing to others with the words of our mouth, knowing that in this way we were made in the image of Christ. So pay attention this week to what comes out of that so very small instrument, mindful that life or death dwell in it.

Thursday

Not only are the words we speak into our situations, ourselves, and those around us important, but the words of others that we allow to be spoken to us are also of incredible value to our well-being.

The book of Job is known for many things, not least of which are the three "friends" of Job who come to him at his most heartbreaking season and heap on more heartbreak.

Look through **Job 4-15**. Who are his three friends and what are their messages to him?

_____

_____

_____

In **Job 16:1-4**, what did the words of his friends do to him?

_____

_____

And then what is God's response to Job's friends in **Job 42:7**?

_____

_____

Take friend inventory today. Honestly evaluate the amount of life they speak into you and prayerfully consider what action to take if any of them don't use their words to uplift and encourage.

Friday

We don't need people in our lives like Job had. We want to be surrounded by those who love us well, challenge us, and encourage us.

It is also vital in our lives that we have friends in our lives who believe the truth of God's word. Who will stand in faith with us to see His promises fulfilled in our lives.

Read **Proverbs 27:17**. What does a good friend do?

_____

_____

According to **Proverbs 27:5-6**, what happens when a true friend speaks life to you?

_____

_____

Think back to that friend inventory you took yesterday… consider sending a note or text message to the life-giving, good friends of yours thanking them for the role they play in your life.

Saturday Surrender

> **"Become wise by walking with the wise;**
> **hang out with fools and watch your life fall to pieces."**
> **Proverbs 13:20 (MSG)**

Severing ties with anyone for any reason is a tough and very uncomfortable thing to do. Maybe the other day when you prayerfully considered the friend relationships in your life you realized there may be one that needs to either change or even be removed completely.

Something like that cannot be done on your own strength or by your own will.

As an act of surrender today, ask the Lord to guide you and give you wisdom regarding how to address that relationship using life-giving words.

Also, surrender today your need to speak. Ask the Lord to enable you to become a "prayerful listener." Ask Him to help you realize that sometimes words are needed and sometimes they aren't. Ask Him to help you not feel the need to finish someone else's sentence, be critical, make it about you or think you always have to have an answer.

Sunday Sabbath

> **"Oil and perfume make the heart glad,**
> **and the sweetness of a friend comes from his earnest counsel."**
> **Proverbs 27:9 (ESV)**

Songs for Your Sabbath

Planetshakers, *We Speak Life*
Anna Boyd, *Your Word*

Whenever I leave times with my life-giving friends, my heart is always so incredibly full. You know that feeling I'm talking about? There isn't much like it. My prayer after those times is that I would be that kind of friend. One that truly speaks and offers life to the people God has privileged me to do life with.

Lord, what a beautiful example You set by using Your words to create, to speak life. May I be ever mindful to wisely choose my words to reflect Yours when speaking into my situations, myself, and those around me. I am so grateful for the life-giving relationships You have blessed me with, too; I ask for Your wisdom in handling any of my relationships that may not be the most life-giving to me. It's only with You that transformation can happen and I surrender those friendships to Your hands, Father, in Jesus' precious name.

Week 32

The Power of Praise

Monday

❧

Read: 2 Chronicles 20:1-30

Good Monday morning.

One evening I was home alone watching a pastor on television right before I went to sleep. He was preaching on praise; I was so captured by his message that by the end of his teaching, I found myself laying there in my bed just worshipping the Lord. When I went to sleep that night, the Lord showed me a powerful revelation in a dream.

There have been multiple times over the years that I know God has spoken to me in my dreams -- I often joke that it's because I'm so hard-headed in the daytime He has to get me asleep for me to hear Him... but in my dream that night, Philly, my parents, and I were taken hostage by terrorists. There were also other hostages there as well. These terrorists held us inside an old silo and were making us march around in a circle; one of the men guarding us was on the floor by us and the others were overhead with their guns pointed down at us. The terrorist on the ground took me by the arm and pulled me out of the circle; I knew immediately that he had pulled me out to kill me. I looked back and I saw the horror and fear on the faces of my family, but inside of me, my spirit was at perfect peace. And in this dream, as I stood outside of the circle with the terrorist at my side, I raised my hands and I began to worship. Right there, swaying back and forth with a smile on my face, I sang worship to my heavenly Father. Then, all of a sudden they began to rain down bullets from above -- yet, not a single bullet penetrated me. Not one. I looked at the terrorist's face next to me and it registered his shock.

When I awoke, I knew immediately the dream was from the Lord. He was revealing a tangible representation of the power of praise that had been spoken to my heart before I went to bed. The Lord was showing me that praise is so powerful a weapon that it can even stop the penetrating bullets of the enemy.

It reminded me of the story of Jehoshaphat in 2 Chronicles. Scripture says armies were coming at him from every side so he called a time of fasting and praying of all his people. As they headed into battle, however, Jehoshaphat did something out of the ordinary for battle: he sent out the praisers first. Remember how that affected the battle? The very armies that were coming to destroy him, instead began to attack one another – not one soldier ever came against Jehoshaphat or his men. The other armies simply self-imploded until they totally destroyed each other. That story ends by saying, "Then there was rest all around." Praise alone can win battles and while God's angel armies war on our behalf, our spirits can be at rest.

Friends, God is worthy to be praised and He will inhabit the praises of His people. So I encourage you today, give Him the praise He is due and watch as heaven comes to Earth and the throne of God takes up residence in the reality of your situation. There is no evil so great, no enemy so powerful that praise cannot turn the situation around and the power of God destroy the very works of darkness.

Read **Matthew 6:9-13** and **Psalm 100:4**.

What is the very first line of the Lord's Prayer? Why do you think when Jesus was teaching us how to pray that He started it the way He did?

_____

_____

_____

When Jesus taught His disciples how to pray, the very first thing Jesus tells them to begin with is, "Hallowed be thy name…" That means you praise God. Praise does two things. First of all, scripture tells us that God inhabits the praises of His people. When we praise, God is there. It brings heaven to Earth. It brings God's purposes to our plan. It creates an atmosphere for God to operate in our lives, unhindered, and work victory on our behalf. Secondly, when we praise Him for who He is, for His attributes, for His goodness, for His holiness, for His ability to be just in our situations, it builds our faith in the God that we serve. When we praise God for all of the ways He's fought for us in the past, for the ways that He's provided, for the ways that He's led, for the ways that He's protected, our faith is strengthened to know if He did it back then, He'll do it again.

How does doing this affect our perspective and response to the other aspects of this prayer?

_____

_____

_____

Tuesday

❧

In **Luke 1:46-55**, Mary, the mother of Jesus, sings a song. What does her song reveal about her heart?

_____

_____

_____

What is the initial response from your mouth when an opportunity comes your way that feels greater than your ability?

_____

_____

_____

What should your response be?

_____

_____

_____

Read **Psalm 105:2**. What are some of the mighty deeds He has done in your life? What happens when these become our focus instead of our own challenges?

_____

_____

_____

_____

_____

Wednesday

❦

Read **Psalm 34:1-3**. Why would the enemy not want us to have hearts of praise? Think back to his lie about God in Genesis 3 that we have studied before.

_____

_____

_____

Flip back a few pages to **Psalm 16:11**. Where is fullness of joy found? What does that mean to you for your life? To live in this kind of joy.

_____

_____

_____

Thursday

❦

Look up the definition of the word 'inhabit' and write it here.

_____

_____

_____

Read **Psalm 22:3** (KJV or ESV).

What are ways that God inhabits your praise?

_____

_____

_____

Take a look at the following verses:

Philippians 4:4
Psalm 34:1

Psalm 71:6
Psalm 119:64

How can you begin to practice a lifestyle of praise?

_____

_____

Friday

Read about the beautiful, sacrificial act of a broken woman in **Luke 7:36-50**.

What did this act of worship speak about her?

_____

_____

What did Simon's response reveal about his heart?

_____

_____

_____

What did her gesture do to the heart of Christ?

_____

_____

_____

Hebrews 13:15 talks about a "sacrifice of praise." Are you willing to praise when it isn't convenient? Praise when life is hard? Praise when answers don't come the way you'd ask or healing doesn't arrive when you desired? Will you praise then? What may God be desiring to teach you about praise?

_____

_____

_____

_____

_____

_____

Saturday Surrender

"Bless the Lord, oh my soul, and all that is in within me, bless His holy name!"
Psalm 103:1 (ESV)

At the writing of this devotion, I was just coming out of a two year-long season of chronic pain. I did everything I could; I saw many doctors and therapists and sought alternative routes to find healing. At one point during that season, I felt led to go on a twenty-one day fast to believe for my healing. I was certain complete and total healing would come on the last day of it. However, the last twenty-four hours of the fast were some of the most painful I had experienced. The pain limited my writing; I couldn't exercise or carry my laundry basket to the laundry room. It required others to pull my luggage through the airport as I walked alongside them. And I had to rely on help to even get my groceries in and out of my car, which left me embarrassed at what others may think.

The disappointment when the pain didn't end at the conclusion of my fast was exceptional. It was during that season, that I first began working on this devotional. It was as if God said, "Praise me anyway." So in my intermittent writing I praised Him, trusting that He was big enough to take my pain away in a moment or give me the supernatural grace to endure it as long as it stayed around while working on my inner man in the process.

Sometimes the terrorists aren't external, they are within. God loves us enough to allow circumstances to come into our lives to deal with those as well. But praise… praise moves our eyes off of ourselves and onto the indescribably big, all-powerful, and loving Father that we have!

Sunday Sabbath

"Around midnight Paul and Silas were praying and singing hymns to God, and the other prisoners were listening. Suddenly, there was a massive earthquake, and the prison was shaken to its foundations. All the doors immediately flew open, and the chains of every prisoner fell off!"
Acts 16:25-26 (NLT)

Songs for Your Sabbath
Shannon Wexelberg, *Right Where I Am*
Michael W. Smith, *This Is How I Fight My Battles*

How easy it is to resort to stressing out about what needs to happen next or what isn't happening that you think should.

But the Bible is full of instances where people chose to rest in the goodness and promises of God. And in the resting, in the praise, that's when He desires to show up and show off. It's God's power that causes breakthrough – not ours.

So rest in that truth this Sabbath. Any prisons you need to be released from, choose praise over pouting and watch the Lord do mighty things when your attention is on Him!

Lord, thank You for holding everything together. You are worthy of more praise than I could ever give. It's not my job to fix, to control, to handle everything that happens to and around me – it's Yours. Even though I can't see the big picture and I don't understand why things are the way they are, I will choose to praise You, because You are my good and loving heavenly Father and it's You who works all things together for my good! Thank You that while I praise, You are fighting my battles. That my praise moves Your heart. Thank you that as I praise, I enter Your presence and everything I need is found in You. Thank You for the privilege of praise and how You move inside of it.

Week 33

The Lord's Promises Prove True

Monday

❦

Read: Romans 4:18-25

Good Monday morning.

If today was the day you got the painful news, the news about your health, or your marriage, or your child, who would you call? Who would you want with you? Around you? Speaking into your story? The friend who perpetually speaks death or despair? Or the friend who even on their worst day can find something to be hopeful for? Me, too… I'd want that friend who has a way of chaining herself to hope.

Abraham was called the "Father of Faith." His story began when the Lord called him to leave his home and everything that he knew, and with this step of faith God would make him into a great nation and all of the nations of the earth would be blessed by him. God also told him that his descendants would be more than the stars of the heavens and more than the grains of sand at the seashore. But at the age of 100, he still had no child. Now, you and I know that the odds of having a kid at that age are slim-to-none -- I mean, he was way past the medication help kind of years, if you know what I mean -- and yet scripture tells us, he *believed* God's word to him.

His story is recorded in Genesis but it is recounted for us by Paul in Romans 4. Verse 18 says this of Abraham, "Even when there was no reason to hope…" Okay, let's stop there just a minute. May I speak to you from this statement? You may be in a situation – whether it be your marriage, a situation with your child, your health, your finances, whatever it might be – and every single circumstance says you shouldn't have any hope, that you need to give up hope. We all know those moments. But what I love about scripture is that, thankfully, we are never left in those hopeless moments.

It goes further still: "Even when there was no reason for hope," listen to this, "... Abraham kept hoping." Don't you love that?! Isn't that one of the enemy's greatest goals in our seasons of disappointment, pain, or struggle, to get us to quit hoping? Because remember, Hebrews 11:1 tells us,

"Faith is the substance of things hoped for, the evidence of things not seen." So as long as there's still hope, there's room for faith. So, is it any wonder that when we've had situations come and go in our lives that have been disappointing or challenging, that the enemy is a master at trying to move us away from hope? We find ourselves saying things like, *I'm not even going to hope for that; I don't want to be disappointed.* Friends, it is thoughts such as these that give the enemy room to have a field day in our mind and in our spirits. It is then that we have to stop the thought and go back to speaking the Word in faith, because *faith is the substance of things hoped for.* We should all have hope.

"Even when there was no reason for hope, Abraham kept hoping — believing that he would become the father of many nations. For God had said to him, "That's how many descendants you will have!" And Abraham's faith did not weaken, even though, at about 100 years of age, he figured his body was as good as dead — and so was Sarah's womb. Abraham never wavered in believing God's promise. In fact, his faith grew stronger, and in this he brought glory to God." Romans 4:16-20 (NLT)

Do you know the glory that it brings to God when people look at you and say, *Honey, bless your heart, I'm so sorry you're still believing for that* and you respond *Oh, don't be sorry for me -- if God said it, it's mine.*? If God said "I will perfect all that concerns you,"[60] then He's going to perfect all that concerns me. If God said that He will work all things together for my good[61], then He will work all things together for my good. "God is not man, that He should lie, or a son of man, that He should change His mind. Has He said, and will He not do it? Or has He spoken, and will He not fulfill it?"[62] God isn't capable of lying because He is divine. The ability doesn't even reside in Him. So when He told Abraham that his descendants would be as many as the stars of the heaven, Abraham believed God's word.

Friend, when I pray I'm rarely like Abraham. Oh how I wish I had a faith that never wavered. I don't. My faith wavers. But what I do in those moments when my faith wavers is go back to the promises of God as we have talked about now for this our fourth week. I go back to the heroes of faith like Abraham who was 100 years old, his body as good as dead, and he still kept believing. The God who promised is faithful to complete His promises. So, during my prayer times, especially when I pray for my family, I have scriptures written out that I pray for them. Worn pages of handwritten and typed scriptures filled with promises. I pray God's promises because remember, they can't return void, God's Word accomplishes what it was sent forth to do.

I hope your faith is encouraged today. Don't lose hope. We don't serve a hopeless God. We serve a God who keeps His word. His promises are true. His word is yes and amen; that's like done and done-er… that's like good and gooder. He keeps His word to us. I do not care how dead, how hopeless, how lifeless your situation may seem. *"Even when there was no reason for hope, Abraham kept hoping — believing that he would become the father of many nations…"* And he did. Just like God promised.

---

[60] Psalm 138:8

[61] Romans 8:28

[62] Numbers 23:19 (ESV)

Find those promises. Dig them out. Pray them in faith. Then trust that God will keep His word. He is always faithful to keep His promises.

⸙

What are the situations in your life that the enemy has convinced you are hopeless and are too hard for God?

_____

_____

_____

_____

Tuesday
⸙

In Genesis 18, a pre-incarnate Jesus visits Abraham and Sarah while they are waiting to bear a son. Read **Genesis 18:1-14** and pay close attention to the Lord's response to Sarah's laughter. What question does He ask in v. 14?

_____

_____

Why is this such an important question, not only for Sarah whose story we know the end of, but for our stories as well?

_____

_____

_____

_____

Remember, God doesn't ask questions because He doesn't know the answer. So with a question like the one here, He is trying to reveal to Sarah, and to us, something about our hearts.

Be mindful of that today and really ask yourself how much you believe God is capable of.

Wednesday

⚜

"It's impossible to please God apart from faith. And why? Because anyone who wants to approach God must believe both that He exists and that He cares enough to respond to those who seek Him."
Hebrews 11:6 (MSG)

What must be present to have a faith that pleases God?

_____

_____

_____

Why can't we please God without faith?

_____

_____

_____

_____

And so ask your heart today, do you truly believe those two things about your God? If so, what is a way you are moving in faith in this season?

_____

_____

_____

Thursday

⚜

Grab your favorite pen or highlighter and open your Bible to **Hebrews 11**.

Underline or highlight the places in each person's story where their faith story was quantified, or what action they took or impact they had as a result of their faith.

What quantifies your faith? What specific promises right now are you willing to believe from your Father that will be declarations of faith?

_____

_____

_____

_____

_____

_____

Friday

~❀~

Hope is a beautiful and powerful thing that we, as followers of Jesus Christ, have to always hold onto because we know that our God fulfills His promises.

Read **Zechariah 9:9-13**. What does it say we are prisoners of?

_____

What does that mean to you?

_____

_____

_____

Read that passage one more time and in the space below write out all the promises of God it contains. Pray them over yourself and your circumstances today!

_____

_____

_____

_____

_____

_____

_____

_____

Saturday Surrender

"Now Faith is the assurance (title deed, confirmation) of things hoped for (divinely guaranteed), and the evidence of things not seen [the conviction of their reality — faith comprehends as fact what cannot be experienced by the physical senses]. For by this [kind of] faith the men of old gained [divine] approval. By faith [that is, with an inherent trust and enduring confidence in the power, wisdom and goodness of God] we understand that the worlds (universe, ages) were framed and created [formed, put in order, and equipped for their intended purpose] by the word of God, so that what is seen was not made out of things which are visible."
Hebrews 11:1-3 (AMP)

Note in this passage all the things faith is and does. Oh what hope that should speak to our hearts! And of all the things faith is, it is not dependent on anything we can do. Faith spurs surrender; it removes even the very desire to be self-sufficient, when we place that faith in the one who framed the very worlds in which we dwell.

That circumstance testing your faith in this season, if you are in Christ, you have a hope unlike any other, friend. Release all the pieces – even the unknowns. In his book, *Crazy Love*, Francis Chan writes, "I am thankful for the unknowns because they make me run to God." Release the unknowns to your heavenly Father today, trusting that He's a God of His word!

Sunday Sabbath

"And if the Spirit of Him who raised Jesus from the dead is living in you, He who raised Christ from the dead will also give life to your mortal bodies because of His Spirit who lives in you."
Romans 8:11 (NIV)

Songs for Your Sabbath
Casting Crowns, *Voice of Truth*
Brian and Katie Torwalt, *Praise Before My Breakthrough*

Think about what this verse means for the things in your life that look dead. We have access to the same life-giving Spirit that raised Christ from the dead!

So, this Sabbath, in your quiet place, dwell on that powerful truth.

Slow down and just sit in the beautiful comfort that is the mighty power of the Holy Spirit. He brings life to seemingly dead situations or relationships. All we do is stand firm on the promises we've been given, confident that as a follower of Jesus Christ, He will work all things for our good according to His purpose.[63]

Lord, thank You for always fulfilling Your promises. Thank You for the reminder that nothing is too hard for You; You are able to breathe life into even the most hopeless looking and seemingly dead situations of my life and of those that I love. I know that because I am in You, I have hope eternal. May I run straight to Your Word at the first twinge of fear, doubt, anger, or desperation. You are God, You are good, and You are in control, Lord, not me. May I live as a prisoner to hope.

---

[63] Romans 8:28

Week 34

The Danger of Double-mindedness

Monday

❈

Read: 1 Kings 17:16-46

Good Monday morning.

There's a story in 1 Kings about a battle between a king and a prophet. King Ahab was the last king of Israel and Elijah was the voice of God in that time and season. Scripture says that Ahab was the most evil of the kings of Israel... and that's saying something because there were some horrific kings in Israel during that time. Ahab was married to a foreign woman named Jezebel. Over and over God had told the children of Israel not to take foreign women as their wives and yet they continued to do so. Now, Jezebel brought into Israel with her the god, Baal. We're told that Baal was identified as the Sun god, or the god of the storm. The Encyclopedia Britannica says he was the god of rain and dew, which is really interesting in light of what we are about to read in this story.

So, here we have this set up in the passage you read: an evil king, a wife who worships Baal, and the voice of the prophet, Elijah. The climax occurs when Elijah asks the people, *"How long will you go limping between two different opinions? If the Lord is God, follow Him; but if Baal, then follow him."*

It's important to understand the confusion of the people. They are children of the living God, yet the king they serve has introduced them to the god of Baal, and now prophets of Baal have swept through the nation spreading their deception. Honestly, this isn't much different from today, is it? Many inside of the church are trying to serve the God of the Bible and the god of their own personal desires. So, it isn't a far stretch to believe this question is the same to us today.

What are you going to choose? The gods of this culture and generation, or the God and Creator of heaven and earth? Joshua, centuries before, had set before the children of Israel the same announcement when they came into the Promised Land, Canaan; "Choose this day whom you will serve… as for me and my house, we will serve the Lord."[64] God wrote the truth in stone, "I will have no other gods before me." When Jesus narrowed the Ten Commandments down to two, He made this same declaration clear in Matthew 22:37, *"Love the Lord your God with all your heart and with all your soul and with all your mind."* Serving two masters never works.

James wrote in James 1:8, *"A double-minded man is unstable in all his ways."* Few things could be as true. Ever met a man who couldn't make up his mind? One day he believes one thing, the next day he believes another. One day he is sure God is good. The next day he is confident God has one goal and that is to screw up his life. It makes everything about him schizophrenic. You can't trust him to make a decision. You can't have confidence in his emotional state. It provides a foundation that is faulty and perpetually at risk of crumbling. That is why Elijah asked the question and why God wrote the truth in stone and Jesus crammed ten commandments into two. No one can live double-minded about what they will believe about God. Either He is God or He isn't. Either He is who He says He is as C.S. Lewis writes, or He is a madman. How could you call yourself God and be anything other, God or crazy?

Friends, we do not live in a day and age that can afford our double-mindedness. If we choose to live there trying to serve God while still trying to hold onto another, we leave ourselves exposed to destruction on every side. The enemy is not playing. He is intentional and conniving, he is stealthy and patient. But God, your God, stops the rain and dew of a false god for three years. Your God drowns the very altar of their pathetic imitation and has these 450 prophets of Baal destroyed. God does not want you limping in life. He wants your feet steadfast and sure. Serving Him wholeheartedly assures that kind of life every time.

In **Genesis 3**, what is the fundamental lie about God that Satan touts Eve with?

_____

_____

What happens when Satan can get us to believe that God is like us — weak, petty, competitive, scheming…?

_____

_____

_____

One thing it does is remove God from the throne of our hearts, making room for us to put something — or someone else — there.

---

[64] Joshua 24:15 (ESV)

Is there another god you have placed your confidence in other than the God of heaven and earth?

_____

_____

What has trusting in that god brought you?

_____

_____

_____

What does trusting in that god make you believe about the one true God?

_____

_____

_____

Tuesday

~✦~

Read **James 4:1-10**.

What does this passage say friendship with the world produces?

_____

_____

_____

How would you define friendship with the world? What does it look like?

_____

_____

_____

According to **verse 7**, what has to happen before we can "resist the devil?"

_____

_____

_____

What does it look like to submit to God? What does that submission produce?

_____

_____

_____

_____

_____

What does James categorize double-mindedness with in **verse 8**?

_____

_____

_____

According to **verses 9 & 10**, what should our response to our double-mindedness be?

_____

_____

_____

Wednesday

In **Matthew 6:24**, Jesus is talking about double-mindedness in relation to money. But it can be related to anything we allow to become a god in our life. It can be exercising, or entertainment, or unbelief. Pick your poison here.

How does Jesus describe double-mindedness here? And what does it always produce?

_____

_____

_____

_____

What is double-mindedness according to **Isaiah 29:13**?

_____

_____

_____

So, then, how do we guard our hearts from double-mindedness? Refer back to the first part of **James 4:8** again.

_____

_____

_____

_____

Thursday
❧

Read **Numbers 13:1-14:23**.

What does **13:2** say God was doing with the land of Canaan?

_____

_____

Even though they knew this, how did the Israelites respond in **14:1-4**?

_____

_____

_____

And what impact does their response have on their access to the Promised Land?

_____

_____

_____

_____

Can you think of a time your response, despite knowing the truth of the promise from God, may have impacted your access to it?

_____

_____

_____

_____

_____

Friday

Digging a little deeper into what we started talking about yesterday — what does **Hebrews 3:12-19** speak to you personally about being double-minded to the promises and character of God?

_____

_____

_____

_____

God had given the Israelites a promise. Yet, they let the unbelief of ten men cause them to miss the Promised Land He had for them.

I can always tell when I have moved away from the Lord: He gets smaller and whatever I am looking at gets bigger. The enemy of our hearts is a master at even getting us to believe that the wretchedness and pain of our past is more attractive than the beauty and power of our future! This one report of doubt caused them to think that their bondage in Egypt looked better than the freedom of Canaan. Because of that, Canaan was lost to everyone in that generation except the two men, Joshua and Caleb, who believed.

That, my friend, is what is lost when we live double-minded.

What destiny and promise are you willing to thwart by staying in your double-mindedness about the goodness, bigness, or power of your God?

Saturday Surrender

"Therefore, my dear brothers and sisters, stand firm. Let nothing move you. Always give yourselves fully to the work of the Lord, because you know that your labor in the Lord is not in vain."
1 Corinthians 15:58 (NIV)

Friend, I've said it before and I will say it again — **nothing** is lost in surrender and so much can be missed without it.

We can't pick and choose what things we're going to give to God and what things we're going to hold onto. He is an all-or-nothing God.

So are you all in or are you not in at all? Spend some time today meditating on what was lost by the Israelites with their double-mindedness and what God is speaking to you.

Sunday Sabbath

"You will keep in perfect peace those whose minds are steadfast, because they trust in You."
Isaiah 26:3 (NIV)

Songs for Your Sabbath
Hillsong, *I Belong to You*
Hillsong, *With All I Am*

Read that verse above a couple more times — slowly, soaking in every word.

That's a powerful verse, isn't it? Oh, how encouraging and comforting that promise should be to our hearts!

By not being double-minded but steadfast, trusting that God is who He says He is, He *will keep us in perfect peace.* When you begin to feel yourself wavering, your confidence beginning to shake, remember that your God can be trusted and that He provides perfect peace in response to your unwavering trust in Him.

Sit in that truth this Sabbath… mull over that verse, chew on those words just a bit longer… let them settle into the depths of your heart today…

Father, thank You for being unchanging, even though I may not always believe You are. Forgive me for choosing to believe lies about You and for placing anything other than You at the throne of my heart. Help me to maintain a posture of surrender so that my mind would be firmly focused on You and Your plans for me, not wavering and easily deceived by the schemes of the enemy. Help me to quickly recognize a lie from him and immediately turn to Your steadfast truth.

Week 35

Oh, How as a Bride You Loved Me

Monday

Read: Jeremiah 2:1-13

Good Monday morning.

I've learned there's a difference between a bride and a wife and a groom and a husband. When I was a bride, Philly never heard one comment about his driving. Now that I'm a wife, poor guy, he hears quite far more than he should. When I was a bride, I used to sit down on the sofa with him every Saturday no matter what SEC team was playing. Now that I'm a wife, I go to the other room and watch Hallmark movies unless it is the University of South Carolina playing. When I was a bride, I thought all his jokes were funny. Now that I'm a wife, well…. I think you understand where I'm going with this and there are a few I could tell on him as well.

In scripture, God often refers to Israel as His *bride*. In the book of Jeremiah, where you read today, He begins this way, "I remember the devotion of your youth, your love as a bride, how you followed me in the wilderness, in a land not sown." Even for God, a bride often holds a different kind of love. It's as if God was saying, w*hen you were a young bride you'd go with me anywhere. Even if I wanted you to go to the wilderness with no idea of where we were headed.*

The writer goes on to write, "What wrong did your fathers find in me that they went far from me, and went after worthlessness, and became worthless?"

Wow. What sobering statements. This passage makes evident to my own heart that anytime my heart moves away from being the bride of Christ it opens itself up to then moving towards things that are worthless with the danger of becoming worthless, myself. That is why guarding our hearts is so important. That is why creating space to regularly be with and enjoy Jesus whether in worship, or prayer, or reading His word, or simply being quiet in His presence, keeps our heart desiring to be with Him even more. The same thing is true in the natural that is true in the spiritual. One of the things that makes my heart melt is seeing older couples walking hand in hand and imagining the shared history, the knowing, and the memories. It is one of the things I have grieved in the loss of my first marriage.

Marriages should only get more beautiful, more loving, more kind, more enjoyable with time. Yet, we have seen through our ministry and friendships many marriages failing well after the twenty year mark. It is because we move away from the things that keep us brides, if you will, and we listen to the accusing lies of the enemy believing grass is greener somewhere else. Accusation is the enemy of any relationship.

Accusation also often causes us to forget the good we have experienced. The Lord even challenges this in verse six. When we move our hearts away from that which creates love, it is very easy to forget all the beautiful things that have happened as well. It's easy to forget the places God has delivered us from, the times He has salvaged us from ourselves and our own mistakes or from the mistakes of others, or to forget the times He's made a way through seas that in the natural were impossible to part. This aspect of our relationship with Jesus, our Bridegroom, can be so easily forgotten when we move away from our first love and towards accusation instead. The same is true in our marriages.

In verse 11 He reveals the heartbreaking results of the path they've chosen. They exchanged their Glory, which was Jesus, for something that had no value whatsoever. Isn't this what happens in our own marriages or in our relationship with the Lord whenever we move away from "first love" things? It's important to remember we are always moving towards something and we can commit adultery on Jesus as easily as we can our spouse. In fact, anytime we give something a more exalted place in our heart than Christ, we are committing adultery. And anytime in our marriage we allow a relationship to have a greater voice in our marriage than our spouse, then we are in dangerous territory as well.

"For my people have committed two evils," He says in verse 13. First, "they have forsaken me, the fountain of living waters." Remember, Jesus told the Samaritan woman, if you drink of me you'll never thirst again; I'm a well that will always satisfy. And there she was, drinking from man after man after man. Yet, now she was encountering the Living Water Himself. Whenever you or I move away from being a "bride" we are forsaking Jesus.

Secondly, He says they've, "hewed out cisterns for themselves, broken cisterns that can hold no water." Oh, my friend, this is what the ultimate battle is between: our self-sufficiency and our surrender. I heard someone say recently life is only about two things: surrender and obedience. Self-sufficiency is such a sham, such a mirage. And what a sad, yet true, picture that is of self-sufficiency hewing out a cistern for ourselves yet being unwilling to admit that it is broken and can hold no water.

I don't know where your heart is. I don't know if you've tried to dig your own wells and are living in self-sufficiency or selfishness both in your marriage or with Christ, forgetting the days of being a bride or groom, but God is calling you back to your first love today, back to a place where you would trust Him no matter where He would lead you. Hear me today, sweet friend, do not miss or resist His precious pursuit of love… we should all be brides and grooms until Jesus comes.

What is the danger of an "I can do anything I want" mindset, according to **1 Corinthians 6:12**?

_____

_____

_____

Does anything master you now that is worthless or unprofitable? That has no value? That produces nothing of lasting fruit, but could even move your heart from the heart of your Father?

_____

_____

_____

_____

Tuesday

Look up the words **idol** and **idolatry** and write down their definitions.

_____

_____

_____

_____

Read **Exodus 20:3-5**. What does this make clear?

_____

_____

_____

Is there anything in your life right now that could be considered an idol or idolatry? If so, what does this do or has it done to your relationship with Christ?

_____

_____

_____

_____

Wednesday

If you are married, what are some ways that you acted or treated your spouse in the early days that you may no longer do? If you aren't married, what are ways you think may change over time? Why is that?

_____
_____
_____
_____

What does God have against the church at Ephesus, according to **Revelation 2:1-5**?

_____
_____
_____

How does He tell them it is to be restored?

_____
_____

What was your relationship like with the Lord and with others when you first came to a saving knowledge of Jesus Christ?

_____
_____
_____

What is that relationship like now?

_____
_____
_____
_____

If you have lost your first love, how could some of these things help you come back to a place of first love?

_____

_____

_____

_____

Thursday

Read **Psalm 103:2, 106:7**.

What happened when they forgot what God had done?

_____

_____

_____

Spend some time today listing the things God has done for you over the last year. If you cannot think of anything, then I would ask God if there is any rebellion in my heart and if so, to reveal it. Because it is our sin that separates us and makes it harder to hear His voice. Remember, "My sheep know my voice." He is speaking and working all around us.

_____

_____

_____

_____

_____

_____

Friday

Read the story of the Samaritan woman in **John 4:1-26**.

Underline the things you see in this story that reveal who Jesus is and reveal the broken cisterns of the Samaritan woman.

What does her decision to make Jesus her first love and become his bride do for her story?

_____

_____

_____

_____

_____

What is your story missing and what might others be missing because you are living in self-sufficiency instead of surrender?

_____

_____

_____

_____

_____

Saturday Surrender

"And you must love the LORD your God with all your heart, all your soul, and all your strength."
Deuteronomy 6:5 (NLT)

We are willing to do some pretty irrational things in the name of love. Drive long distances. Spend money on things we probably shouldn't – or wouldn't spend otherwise.

When we really love someone, we're more willing to put our own comfort and needs aside in order to love them well; it's easier to make certain personal sacrifices as acts of love. Think about what you've surrendered in order to be with someone you love and how easy it was to do that. Your heavenly Father desires that same heart of self-sacrifice in your relationship with Him.

So take some time today to ask Him to show you if there's anything you may need to be willing to sacrifice in the name of truly loving Him well with your entire being. Or anything you may need to surrender to love your spouse as they should be loved.

Sunday Sabbath

"I am my beloved's and my beloved is mine…"
Song of Solomon 6:3 (NIV)

Songs for Your Sabbath
Jonathan and Melissa Helser, *First Love*
Darlene Zschech, *First Love*

Oh, what a freeing truth, friend, to know that you and I are *His* and He is *ours*…!

Meditate on what those two things mean for you today. Rest this Sabbath knowing how much you are loved and adored; knowing that you don't have to work to earn His affection — you already have it. Your heavenly Father takes such delight in you and you can trust that His love for you is more than enough!

Lord, I am so very grateful for Your deep, sacrificial love for me. Oh, how as a bride You loved me… and continue to love me. May my heart's response to Your love always be one of surrender and willing self-sacrifice not from a place of obligation but out of a longing to love You in return. Show me where I might be trying to dig my own cistern and help me, in that, to turn to You, the fountain of living water. Then, Father, help these be manifested in my own marriage. Allowing me to love well as long as my spouse is here to love.

Week 36

Not Even a Sparrow

Monday

Read: Matthew 10:29-31

Good Monday morning.

One afternoon on my way home I was listening to talk radio. In less than ten minutes my pulse had increased and I felt my heart beat in my fingers. By the time he was done talking, the show's host had me convinced that I needed to go take all my money out of the bank and use most of it to buy gold and put the rest under my mattress, as well as get a whole bunch of prepackaged food to provide for me and my family for a year. My anxiety had increased to such a level that I was about to turn around and go get a [very large] McDonald's Coca Cola to be able to relax. It reminded me of Y2K and the fear that settled in then that left me with enough toilet paper for a year!

In the middle of this onslaught of pulse-racing, fear-driven information, though, I realized what was happening in my heart. Through the years, I've really tried to learn to be a student of my heart; a byproduct of spending years with a very shut down heart that needed to be reclaimed (as we talked about last week), and one of the things that had it shut down in such an extreme measure was fear. Now, anytime I feel that pulse-racing anxiety level rise, I will stop and ask the Lord what He's asking of me and I'll make sure that I'm being directed by Him instead of driven by fear.

And so I did just that. On that winding Tennessee back road, I settled my heart and my spirit and I asked the Lord a question. I said, "I don't know what times are facing us Father, but You do. So, what are You asking of me? What are You asking for me to do in this season?"

Right after that prayer was whispered, a bird flew down and hit the front of my bumper. I saw feathers fly and I thought, oh my goodness, I just killed Tweety! I looked back in my rearview mirror and I saw little Tweety flapping his wings and all of a sudden he just took right off back in flight. As soon as he flew away and I realized he wasn't dead, this passage of scripture came to my mind: *"Are not two sparrows sold for a penny? Yet not one of them will fall to the ground outside your Father's care. And even the very hairs of your head are all numbered. So don't be afraid; you are worth more than many sparrows."* (Matthew 10:29-31 NIV) In that moment I knew the Lord was answering my questions. He assured me that I'm not to fear because He's got even the hairs of my head numbered. He had just seen what happened to one of His birds and I knew I could be confident that He had me.

Friends, I don't know what this next season holds for us as a nation, as individuals, for our story as a whole, or for the individual pieces of our lives. I can tell you this, though: I'm not placing my trust in a government or any other human leadership nor am I in the money in my bank account. I am placing my trust in this God of the universe who turns the hearts of kings whatsoever way He will[65] and who promises that not one sparrow falls from the sky without the Creator of heaven and earth taking notice; yet, we are of more value than *many* sparrows.

May fear not rule our hearts. I'm not saying we can't be prepared in some measure but we are to "fear not," knowing that our Father in Heaven who watches sparrows is more than capable of taking care of you and me.

Are there certain fears hanging onto you a little too tightly right now? What are they? An uncertain financial future? The political, social, or economic state of our nation? The fear of the health crisis? Or the fear over what is happening in your family? Maybe it's a fear of failing at something or being rejected? Just list them below and we'll unpack how to face them as we go throughout this week together.

_____

_____

_____

_____

_____

_____

_____

Tuesday

There are healthy fears to have. Those are the ones that are wired in us to keep us safe from harm – fears of heights and dangerous animals, the fear of questionable strangers we're taught as children. At some point, for many of us, those healthy fears morph into deeper fears which end up

65 Proverbs 21:1 (ESV)

being the funnels through which we make many of our decisions – like me wanting to turn all my money into gold and begin hoarding food.

But what one command is the most repeated command in all of scripture? *"Fear not."*

Why do you think God would choose that command to be the one to be spoken more than any other?

_____

_____

_____

Read **2 Timothy 1:7**. You may even already know this one by heart. What does it say God has given us instead of a spirit of fear?

_____

"Power" in Greek means "force, miraculous power, ability, abundance, might and strength."
"Love" in Greek means "affection or benevolence."
"Sound mind" in Greek means "discipline, self-control."

Now considering these words, what is God inviting you into instead of fear?

_____

_____

_____

Boldly speak these truths into those fears you wrote about yesterday. Speak the truth of God's love, provision, and grace in power!

Wednesday

Read **Deuteronomy 1:19-36**. You've most likely heard this story before. Moses is giving an account here of how the Israelites responded when the 12 spies went to the promised land and came back to give their findings to the children of Israel.

In verses 20-21, how does Moses direct his people to respond? And why does he tell them this should be their response?

_____

_____

But what does their response actually end up looking like? (vs 26-28)

_____

_____

Not only does Moses reiterate the command to not be afraid but he speaks to them in regards to both their past and future. What does he say in verses 30 and 31?

_____

_____

_____

He reminds them of God's faithfulness! Now, that's an entirely different lesson right there… what in your past that God has done helps to remove your fear in your present situation? Oh, the gift of remembering...

_____

_____

_____

_____

But how did they respond? (v 32) How, then, did God respond? (v 35)

_____

_____

Take a moment to really take in the reality of what they allowed fear to steal from them. Because they were so wrapped up in their fear, an entire generation missed out on experiencing the biggest, God-purposed and promised victory they would ever encounter. **So much is lost in fear.**

What victories, what blessings, what breakthroughs, what promises from the Lord, might you miss out on because you're allowing yourself to be led by fear?

_____

_____

_____

_____

_____

_____

_____

_____

Thursday

God knows fear is part of the human condition. In fact, when God came looking for Adam after he and Eve ate of the fruit of the tree, how did Adam respond when God asked where they were? **(Genesis 3:10)**

_____

Adam had never known fear until he sinned. Now, because of that, we all do. But relationship with Jesus Christ is all about moving us from fear to faith. Faith is a confident trust in Jesus Christ who is holds everything by the words of His mouth and who has already won the victory for every situation that we face.

Read **Hebrews 11:1** and explain what it describes faith as in your own words.

_____
_____

Jump ahead a few verses to **Hebrews 11:6**. What does it say a lack of faith prevents us from being able to do?

_____
_____

It's not just "slightly challenging" or "really hard" or "doable;" it is _impossible_ to please, to honor, God without faith. We can't live the life God has called us to live when we choose fear over faith.

"There's freedom on the other side of your fear." – Christy Wright, Business Boutique

What would real freedom from your fears look like in the way you live? In the relationships you have? In the way you give?

_____
_____
_____
_____
_____

Friday

Now, don't get me wrong. I'm not saying faith is the absence of fear. I'm definitely not saying that you aren't allowed to be afraid when exercising your faith. There are so many accounts in the Bible of people who were afraid – whether it clearly says it or not – and chose to still move forward in faith.

Are you familiar with Esther's story? I do encourage you to read the whole thing if you haven't; her book of the Bible is tucked right between Nehemiah and Job… she literally risked her life, she pushed past even the fear of death, to save her people, the Jews, from genocide. Because of her faith and obedience, not only was her life spared and her people saved, the king also showed exceptional favor towards them all.

When was the last time you were afraid to do something you knew was the right thing to do?

_____
_____
_____
_____
_____
_____

Did you follow through? Whether you did or didn't, how did you feel about your decision?

_____
_____
_____
_____
_____

Read **Psalm 27** and underline as you read all the ways in which your God is with you and be encouraged today, friend…

Saturday Surrender

"Don't be afraid of those who want to kill your body; they cannot touch your soul. Fear only God, who can destroy both soul and body in hell."
Matthew 10:28 (NLT)

We have a choice of where we place our obedience. We can obey the lie that fear will keep us safe or we can obey the truth that obedience in faith produces freedom.

The fears you have written about this week are getting you nowhere fast. Choose today to surrender them to the Lord – the only One capable of replacing any fear with faith, life, and security!

Sunday Sabbath

"In peace I will lie down and sleep, for you alone, O LORD, will keep me safe."
Psalm 4:8 (NLT)

Songs for Your Sabbath
Chris Tomlin, *God of Angel Armies*
Matt Redman, *You Never Let Go*

A heart plagued by fear is a heart of unrest. Quiet your soul this Sabbath. Feel the arms of your heavenly Father embrace you, enveloping your heart in safety and security in the way that only He can. Don't resist His wooing, friend. There is no fear, no concern or doubt He can't handle. Don't let your fear cause you to miss out on the freedom, the victory, He is inviting you to experience…

Lord, I have let my fear control my decisions for far too long. I have let it steal too much from me. But not anymore. Father, I ask that this Sunday be a marker day for me. I ask that just as Moses knew You had given a promise, I place a stake in the ground believing Your promises for me. I choose to walk in faith, confident in Your plans and purposes. You are my audience. My heart's desire is to please You and You alone and You see me and care for me and will protect me even as You do the sparrows.

Week 37

Twelve Baskets Left Over

Monday

Read: Mark 6:30-44

Good Monday morning.

Have you ever noticed that there are seasons in life where you kind of think you're dependent on God and others where you know you are utterly dependent on Him? I'm sure many of you said, "Amen," right there. In fact, you might even be in one of those situations right now. Or maybe you have just come out of one. I've learned God loves me enough to keep me in situations that perpetuate my awareness of dependency on Him.

The disciples had a lot of those moments, too. One of them is recorded in Mark 6. This story happens right after Jesus has begun to send the disciples out two by two. The disciples had returned to tell Jesus some results of their new adventures and Jesus encouraged them to get away and rest for a while. However, getting away from the crowds was never an easy one for Jesus. So by the time they arrived to their solitary place, it was anything but solitary. Men and women and families covered the hillside. Jesus' compassion could not refuse their hunger and He began to teach them. Eugene Peterson picks up this story in the MSG translation this way, beginning in verse 35, "When His disciples thought this had gone on long enough, it was now quite late in the day and they interrupted, 'We are a long way out in the country and it's very late. Pronounce the benediction and send these folks off so they can get some supper.' Jesus said, 'You do it. You fix supper for them.'"

You know what I've learned? Our faith grows best in those moments when Jesus makes *our* need greater than *our* supply. In other words, He knows how to keep us dependent on Him. When the need is too big, too great, or too extreme for us to handle on our own, that's when He has set us up perfectly to show us how big and great and extreme He is capable of being.

The disciples were shocked. Wouldn't we be? After all, they were doing what we do so often, looking at our circumstances through natural eyes, forgetting that our God never looks at things from a natural perspective. He is incapable of looking at things from a natural perspective because He is supernatural.

Jesus told them to get to counting. They did. The percentages did not look good. But Jesus just continued acting in a way that expected a miracle. And a miracle is what they got. So much fish and bread that there were twelve basketfuls left over.

So much exists in this small story about supply, need, breaking, and blessing. The disciples were just beginning an entirely new aspect of ministry. Now, Jesus was showing them something vital to real ministry. First, you must recognize that only Jesus can meet the need. Second, you must realize that our need moves Him to compassion every time. Third, we can never be truly given, given in a way that can multiply in the hands of God for other's blessing, until we have first been broken. But once we are broken, God can give us out and move through us in ways that are abundant.

At what moment in your life have you needed God's most extravagant supply? How did that supply come?

_____

_____

_____

_____

Tuesday

Read **Genesis 22:1-14**.

At the beginning of this passage, what does it say God did to Abraham?

_____

_____

How is genuine faith created according to **1 Peter 1:7**? So what was God after in Abraham?

_____

_____

The disciples were about to begin what would require extraordinary faith. History records that every disciple would be killed for his faith in Christ, except John who was banished to the Isle of Patmos for his and is said to have died there of old age. Part of what gave each one of them a faith so great to trust God in the face of their own death were the countless times they saw God do miracles like these. That is why it is so important that you and I recall the moments in our own lives when we have seen God do extraordinary things.

In **Genesis 22:14** what was Abraham's revelation of who God is and was to him?

_____

_____

_____

How has God been Jehovah Jireh, the Lord God who provides, in your life?

_____

_____

_____

Wednesday

What was the first thing Jesus did to the bread before He gave it to the five thousand men and their families in **Mark 6** (in the MSG translation from Monday)?

_____

This helps us see that when God blesses something it means it is going to do more than it could in our hands. It is going to be used for supernatural, other-worldly purposes.

List the different ways God defines blessing as shown in **Matthew 5:1-12**.

_____

_____

_____

_____

_____

_____

_____

How does this blessing differ from how you see blessing? So, then, what does this help you see about God in relation to your understanding?

_____

_____

_____

_____

Thursday

~❦~

What was the second thing Jesus did to the bread before He gave it to the five thousand men and their families in **Mark 6** (in the MSG translation from Monday)?

_____

None of us can ever be given away until we have first been broken. Ever.

In what ways has God allowed you to be broken? Have you surrendered to that breaking or run away from it?

_____

_____

_____

_____

_____

In one of my favorite books, _Broken in the Right Place, How God Tames the Soul,_ Alan E. Nelson writes about what happens often when we resist brokenness. "Brokenness in the right place is thwarted when I see the difficulty, feel the pain, and sense the need to reevaluate things, but instead choose to try all the harder... Our self-help culture has given us the idea that we can fix all our problems. We have become our own gods... human activity must never be a substitute for godly power."[66]

How have you tried to become your own god? What has this caused?

_____

_____

_____

_____

_____
[66] Thomas Nelson, Inc. 1994 p 83

Friday

~⋘~

What was the last thing Jesus did with the bread in **Mark 6:41**, after blessing and breaking it?

_____

Remember, the disciples were just beginning their ministry. They were just beginning to see and understand what it meant to be given out. So who was God building their faith in?

_____

_____

What did Jesus allow the disciples to see about their own human abilities in the face of this inexhaustible need? What is your need trying to reveal to you?

_____

_____

_____

_____

_____

How does this story end? What do those leftovers speak to your heart about Jesus?

_____

_____

How might Jesus want to serve you up? What, if anything, in this season might cause you to miss it?

_____

_____

_____

_____

_____

_____

Saturday Surrender

**"Unless the Lord builds the house,
they labor in vain who build it..."
Psalm 127:1 (NASB)**

As born again believers and followers of Jesus, you and I are blessed. We must surrender to His holy breaking in order to be able to be completely whole, alive, and giving of ourselves. I know it makes no logical sense – but our God doesn't operate within our standards of logic and I couldn't be more grateful!

So, what may be hindering you from being completely broken in His hands? Once you recognize it, ask the Lord to remove that barrier.

Is it fun?
Not a bit.
Is it easy?
Not at all.
Is it worth it?
You better believe it.

Sunday Sabbath

**"God saved you by His grace when you believed. And you can't take credit for this; it is a gift from God."
Ephesians 2:8 (NLT)**

Songs for Your Sabbath
CeCe Winans, *Broken and Spilled Out*
Elevation Worship, *Give Me Faith*

No amount of our own effort or doing could ever save or sustain us. It's only by God's extravagant grace and His love for us. Period.

And it is only in truly understanding this truth and recognizing how dependent on Him we are that we can encounter life-giving freedom — another beautifully illogical aspect of relationship with Jesus.

With that in mind this Sabbath, as you find yourself in your quiet place again, ask yourself and the Lord if an understanding of His grace is something you have and are aware of how much your thriving and success depends on God's strength and abilities, not your own.

Remember the children's song, "He's got the whole world in his hands…?" He does. He's got your world, And He's got my world. And we can rest assured today that He will not even come close to letting them drop.

Father, break me. I want to be complete in You. I want to be able to give of myself in such fullness that only comes from You. Show me what it looks like to lean into Your holy breaking so that I can not only be utterly dependent on You but so that I can be offered up to others however they may need—knowing that just like You provided for the disciples and the families on the hillside that You will provide for me.

Week 38

Do We Trust God Enough to Give?

Monday

Read: Matthew 6:19-21

Good Monday morning.

In an article I read on relevantmagazine.com, Pastor Mike Holmes shared that tithers make up only 10 to 25% of a normal church's congregation and only 5% of the US actually tithes. He said 80% of Americans only give 2% of their income. So, if you read this title of this week's musing and every muscle in your chest tightened and the vice grip almost took your breath, then my prayer is that you will truly dig into what God may be inviting you into this week.

Don't run. It is not a punishment. It is a beautiful invitation.

Prayerfully ask the Lord to help you hear whatever He desires you to hear.

That first statistic that only 10 to 25% of Christians tithe, should be a heartbreaking statistic to every believer. Being a giver, at its root, is a heart issue. One of the very first verses of scripture that any of us learned -- whether we were raised in church or not -- was probably John 3:16, *"For God so loved the world that he gave His one and only son…"* God gave *extravagantly*. He gave His first and He gave His best. The power in that gift is its extravagance and should communicate to our hearts that He understands giving. No one has ever done it like our God has.

Yet, the enemy has so distorted the concept of giving. He's caused us to believe that it's all churches ask for or it's all televangelists want. Well, you know what? Their motive is their heart issue. However, I've never seen a church's electric bill get paid by prayers. And I've never seen a minister of the gospel who gets to spread that message via the airwaves accomplish that by wishing. It takes dollars. And we will gladly go into a restaurant and pay for service, or go into a store and pay for a product, but when it comes to thinking that the gift of the message of the gospel isn't in need of funding it is a faulty way of thinking at best and a stellar deception of the enemy at worst.

Honestly, I've been raised in church my entire life and because this is the way Satan has deceived people into thinking, most pastors are afraid to even talk about giving. But what we need to realize is that ultimately the issue isn't one of the "asker" but one of the "giver." It's not about you and the preacher. It is ultimately about you and God. And each and every time, our perspective of giving reveals something undeniable about our hearts. Now, what if instead of viewing giving as something God is wanting to take from us, we reframed it to realize it is something holy that God is inviting us to be a part of? When we give to people, when we give to ministries, when we give to our church, we are partnering with the work of the Kingdom of God and there is no greater privilege.

Jesus tells us in the Sermon on the Mount in Matthew 6, "Do not lay up for yourselves treasures on earth where moth and rust destroy and where thieves break in and steal. But lay up for your-selves treasures in heaven where neither moth nor rust destroy and where thieves do not break in and steal. For where your treasure is, there your heart will be also." That doesn't mean we're not to save, steward our resources, or get out of debt -- we're to do all those things. But we are not to store up for ourselves treasures here on earth, meaning allowing our stuff to become our treasures, because one day we are going to be gone and our stuff is going to stay right where we left it. Instead, we are to store up for ourselves treasures in heaven. Real heart treasures are in the eternal things that we invest our time and our resources in. The heart treasures of the people that come to know Christ by the work of our church or a ministry. Things that when everything in our home has passed away, remain. Souls. Lives. People.

Jesus goes on to say, "where your treasure is there your heart will be also." So, there it is again. Money is a heart issue. Where we pour our treasures is what owns our heart. Philly says it like this so often, "Your money follows your heart." It's true. What we give to has our hearts. So when we're not givers, when we're afraid to give, it reveals two things. First, it speaks of a lack of surren-der. We simply haven't surrendered everything to the Lord. Second, it reveals our unwillingness to acknowledge that every good and perfect gift comes from the Lord; He is the provider of all things -- we don't have anything separate of Him. The fact that we have resources at all is because He is good and provides them. So, if we're not giving, then we need talk to the Lord about what needs to be surrendered in our hearts.

Finally, it reveals a lack of faith in our God. God is faithful and is faithful to keep His word. He talks over and over about giving; and each time it comes with a promise. He says in Proverbs 11:25, *"A generous person will prosper. Whoever refreshes others will be refreshed."* I have to be honest with you. In those moments when I have given to something or to someone and I have been able to see the impact of that gift, whether it's on their face or I've heard it in their words, that is refreshing to my heart. It is a privilege to partner with the Lord in that way. That same scripture also says that, "generosity breeds prosperity."[67] Why? Because God can trust generous people to let His resources flow through their hands to get to the place He desires those resources to be. He says, "Give and it will be given unto you. Good measure, pressed down, shaken together, and running over will be

---

[67] 2 Corinthians 9:6

poured into your lap. For with the measure you use, it will be measured back to you."[68] God is faithful to give as we give so that we can then give again; giving is an invitation to our hearts to encounter the faithfulness of our God. He loves to show off His faithfulness!

Friend, we are not to live with a mindset of scarcity. We are to live with a heart of surrender that knows that the reason we have anything is because God is so exceptionally kind. We are to give out of those resources; we are to partner with Him in our giving.

Where your treasure is there your heart will be also…

So I ask you today… where is your treasure? Because there you will find your heart.

Take a few minutes to just reflect on your own heart towards giving and your current giving practices. What motivates you to give or prevents you from being more generous?

_____

_____

_____

_____

_____

Like I said earlier, this is an area of our hearts we all need to dig into. Be honest with yourself and with the Lord as we dive into this topic this week.

Tuesday

Read **Genesis 4:1-12**.

What was the difference between Cain and Abel's offerings? Why was God's heart moved by Abel's but not by Cain's?

_____

_____

_____

_____

---

[68] Luke 6:38-39

Why did God ask Cain why he was so angry? (Remember what we've talked about before regarding why God asks questions)

_____

_____

_____

What happens when we ignore God's instructions?

_____

_____

This account is the first time the act of giving is ever seen in scripture. It holds within it the "law of first mention."

The "law (or principle or rule) of first mention" is a guideline for studying scripture. The law of first mention says that, to understand a particular word or doctrine, we must find the first place in scripture where that word or doctrine is revealed and study that passage. The reasoning is that the Bible's first mention of a concept is the simplest and clearest presentation; doctrines are then more fully developed on that foundation. So, to fully understand an important and complex theological concept, Bible students are advised to start with its "first mention."[69]

So, if we use this principle in this passage in Genesis, we see clearly that in this moment giving to the Lord from what we have is about the attitude of our heart.

Wednesday

What does God say we can do to Him in giving of our tithe according to **Malachi 3:10**?

_____

_____

In what ways does God desire to bless us besides financial provision?

_____

_____

_____

_____
[69] https://www.gotquestions.org/law-of-first-mention.html

Many look at this passage in Malachi and argue that it is an Old Testament passage so tithing is not relevant to today. Of everything Jesus taught on in the New Testament, though, giving was His most talked about topic.

With that in mind, I daresay if we take into account all that Jesus said about giving, then we would probably find ourselves desiring to give far more than 10% away.

Read 2 Corinthians 9:6-15. What does the law of sowing and reaping say? Give an example of how you have seen this played out in your own life?

_____

_____

_____

_____

Who actually provides our supply? How does this make you look at your resources differently?

_____

_____

What does **verse 9** call our giving?

_____

What does **verse 11** say our generosity does?

_____

_____

Thursday

Read **Hebrews 11:4**. According to this passage of scripture what does giving reveal? And in whom is it revealed?

_____

_____

_____

So then, wouldn't it make perfect sense if giving and our attitude toward it reveals the faith we have in God, then the enemy of our hearts would do everything in his power to give us a distorted view of what giving actually is? What are some of the things you've found yourself believing about giving (giving to your church, to the preachers you see on television, to the person standing on the curb with a cardboard sign…)?

_____

_____

_____

_____

Friday

Take a look at the following passages of scripture:

Psalm 50:9-12
James 1:17
Psalm 24:1
2 Corinthians 9:10

How much of creation and the available resources are ultimately God's?

_____

_____

So when it comes to the resources we have, what's our role?

_____

_____

What, then, could be some reasons and ways Satan, the thief who comes to steal, kill and destroy, would steal from us the beautiful gift of having a giving heart that holds its hands open?

_____

_____

_____

_____

_____

Saturday Surrender

**"Honor the Lord with your wealth
and with the firstfruits of all your produce;
then your barns will be filled with plenty,
and your vats will be bursting with wine."
Proverbs 3:9-10 (ESV)**

God is a Father who wants us to love and trust Him with all of our heart and soul and mind and strength. We cannot be fooled into thinking that there is nothing wrong with our trust if we can be givers in every other way in our life except in our financial resources.

Giving is a faith and surrender issue. Ultimately in this life there are two things as believers we should always be doing: surrendering and obeying. It is in those two acts that we enjoy all of the beauty our loving Father desires to give.

Where might you be holding back with regards to your generosity? How willing are you to share of not only your financial resources but also of your time and energy? Some of us believe as long as we are giving financially, we won't be required to give of our time or energy. Surrendering those things is an act of obedience to the Lord. Ask Him today to show you if there is anything – fear, pride, selfishness, desire to be in control – that is hindering you from being more generous with the resources He has so lovingly entrusted you with.

Sunday Sabbath

**"Look at the birds of the air; they do not sow or reap or store away in barns, and yet your heavenly Father feeds them. Are you not much more valuable than they?"
Matthew 6:26 (NIV)**

Songs for Your Sabbath
Hillsong, *The Stand*
Lincoln Brewster, *Surrender*

Will you accept your heavenly Father's invitation to trust Him, to test Him, and to watch Him pour out His extravagant blessings? He doesn't want to take anything away from you – that's impossible because anything in your possession is ultimately His, anyway. He wants you to actively and willingly participate in the bigger story of bringing the Kingdom of heaven to earth. What better way to do that than to step out of the way and let Him do what He desires to do? And, so, in your quiet place today, meditate on that beautiful truth. God sees you. He sees your heart. He knows what you need better than you do. Enjoy Him in this Sabbath. Tomorrow will take care of itself.

Lord, thank You for being such a generous Father. Show me any places in my heart that lack a posture of generosity that reflects You. I know You are Jehovah-Jireh, the Lord God who provides, and all the resources I have, I only have them because You choose to trust me with them. Please cultivate in me a heart that has only the deepest and sincerest trust in You and Your word. You are in control – not me.

Week 39

War Room

Monday

Read: Romans 8

Good Monday morning.

If I were to say the words "War Room" to you, I'm sure you would know exactly what I'm talking about. It was a movie that really captured the Church and our culture at the end of 2015. I remember when we left the theatre, Philly and I were talking about its impact and I asked him, "Can you imagine how many people are going to run home after this movie, clean out closets, sweep hidden corners, maybe even build buildings and create their own war rooms? I wonder if in two months, or six months, a year, or even decades down the road if the very trajectories of lives changed will be pinpointed back to this movie because of prayers that were prayed in war rooms people went home and made. I really think we will see that happen.

I also had another thought in regards to this movie. My heart went out to those who had war rooms for years before they ever saw the movie; they prayed prayers, stood in faith, believed for the marriage to be restored, for the child's healing to come in their physical body, the home not to be lost and yet things didn't happen the way they had prayed. I had that thought because I experienced that, I believe, in my own life. I had a "war walk," if you will, around this little area in my home... I like to walk when I pray... and I prayed for years for my marriage to be healed, restored. After 13 years, I walked through the heartbreaking loss of divorce. It was definitely not the answer to the prayer I wanted and I realized that in life, answers to prayers do not always come the way we desire.

Inside of that reality we have two choices. Our first option: quit praying. We can end up believing the lie that somehow if God didn't answer our prayer the way we desire, then He isn't for us. We call that the lie of the disappointed heart. Or our second option: we can choose to trust God even when His ways are higher than ours and His thoughts not understandable to us.

I have learned, as I'm sure you have as well, you can't make decisions and choices for other people. But I have also learned that God may be doing something that in our finite human way of thinking we cannot comprehend. Romans 8:28, which many of us know so well, is translated in the Wuest translation this way: *"And we know with an absolute knowledge that for those of us who are loving God, that all things are working together resulting in good for those who are divinely summoned ones according to His purpose."* Friends, there are fewer more life-giving thoughts in this broken, fractured, and hard world than this truth of God's word. **All things** are working together for the good of those who live in relationship with Him! You might just need to sit in that for a moment. So if we're praying a prayer, trusting the Lord, believing for something and we're asking God from a sincere heart, then we can trust that God loves us enough because He knows our love for Him and He is working everything out for our good even when the answer doesn't come the way we desire.

Sometimes the good work that God is working out may even come in the form of delays or even denials at times. Paul was denied. Three times he asked for his "thorn" to be removed.[70] Though scripture does not tell us what this thorn was, it does tell us that God said no. But He didn't just leave Paul there. No, He came with the words that give each of us indescribable hope in the middle of life's greatest pains. He said, "My grace is sufficient for you. My strength is made perfect in your weakness." Sometimes what God is working out is something *in* us. Sometimes He's trying to build our faith or build our endurance or build our grace or build our forgiveness.

Sometimes the good work is about him doing something in someone else or for someone else. In Joseph's story, he was sold by his brothers, served as a slave, then falsely accused of rape, sent to prison, then forgotten after he interpreted dreams for other prisoners... want to talk about not understanding what God is doing... but in those thirteen years, God was working Joseph out of Joseph. He was also bringing Joseph's brothers to their needs of humility and surrender. When they arrived before Joseph again, these very brothers who sold him, he said to them, "You meant it for evil, but God meant it for good."[71] The good work done in those thirteen years saved the tribes that would birth and lead the nation of Israel. Because, in his book, *The Bait of Satan,* John Bevere makes the point that if Joseph had not been a man free of offense, then when he had his brothers in front of him, he could have very well killed ten of the twelve tribes of Israel from which all of God's promises for Israel were to be birthed through.

See, God's plan is often about so much more than us. It's about generations to come. Maybe He's doing work through our prayers for others, and so it takes time or will look a different way. But this is what I know: God is faithful to His Word. And His Word says that **all** things work together for the good of those who love Him.

So don't forsake a war room when the answer doesn't turn out the way you think it should or hoped it would... but, you build that war room. You build it in your car, in the carpool line; if

---

[70] 2 Corinthians 12:7-9

[71] Genesis 50:20

you have to, you build it on your commuting route to work or you build it over the island in the middle of the kitchen when you're fixing dinner... A war room can be found anywhere. I have said many times I would rather have prayed the prayer and still not gotten the answer I thought I should get than to have never prayed the prayer at all.

Friends, God is faithful to every prayer that we pray. Scripture says it goes up before Him as a fragrant aroma... your prayers, my prayers... and He is faithful to work a good work on our behalf.

In **Romans 8:28**, for whose good is God working all things?

_____

_____

It is important to realize that the promises in God's word are not for those who are living outside of relationship with Jesus. If you are walking in relationship with God today, know that even though you may not see or understand right now, He sees where you are today – whether there by your choice, by someone else's choice, by an attack from Satan, or by the very directive of God Himself – and no matter how you got there, He is working good.

What is it in your life currently that you may be having a hard time seeing how any good can come of it? What does the truth of this passage do for this specific place you are?

_____

_____

_____

_____

_____

Tuesday

I want to sit a little bit longer in **Romans 8:28** – there's one more thing there I want to make sure we talk about.

Think back to a time during your childhood or as a teenager when you really wanted something or to go somewhere and your parents or someone in authority over you wouldn't let you. Write below about that experience and how it made you feel.

_____

_____

I'm sure some of us may have been a bit more rebellious than others, but whether you obeyed or not, you're probably far enough removed from that experience now to understand why your parents weren't allowing you to have what you wanted. What was it for you? Were they protecting you from something? Teaching you something? Did they have something better planned and waiting for you?

_____

_____

_____

_____

Most often when we were young, our definition of 'good' for ourselves, like the staying up later, or the eating that extra dessert, or dating that person, didn't match up with our parents' or authorities' definition of 'good' for us. It's the same way with God. God's definition of 'good' for us isn't always the same as ours.

Reading Romans 8:28 with that perspective should shift our heart's posture. He isn't trying to punish or withhold anything from you. Instead, He is inviting your heart to see that He actually might be protecting, teaching, or providing for you.

Wednesday
※

Just like God's definition of 'good' for us doesn't always match ours, His picture of war is usually different, too – which we'll unpack these next couple of days. First, let's talk about our approaches to battle. Max Lucado said one time in a sermon at Gateway Church, "Every battle at its root is a spiritual battle." And Ephesians 6:12 says, *"For we do not wrestle against flesh and blood, but against principalities, against powers, against the rulers of the darkness of this age, against spiritual hosts of wickedness in the heavenly places."* Keep that in mind as you ponder your answers the next few days.

Read **2 Chronicles 20:1-4**. How many nations were waging war against King Jehoshaphat?

_____

Of course he was worried, wouldn't you be? But what does verse three say were his first two courses of action? Why are these important weapons in the battles we face? Would they be someone's *normal* response to a challenging situation?

_____

_____

_____

When there are multiple assaults coming at me from different directions, I'll be the first to admit that my heart's immediate reaction isn't always the same as King Jehoshaphat's. But we have so much we can learn from him in this. Read his prayer in **2 Chronicles 20:5-12**. What about this prayer stands out to you?

_____

_____

_____

_____

How might you reflect Jehoshaphat's posture of surrender and complete dependence on the Lord as you walk through battles you face?

_____

_____

_____

Most often, we want to develop a plan of attack, create a strategy, figure it out ourselves, in order to fight our battles; either that or we retreat, afraid of the wounds that fighting might inflict upon us. Nonetheless, our first move should be neither. Assuming a posture of surrender to the Lord will set us up for success through and with Him, which we'll talk more about tomorrow.

Thursday

Let's take a look back at what happens next in Jehoshaphat's story… we left off yesterday with him telling the Lord that he had no idea what to do, that his eyes were on God. Well, then someone spoke up. Read **2 Chronicles 20:14-17**. What stands out to you about what Jahaziel said?

_____

_____

_____

_____

My ears and spirit always pay extra close attention when I see things repeated in scripture. What does the Lord say twice as He's speaking through Jahaziel?

_____

_____

Thinking about what you're facing in your story, what might these words mean to you?

_____

_____

_____

_____

Jump down and read verses 21-23. The men appointed to praise - where were they positioned when heading out to confront the enemy?

_____

Logically, does that make any sense? Why is that significant?

_____

_____

_____

What ended up happening to the three armies who had initially waged war on Judah?

_____

_____

_____

So we see here that even in war, God makes things happen in ways we could never begin to imagine. When we submit to Him through prayer, fasting, and praise, then we are able to see Him accomplish things on our behalf we never thought possible!

Friday

On Monday, we talked about the two options we have: to stop praying or press in harder in prayer. Even though we may be fully aware of the benefits of choosing to press in, that doesn't make the decision any easier.

Before Jesus is taken to be crucified, He goes away to pray and takes Peter, James, and John with Him. What does He tell them in **Matthew 26:41** before He goes away a second time to pray that evening?

_____

_____

And what does **1 Peter 5:8** tell us to watch out for?

_____

Did you ever watch those videos in school where the lion or the cheetah is scoping out a herd of zebras or antelope? When they go in for the kill, which ones tend to be the ones that get caught?

_____

_____

Peter is warning us. He's encouraging us to be diligent in our pursuit of our relationship with Christ lest we become feeble and weak, susceptible to the lies and schemes of the enemy of our hearts.

No, it isn't always easy, but choosing to press in, pray, fast, and praise, even in the middle of the war, will always be worth it.

Saturday Surrender

"Because even if he killed me, I'd keep on hoping... Just wait, this is going to work out for the best – my salvation!"
Job 13:15-16 (MSG)

Ultimately it all comes back to this – because we do not always know how God will answer. We approach thought from human perspective, not our Creator's perspective. We look at life from our small, narrow lens while God has the twenty thousand foot view, able to see all that we cannot.

That's why self-sufficiency is so dangerous and why surrender is so vital.

Those seemingly hopeless situations you wrote about on Monday – take the time today to truly surrender those to your heavenly Father. Friend, there is always hope, no matter how dark and hopeless things may seem.

Sunday Sabbath

"Don't worry about anything; instead, pray about everything. Tell God what you need, and thank Him for all He has done. Then you will experience God's peace, which exceeds anything we can understand. His peace will guard your hearts and minds as you live in Christ Jesus."
Philippians 4:6-7 (NLT)

Today in your time with Jesus, and honestly, I'd encourage this to become a practice daily in your quiet time, take some time to soak in some worship music.

Two songs I'd recommend specifically for today are:
Michael W. Smith, *Surrounded (Fight my Battles)*
Mercy Me, *Even If*

Only upon surrendering our finite perspective can we encounter a peace unlike anything this world can offer. True surrender yields supernatural peace. Seek that peace this Sabbath. Rest in the promise that your God is working all things for your good – the good that is what He knows is best for you…

Lord, thank You for being so active in my story in ways seen and unseen. Your definitions of things like what is good for me and what war looks like are far from what I would expect and honestly beyond what I can at times understand – but for even that I'm grateful. I trust You, Father. I choose to press into Your presence even harder when I don't understand what is going on, knowing that You are now and always working ALL things together for my good.

Week 40

A Faith That Endures

Monday

Read: Luke 18:1-8

Good Monday morning.

Have you ever wondered why Jesus asks questions? At the end of this passage Jesus closes with a question… omniscient Jesus asking a question. Surely it isn't because He doesn't know the answer. But He does this often. In fact, in Genesis 3, God asks Adam, "Where are you?" Then the very first words that we read spoken by Jesus are when He's twelve and He's found in the temple; His parents come back to get Him and He asks, "Didn't you know I'd be about my Father's business?" This pattern with God and Jesus found over and over in scripture is clearly not because they don't know the answer. Instead, they're asking questions so that whomever they're speaking to, be it in scripture or be it in the quiet of our own souls, will recognize what truly is happening in their own hearts.

So, at the end of this story in Luke 18, Jesus poses a question: "When I come back, will I find faith on the earth?" Now, that question has always struck me. Of all the things Jesus could have asked if He would find when He returns, He's asking if He's going to find faith? In other words, persistent, enduring people who are unwilling to back down, run away, leave, or forsake Him. He's asking, *Am I going to find faithful, enduring people when I come back to Earth?*

It's evident in this day and age the bombardment and assaults that our hearts and lives are under. We've watched persecution of the most heinous kind on believers' lives in other nations for centuries, but the last few decades it seems to have heightened. From the decades of North Korea being the worst place for believers to the slaughter of believers in Nigeria, to the traumatic image that is hard to shake loose of the Coptic Christians being paraded on the beach by Isis fighters prior to the insidious taking of their lives, mockingly displayed to the world… to the Christian leaders assassinated in Mexico in a rare form of violence there. Yet, now, even here in America, we are feeling the impact of persecution for our faith. Our social media is being stalked and pulled for hate speech that is simply truth coming from the Word of God. Our morality is being challenged in the Supreme Court and state and local governments are attempting to pass bills to make the truth of the freedom of the Word of God against the law. We are nowhere near what the Church as a whole is currently dealing with and has suffered for centuries globally. We are only nibbling on an appetizer of persecution. So, it forces us to ask ourselves, what would we do under the weight of life-threatening kind of persecution?

I mean, after all, we'll run away from a relationship with the Lord on far lesser things than guns held to our head. We'll run away when someone at the church offends us or our prayers aren't answered the way we thought they should be answered. So doesn't it make this question far more sobering? Because it remains the question for us today: *When I come back, are you still going to be people of faith? Are you still going to have enduring spirits? Or are you going to have rejected your faith because things got difficult or challenging? Because you were unfriended by some on Facebook? Because YouTube quit showing your videos? Because family members no longer wanted to share your belief system? Because other churches view you as intolerant and misguided and holding onto "2000-year-old letters that have now made you irrelevant?"* [72]

Friends, this isn't a season for sissies. This is a season for sold out believers who have enduring faith. Faith that is persistent. Faith that is unwavering. Faith that is bold. May we declare loudly to our Lord and Savior who paid the price of our pardoning with His very blood, "Yes! A thousand times, yes! When you come back you will find my faith right here, waiting for you."

Being completely honest with yourself and with God, on a scale of 1-10, how firm would you say your faith is in God and the unwavering truth of His word in the season you currently find yourself? Why?

_____
_____
_____
_____
_____

Read **Hebrews 10:35, 36**. What word is used in describing what is needed in doing the will of God? Why is this so needed now in this life?

_____
_____
_____

[72] Rob Bell from Interview on Oprah Winfrey Super Soul Sunday

What do righteous people have to live by, according to **Hebrews 10:37-39?**

_____

_____

Tuesday

Let's dig a little deeper today in Hebrews -- read **Hebrews 10, verses 37-39** again. What does this say is coming and what is needed for the coming?

_____

_____

_____

How does this bring us back to Jesus' initial question of His disciples that we read yesterday?

_____

_____

_____

What happens if we don't move with perseverance and, if instead, we shrink back? What would this mean to your heart?

_____

_____

_____

Then what is this final faith declaration that Paul gives at the end of this passage in Hebrews? What does "preservation of your soul" mean?

_____

_____

_____

_____

What place in your life do you need right now to begin to set your faith strong in and begin to make this **verse 39** declaration over your own life and what are some ways you need to do it?

_____

_____

_____

Wednesday

❦

Read **Matthew 10:16-23**. What does this passage speak to you about the culture you live in? How to respond to it? How to trust God in it?

_____

_____

_____

Revelation 2 & 3 are letters the apostle John was given through divine revelation for the churches of that time and the body of Christ today. Read **Revelation 2:1-5 (AMP)**. What does the church have that Jesus acknowledges and commends? But what is lacking? Why is keeping your "first love" essential in maintaining your faith?

_____

_____

_____

How was Abraham's faith increased according to **Romans 4:19-22**? Where do you need to simply trust God more?

_____

_____

_____

Knowing the truths and promises in these verses should definitely increase our faith. We can look forward to being blessed and favored when we remember to keep our faith in God's Word.

Thursday

※

Read **James 1:2-3**. What is it that the testing of your faith actually produces?

_____

_____

So what are you going through right now that is actually growing your faith? What do you feel God is trying to produce in you by what you are going through?

_____

_____

_____

What areas do you need to move in greater obedience?

_____

_____

_____

_____

Friday

※

What does **Romans 12:3** say we are all given in regards to faith?

_____

_____

So if we are all given a measure of faith, how does our faith grow? Take a look at **Romans 10:17**. How are you utilizing these things now to grow your own faith?

_____

_____

Nothing in our life grows our faith more than hearing the Word of God, both by reading it in scripture and by hearing it taught by God's messengers. This is why it is important that you are pouring the Word of God into you.

If you struggle with this or have never done it before, then I encourage you in three areas:

1.   Pray and ask God to increase your hunger for His Word and then begin to read it. Get a Bible with good commentary and develop a way of studying that speaks to your heart. Pray before you read. Then as you read, keep a journal close by to write down questions or thoughts that you have about what you've read. Then pray when you are done. Don't rush to read the Bible; if you stay on a verse for a week that is okay. If you read through a book of the Bible in a week that is okay too. Just as long as you are reading to understand and allowing it to speak to you as you read.

2.   Find someone to walk with you and help unfold scripture to you. That could happen in a Bible Study at church or in a small group or in a one-on-one mentoring time.

3.   Listen to podcasts of ministers that teach the truth of God's word or listen to them on television. Purchase books with sound Biblical teaching. They are gifts from God to the body of Christ.

Saturday Surrender

"We also pray that you will be strengthened with all His glorious power so you will have all the endurance and patience you need. May you be filled with joy, always thanking the Father. He has enabled you to share in the inheritance that belongs to His people, who live in the light."
Colossians 1:11-12 (NLT)

Just as a tree doesn't bear fruit immediately after it's planted, our measure of faith doesn't automatically come strong and unwavering. The only way a tree can grow and get to a point of producing fruit is by being properly tended to and withstanding all the storms and temptations that could potentially destroy it.

In fact, the real strength of a tree isn't truly known until the storms or tests come… the same is true of our faith. Standing firm through the things that could wreak havoc on our faith while also feeding it with the Word will yield a level of belief and trust in the Lord that can endure anything.

Are there strong winds beating down your faith?
Is pestilence slowly gnawing away at it?
Is a lack of rainfall causing your faith to dry up?

Take heart, friend, and know that your willing endurance does not go unnoticed.

Sunday Sabbath

**"He gives strength to the weary
and increases the power of the weak.
Even youths grow tired and weary,
and young men stumble and fall;
but those who hope in the Lord
will renew their strength.
They will soar on wings like eagles;
they will run and not grow weary,
they will walk and not be faint."
Isaiah 40:29-31 (NIV)**

Songs for Your Sabbath

Mercy Me, *Even If*
Lauren Daigle, *Trust In You*

Enduring is difficult. It can be exhausting as well. We can even find ourselves asking if it's really worth all the work.

But we know we have the promises of God to cling to and He says He will renew our strength; He will increase our power. Our firm grounding in faith will be met with God's steadfast love.

So as you're in your quiet place today, let your heart wander to the strong, peaceful arms of your Creator. He sees you. He knows the challenges you face. Take the time today to just stop and be present with Him – let Him refuel your heart so that you can confidently enter this next week with an even stronger, bolder faith than you've ever had before.

Father, thank You for the measure of faith You have given me. Thank You for being a God who keeps Your promises and is more than worthy of receiving my full faith. I so desperately desire to follow You with pure, reckless abandon – unwavering in my faith in and dedication to You. Help keep my eyes on You as my faith is tested and let me be always mindful of Your detailed love for me even during those challenging seasons.

Week 41

Been Thinkin' 'Bout Home

Monday

Read: Revelation 21:1-7

Good Monday morning.

Recently, I heard that some of the final words of a friend of mine before he passed away were, "It's more beautiful than I ever thought." I don't know about you, but I think he was seeing home.

One of my earliest memories is of riding to school with my dad; I think I was in kindergarten. I said to my dad, "Dad, when we get to heaven is mom's fried chicken going to be there?" Now, if you've ever had my momma's fried chicken, you would want to know the answer to that question, too! My dad, in a way that's so evident of a father's sweet love for the heart of his child, said to me, "Baby girl, if you love your mom's fried chicken it will be in heaven." You can debate the theology of that if you want, but I know what he was speaking to my heart in that moment.

Since I was a child, I have had a deep fascination with and longing for heaven. A couple years ago I read the book, *Heaven*, by Randy Alcorn and that desire increased. Because of my overactive imagination I spend a great deal of time imagining what heaven will look like, be like, feel like, sound like. One of my hopes is that when we arrive, God will get out the heaven-scaled IMAX and He'll unfold all of history from the beginning, starting with creation, when He formed the world, and He'll go all the way to our story. And we'll get to see all the beautiful ways He protected and cared, loved, shepherded, and shielded us in our stories... we'll get to experience the beautiful love story between a Father and His child.

But, interestingly enough, not everyone feels that way about heaven. Many people, and my husband was one, have a different perception of what it's going to be like. Philly and I were on a trip years ago and I was sharing with him all these beautiful things about heaven and he said, "Babe, I've just seen heaven as flying around and singing... it just hasn't been a place my heart has been drawn to." I was stunned! Who doesn't think and talk about heaven? But I have learned… lots. Randy Alcorn talks about Philly's perception and many others in the beginning of his book. He believes that it's one of the greatest lies propagated to our hearts that if the enemy can create heaven to be a place that we don't want to go, then why would we want to tell anybody about it? And, yet, our hearts were created for this home.

In fact, think about your last vacation. You may have been gone for a week or two and at some point, you may have said or thought about how ready you were to get back home. There is something about home. That's why, in this life, we are continually searching and trying to create "home." That's why even the most incredible things we've ever experienced... that European vacation, or that recent family getaway to the mountains ... there is still longing. That's because the longing is for our ultimate home.

Ecclesiastes 3:11 says, "I put eternity in the hearts of man." We were created to serve Jesus, to be in a love relationship with Him so we can enjoy eternity with Him. And he tells us in John, "Do not let your heart be troubled (afraid, cowardly). Believe [confidently] in God and trust in Him, [have faith, hold on to it, rely on it, keep going and] believe also in Me. In My Father's house are many dwelling places. If it were not so, I would have told you, because I am going there to prepare a place for you. And if I go and prepare a place for you, I will come back again and I will take you to Myself, so that where I am you may be also."[73]

Friend, I don't know about you, but I have a longing for home. It is a beautiful place waiting on you and me and Jesus will be there.

When you think of heaven what emotions or images does it stir up inside of you?

_____

_____

_____

Tuesday

What does it mean, that "He will swallow up death forever," in **Isaiah 25:8-9**?

_____

_____

_____

_____

[73] John 14:1-3 (AMP)

Read the following passages:

Matthew 6:19-21
Hebrews 13:14
2 Corinthians 5:1

What treasures have you placed here that you may need to redirect? Ask Jesus to reveal to you what heavenly treasures you need to be storing in this next season.

_____
_____
_____
_____

Wednesday
❦

Read **Revelation 21:1-7** and **Hebrews 11:10**.

Have you ever considered that it is God who is designing our home? Have you ever realized that the Lord is going to make the earth new? And that there will also be a New Jerusalem that will come down from heaven itself?

Isn't that beautiful?

What do these different revelations about heaven and what it will bring mean or speak to you?

_____
_____
_____
_____
_____

Thursday
❦

Let's revisit **Revelation 21:1-7** again today.

He says here that He will wipe every tear from our eyes. What is the greatest loss, challenge, or experience that has brought you your greatest flood of tears? What does it mean to you to know that you will never shed tears over any kind of pain again?

_____

_____

_____

_____

_____

If God is going to one day make "all things new," what are some of the ways on the earth and in your life that will be impacted by that truth?

_____

_____

_____

_____

What does it mean to you and your story that God is the Beginning and End of it?

_____

_____

Friday

Write down the descriptions of heaven itself in **Revelation 21:18-25** and in **Revelation 22:1-5.**

_____

_____

_____

_____

What do these things speak to your heart about your Heavenly Father?

_____

_____

_____

_____

Spend some time today just imagining this indescribable beauty and meditating on what that beauty means to you about God and His heart for us.

Saturday Surrender

**"And there came a voice from above the expanse over their heads. When they stood still, they let down their wings.
And above the expanse over their heads there was the likeness of a throne, in appearance like sapphire; [a] and seated above the likeness of a throne was a likeness with a human appearance. And upward from what had the appearance of His waist I saw as it were gleaming metal, like the appearance of fire enclosed all around. And downward from what had the appearance of His waist I saw as it were the appearance of fire, and there was brightness around Him. Like the appearance of the bow that is in the cloud on the day of rain, so was the appearance of the brightness all around.
Such was the appearance of the likeness of the glory of the Lord. And when I saw it, I fell on my face, and I heard the voice of One speaking."
Ezekiel 1:25-28**

What does the thought that you will one day come face to face with God do to your heart?

This is an important question.

If fear or dread were stirred in you by that question, then it is because of one of two things. Either you do not have a personal relationship with Jesus Christ or it could be that you have a misguided and unhealthy understanding of God and heaven.

The first requires repentance and surrender — and, oh, the beauty that salvation brings. It opens us up to the abundant life God created for us even while we are still living *on* this earth while living *for* another world. And God has set this devotion before you today to create an understanding that He created you to live eternally with Him.

If, however, it is a misunderstanding of the beauty of heaven and what it truly will be, I highly recommend Randy Alcorn's book, *Heaven,* or, *The Heaven Answer Book* by Billy Graham. God doesn't want you dreading what is the greatest gift of the Christian hope! It is that hope that gives us a joy in sharing the hope that we have.

Sunday Sabbath

**"For God so loved the world, that He gave His only Son, that whoever believes in Him
should not perish but have eternal life."**
John 3:16 (ESV)

Songs for Your Sabbath
The Katinas, *I Wanna See Heaven*
Buddy Greene, *I Don't Belong*

Eternity does not begin the moment you draw your last breath here on this earth. It has already begun and we have access to the promises of the Word and fruit of the Sprit here and now, as long as we have accepted the gift of salvation and walk in right relationship with Jesus Christ as our Lord and Savior.

What a freeing truth that is, this Sabbath, friend…

And, so, I know I offered a prayer early on in our journey together, but I want to do it again today. If you have never trusted Jesus with your heart, I encourage you to pray a prayer, surrendering your heart to Him. In fact, let's do it together…

Lord, I come to You right now, asking You to forgive me of my sins. I accept Jesus, this One who has left this earth to prepare a home for me. I accept Him as my Lord and Savior. I surrender my heart to You. Come and live inside of me and make my heart Your home until we are together again. Now Father, I ask that my life be lived for Your glory and Your purposes. That my will be surrendered to Your will and Your life be reflected in mine.

If you prayed that prayer in faith, believing Jesus has entered your story, He has entered your heart and He has prepared a home waiting just for you. If you need resources for your growth in Christ write us and we will help you become a true disciple of Christ and grow in your relationship with Him. Your growth in Him is an outward expression of a genuine transformation on the inside.

If I don't meet you on this side, I'll look forward to meeting you on that side, when we will be together one day with our Father, with the bridegroom, and we will finally be home.

Week 42

Finding God in the Quiet

Monday

Read: Psalm 131

Good Monday morning.

One of the things I look forward to the most about our Weekend Experiences is the invitation we give our attendees to unplug. The permission and expectation to completely remove the distraction of technology: no emails, no Facebook... well, it's such a peaceful gift. The reason we ask is because we've learned that when you can give your heart a place to rest, you give the Holy Spirit a place to speak. However, a lot of our attendees enter that moment with severe anxiety; some of them choose to participate and some of them resist. I will tell you this, though, one of the things we often hear on Sunday afternoon on their way out the door from those that choose to trust us in this invitation is, "I have so enjoyed this time away from all those pulling distractions."

The wisest man the Bible says ever lived was King Solomon. One of the books he wrote is Ecclesiastes and in Ecclesiastes 3, in the "there's a time for everything" section, he says there's "a time to be quiet and a time to speak."[74] Did you know that? There's actually a time where our hearts need to learn how to be quiet -- and I'm not just talking about keeping your mouth closed. I'm talking about a quieting of your spirit and your heart. Psalm 131:2 (NLT) says, *"I have calmed and quieted myself, like a weaned child who no longer cries for its mother's milk."* I love that passage of scripture. You know what it looks like when a mom walks in the room to a child who hasn't been weaned... the baby starts flailing and going crazy. But when a child has been weaned and mom walks in the room, that same mother can take that little one and lay its little head on her chest and it can be as calm and quiet as a picture. There's something holy about quiet. I think that's why the enemy fights so hard to keep us perpetually distracted, living with a constant influx of noise.

I learned something a few years back. It was about a year after my divorce and the Lord was

---

[74] Ecclesiastes 3:7

depositing a new vision in me. I was getting away to a friend's cabin for a few days to pray and write down what the Lord was giving me and see what He would reveal. I had my whole car trip ready... I had my Coca-Cola, I had my music playlist all set, I had the talk radio queued up... I had what I was going to do all planned out, because I'm a planner and that's what planners do. I got in the car and I heard the Holy Spirit speak to that still small place in my soul. He said, "Don't turn the radio on." And I was like, "Um, I've got 4 hours of driving ahead of me... don't turn the radio on?" He said, "I just want you to be quiet... I want to speak to you."

Well, I have to be honest – it took me the first 30 minutes to even cultivate a heart of gratitude because I was not happy. But when I finally settled into the fact that He was inviting me into something and quieted the internal noise, it was like a supernatural download for the next three and a half hours. By the time I got to the cabin I didn't have to pray and seek and figure it all out because He had given everything to me already! All I had left to do was to write it down. So I wrote down the entire program of the event – down to the song selection. I even cut my trip short and headed back home. Everything the Lord deposited in the quiet ended up becoming the VBS for women event that we had the privilege of putting on for eight years in Tennessee and for many years in South Carolina.

Friends, there is a holiness in quiet. It's an invitation to your heart to hear from the Lord. We cannot hear from Him in a world that is perpetually drowning His voice out with noise. What if, in a few car rides this week, you didn't pick up the telephone or turn on the radio? What if, when you woke up first thing in the morning, you didn't flip the news channel on to hear the talking heads? What if tonight you didn't have to drown your sleep out with the noise of a television? What if you just calmed and quieted your spirit so that you could hear what a most holy God wants to speak to you? Let me tell you something, if you quiet your heart and you ask Him to speak, He will speak. Enjoy the quiet... God will be found in it.

I'm sure you're fully aware that quiet is hard to come by. What are some of the 'noises' in your life?

_____

_____

_____

_____

Tuesday

Let's spend some time these next couple of days on what an external quiet looks like.

One of the biggest noises we have vying for our attention is screen time. If you had to put a number on it, how much time would you say your eyes spend looking at a screen each week? That includes time on your phone, watching television, and time on a computer – that aren't for educational or professional use.

I'm sure if you were to compare that number to the amount of time doing the same things 5-10 years ago, there would be a pretty significant difference. Times have changed. Our culture has shifted.

In his book *12 Ways Your Phone Is Changing You*, Tony Reinke refers to a growing aspect of business and marketing called "captology" or "computers as persuasive technology." A captologist's primary goal is to impact and even change consumers' behavior patterns by learning how to capture their attention with smart phones. Kind of scary, if you ask me.

He goes on to refer to an influential voice at the University of Virginia, Matthew Crawford, who has stated, "The media have become masters at packaging stimuli in ways that our brains find irresistible, just as food engineers have become expert in creating 'hyperpalatable' foods by manipulating levels of sugar, fat, and salt… **distractibility might be regarded as the mental equivalent of obesity.**"[75]

How has your life been affected by screen time? How have your relationships been affected? How has your relationship with the Lord been affected? This can be positive or negative. I'd encourage you to even draw a line down the middle so you can compare.

Wednesday

Another loud "noise" in our lives is the overcommitted schedule. We won't (or we can't) seem to say "no." It's almost as if we wear busyness as a badge, when in reality, it's a form of bondage keeping us away from the quiet our Father so sweetly invites us into. It's also a lie the enemy propagates at our heart that "God needs me."

---

[75] Tony Reinke, *12 Ways Your Phone Is Changing You* (Crossway, 2015), 82-83, emphasis added.

Read **Acts 17:24-25** in the Amplified translation, if you can. What does God need? Why?

_____

_____

Right, He needs nothing. He *desires* us. That's why He made us. But we should never be so arrogant as to think He *needs* us. With that in mind, take a look at your schedule and even some of the requests for your time currently sitting on your plate.

Prayerfully ask the Lord if any of those things could be removed or said no to? What do you hear?

_____

_____

_____

How does the idea of saying no make you feel? Free? Afraid? Guilty? Like the other person may think poorly of you? Like God may not be pleased with you?

_____

_____

_____

Read **Colossians 3:22-23**. What does this speak to your feelings above?

_____

_____

Friend, hear me today: you are only responsible for the condition of your heart. If you need to lovingly say no and decline something, that's perfectly okay. You cannot assume responsibility for how someone else responds or perceives you, nor can you take on a task because you think God needs you. He desires you like crazy, but He does not need you.

Thursday

Read **Psalm 23:2-3**. Read it slowly. Envision what David is describing. How does that scene make you feel? What words come to mind as you picture this?

_____

_____

It's a peaceful and relaxing picture, isn't it? Do you think the peace and quiet this scene offers is available even in the midst of our daily chaos? I'd submit to you that it truly is.

Take a look now at **Matthew 8:23-26**. What was Jesus doing during the storm?

_____

_____

I often say that if Jesus is shown doing something in scripture, how much more, then, should we be doing it? In this account, during the worst part of a storm, He was sleeping; He was quiet. If His faith in His Father was that steadfast that He felt safe to sleep during a "furious storm," how much more, then, should our souls also rest in the quiet?

What might it look like for you to seek and experience an internal, soul quiet even during a storm you might be going through? Intentional times of prayer, fasting, and scripture reading? A deeper trust and surrender to God's sovereign will? A change of heart towards a particular person or situation?

_____

_____

_____

_____

_____

_____

_____

Friday

After a week of considering quiet and changing all the noise we let into our life, what are some of the thoughts or changes you've encountered or made already this week?

_____

_____

_____

_____

_____

_____

Read **Isaiah 30:1-15**. What are the hearts of the people God is speaking to?

_____

What does **verse 15** say will bring their salvation?

_____

_____

Friends, real heart rest is found in trusting God. Rebellion is a movement to self and the desires of its own way. When you and I perpetually resist quiet, we are resisting what our heart needs most. Because it is in quiet and confidence that true strength is found. Jesus wouldn't invite us into quietness, into "being still and knowing He is God," if it wasn't what our soul needed most. Don't resist it. Run to it. For it is where your real freedom is found.

Saturday Surrender

"Don't copy the behavior and customs of this world, but let God transform you into a new person by changing the way you think. Then you will learn to know God's will for you, which is good and pleasing and perfect."
Romans 12:2 (NLT)

Our modern society's norm is full of distraction. Full of noise. Getting caught in that flow, surrendering to that standard, we miss things. We miss out on the detailed displays of God's love for us. We miss out on deep, meaningful relationships. We miss out on opportunities to extend the love of Jesus.

May we be people fully surrendered to the things God is asking of us. Not the things that we put on ourselves. Because His yoke is easy and His burden is light.

We can only truly come to that place, though, when we embrace the beauty of His invitation into the quiet…

Sunday Sabbath

"Be still before the LORD and wait patiently for Him…"
Psalm 37:7a

Songs for Your Sabbath
Alex Boye, *Be Still and Know*
Hillsong, *Be Still and Know*
Selah, *Be Still My Soul*

Welcome to another Sabbath... another invitation into the Lord's presence to sit and enjoy the quiet, the stillness...

Moving forward, may we be ever mindful to intentionally remove ourselves from both internal and external distractions, keeping our eyes fixed on the One who loves and desires and cares for us, who is worth every ounce of our attention.

Lord, thank You for inviting me into the quiet. Thank You for the peace and the restoration it brings to my soul. Father, help me to live a life not branded by the badge of busyness but sealed with the marker of Your Spirit and overflowing with Your grace. May my eyes ever be fixed on You and may I ever remember that You created me because You desire me not because You need me. What a wonderful reminder on this Sabbath. May it be branded on my very soul.

Week 43

The Heart of Our Nation

Monday

※

Read: 1 Timothy 2:1-2

Good Monday morning.

In 2017, I had the privilege of going to the Capitol with a group of women in ministry leadership that have been friends for the better part of a decade. As we walked through security on the West Side of this truly awe inspiring structure and entered the small but ornate entry, we walked the quiet hallway to the small room that had been set aside for us; the awesomeness of the place was not lost on me. A few minutes later, the Senate Chaplain joined us for a private message and prayer time. He shared that he was asking God to bring revival to our nation and to let it start right under that dome. There was a resounding agreement from everyone in the room.

About this time every year, our nation has an election of some kind. As this time rolls around I am reminded again both of the responsibility and privilege it is to pray for our nation, as stated in your passage today. Praying for our nation and its people and for our leaders and for all of those in authority no matter their political party opens up to the people of that nation the opportunity to live in peace. Yet, at least in America at this time, peace seems like a foreign commodity.

As I take a look at where we are as a nation, I'm aware of quite a few different things. The first is that we are a nation in exceptional debt — over 23 trillion dollars as of the time I'm writing this. (It's probably silly to even put it in at this point as it will be obsolete before I finish writing this page.) Yet, scripture tells us that the borrower is slave to the lender[76] and that wherever your treasure is there your heart will be.[77]

---

[76] Proverbs 22:7 (NIV)

It's also a season where we face a racial division like I have never known in my lifetime. But scripture tells us, "as far as it depends on you, live at peace with all men."[78] But so many believers spread comments and beliefs across social media that are critical mass atomic bomb weapons fostering the very demonic seed of division they say needs to end.

Abortion has become a dividing factor in our nation over the last few years that has taken our breath away. We have listened as the head of Disney, a company who has made its wealth delighting the heart of children, no longer want to produce movies in the state of Georgia because they passed a bill that banned abortion once a heartbeat was detected.

The very definition of marriage has been redefined by the highest court in the land.
The courts have tried to legislate something that scripture has clearly defined in Genesis 2:22 (AMP): *"and the rib which the Lord God had taken from the man He made, He fashioned and formed it into a woman. And He brought her and presented her to the man and for this reason a man shall leave his father and mother and cleave unto his own wife and the two shall become one flesh."*

Our very identities are now being questioned, as well. Recently, at two very large universities' freshman orientations that two of my bonus daughters attended, it was made very clear to incoming students that gender identity was subjective to the thoughts and feelings of the individual and that no one was to try to argue with their thoughts or feelings; they completely undermined and ignored the truth that "…God created human beings in His own image. In the image of God He created them male and female He created them."[79]

15% of all Americans today live in poverty. How can this be in America? Yet, why wouldn't it be, if according to *Relevant Magazine* only 10-25% of Christians tithe. They wrote that if believers were to increase their giving to a minimum of, let's say, 10 percent, there would be an additional $165 billion for churches to use and distribute.

The global impact would be phenomenal. Here's just a few things the Church could do with that kind of money:

– $25 billion could relieve global hunger, starvation, and deaths from preventable diseases in five years.
– $12 billion could eliminate illiteracy in five years.
– $15 billion could solve the world's water and sanitation issues, specifically at places in the world where 1 billion people live on less than $1 per day.
– $1 billion could fully fund all overseas mission work.
– $100–$110 billion would still be left over for additional ministry expansion.[80]

---

[77] Matthew 6:21 (NIV)

[78] Romans 12:18 (NIV)

[79] Genesis 1:27 (NLT)

We're told in the Bible that "he who sows sparingly, will reap sparingly and he who gives generously, reaps generously."[81] We're also told that "whatever you did for one of the least of these brothers and sisters of mine, you did for me."[82] We want to blame poverty on others, when, if we are being honest, we could blame poverty on the church alone.

Recently, observer.com did a survey of 100 colleges and universities and found that anti-Semitism in America has risen 45%. And, yet, when God looked at Abraham in Genesis 12, He said "I'll bless those who bless you; those who curse you I'll curse. All the families of the Earth will be blessed through you."[83]

So we do face challenges that we've never faced before. But this I do know — Christians are not haters as it has been projected about us. At least, believers who submit to God before they submit to their denomination, their color, their socio-economic status, or their political affiliation are not the horrible, hate-filled people we sometimes can be stereotyped as. We are lovers of the truth, the truth of God's Word, the truth of Jesus Christ. We're told in John 8:32 (NIV), *"You will know the truth and the truth will set you free."* And the reason we are lovers of truth is because we know that a political party or an election or a bill before Congress has never transformed the human heart. It's never relieved the pain of a broken marriage. It's never relieved a racial divide. It's never relieved a heart and home from poverty. These are heart issues. Only Jesus Christ can transform a human heart or the heart of a nation.

And, yet, I believe we, as a culture, still find ourselves having ""exchanged the truth about God for a lie,"[84] as Paul wrote. Like the old song used to say, "we're living life upside down. Now, what used to be right is now wrong and what used to be wrong is now right." Somehow we are told that we are supposed to change our religious beliefs to accommodate a change in culture. That's not what the Word of God says. God says that He does not change. He said not one jot or tittle of His Word will ever pass away. He said no one is ever to add or take away from His Word. As Christians we're not given the luxury to change our minds based on a change in culture. As Christians the Word of God is our mind! And what a gift it is.

And, so, when I go into a voting booth I go focused on one primary issue. At the end of the day, as a teacher and proclaimer of the gospel of Jesus Christ, will I continue to be able to live out the freedom to speak this Truth of God's Word? Why? Because I know, fundamentally, that it is the only answer to the human condition. John Adams said, "It is religion and morality alone which can establish the principles upon which freedom will securely stand." I firmly believe that to be true. I believe our forefathers knew a great deal about our need for a sustaining faith and the

---

[80] https://relevantmagazine.com/god/church/what-would-happen-if-church-tithed

[81] 2 Corinthians 9:6 (NASB)

[82] Matthew 25:40 (NIV)

[83] Genesis 12:3 (MSG)

[84] Romans 1:25 (NIV)

power of God's Word. And I know that there is only one hope for the world. Matthew said it like this: "And His name will be the hope of all the world."[85]

Friends, if this is an election season, I ask that you would go into it prayerfully — not flippantly, and certainly not ambivalent — but that you would go into it with the primary focus of your heart and your mind being the freedom to teach and proclaim this gospel of Jesus Christ that is the hope for every human heart condition.

⚬⚬⚬

Have you ever prayed for your nation, its leaders, and those in authority? What things have you prayed for or would you pray for?

_____

_____

_____

_____

Does **1 Timothy 2:1-2** awaken or re-ignite anything in you regarding our nation and its leadership?

_____

_____

Tuesday

⚬⚬⚬

What is the power of praying **Matthew 6:10** when it comes to our nation?

_____

_____

_____

What does **Proverbs 21:1** reveal about God and leaders? How does that give you comfort?

_____

_____

_____

_____

---

[85] Matthew 12:21 (NLT)

Wednesday

❦

Read **Daniel 2:21**. Have you ever wondered why someone was elected into a position of authority? What does this passage reveal to you about our God in this matter?

_____
_____
_____
_____

How does a healing of our land occur, according to **2 Chronicles 7:14**?

_____
_____
_____

In your own life, how do you do those things? Are there areas where you need to be more diligent?

_____
_____
_____
_____

Thursday

❦

In what ways can **Proverbs 2:1-8** and **Colossians 4:1-6** guide the way you talk about those in authority, pray for those in authority, and address societal issues in public forums?

_____
_____
_____

Read **Romans 13:1-7**.

How does God see those in authority? How are we told to live according to authority in our land?

_____

_____

How does this passage potentially change the way you view, treat, or pray for those in authority over you?

_____

_____

_____

_____

Friday

Many people do not understand that honoring and protecting the nation of Israel has powerful implications.

Read **Genesis 12:1-3** and **Genesis 32:22-32**.

Abraham was Jacob's Grandfather. So the nation, Israel, that was formed when Jacob's name was changed, was actually birthed in Genesis 12 with Abraham.

What does God say He will do to those who bless and curse Israel?

_____

_____

There are different theological perspectives on Israel and its role: is it the nation specifically (the Dispensationalist perspective) or is it the Church as a whole (Reformed)? Personally, I fall into the Dispensationalist category.

I would encourage you this weekend to do some study in regards to the history of nations and their futures in relation to their relationship with Israel.

Saturday Surrender

"If a kingdom is divided against itself, that kingdom cannot stand."
Mark 3:24 (ESV)

As believers, we are called to respect our earthly authority — even if we don't fully agree with those in power. Our job is to support and lift them up in prayer and trust the Lord to handle everything.

I'm not saying we shouldn't speak up for things we believe in or that we shouldn't be activists for just causes. But ultimately our causes should first be Christ's causes while also seeking unity and not division — because that's exactly what the enemy of our souls wants, division.

If you find yourself regularly stressed about major social, political, and economic issues, that's not healthy, friend. Your Father in heaven wants you to trust that He really does have the whole world in His hands.

Have a conversation with Him today to begin releasing anything regarding those issues from your grasp and let them slip through your fingers into His strong and capable hands, where they belong.

Sunday Sabbath

"For kingship belongs to the Lord, and He rules over the nations."
Psalm 22:28 (ESV)

Songs for Your Sabbath
Tommy Walker, *The Lord's Prayer*
Tauren Wells, *When We Pray*

When we talk about "everything" being God's, that also includes the government. How comforting it is to know that just like God cares about our smallest details, He cares about the issues that face the world governments and He is the One who ultimately is in control — not the president, Congress, or the Senate.

And so as you're sitting in your quiet place this Sabbath, take a few minutes to pray for those the Lord has placed in governing authority in our nation, that they would acknowledge their positions with respect to the ultimate Authority and seek to honor & bring glory to Him. And that our ability to continue to spread the gospel of Jesus Christ, the only thing that brings true healing to anyone, will not be stopped by any scheme of the enemy.

Father, thank You for being present in the midst of apparent chaos in our world. Let me see this world through the lens of you working to reconcile all things to You. I don't understand why our society has the heart it does, but I do know how my heart is to approach issues based on Your Word. Help me to be a voice of truth that speaks words of life about those in positions of authority. Help me to pray for them regardless of whether I agree with them. Help me be a conduit of healing and restoration in Your precious name I pray...

Week 44

The Privilege of God in Us

Monday

Read: John 14:15-31

Good Monday morning.

When my dad was pastoring there was a funny story he used to tell about a little boy. His mom was tucking him in bed one night and this sweet little one was trying to tell her about the scary boogeyman underneath his bed. She, trying to console his fears like so many parents would said, "Baby, it's okay, the Holy Ghost is in here with you, there's nothing to be afraid of." I'm sure you can tell where this is going... so she walks out the door and stands by it as any good parent would, and hears that little voice say, "Holy Ghost, if you're in here don't come out because if you do you'll scare me to death!"

I can't help but wonder and think that many of us still live that way, scared to death of the Holy Spirit and the beauty that He possesses and gives. Yet, there seems to be a great awakening into this third person of the Trinity. There have been many books that have recently come out about Him: Francis Chan's *The Forgotten God*; Robert Morris' *The God I Never Knew*; RT Kendall's *Holy Fire*. Oh, the beauty of this third person of the Trinity.

He is first revealed to us on the beginning pages of Genesis. "And the Spirit of God was hovering over the face of the waters." Then, just as God has finished making all of creation He says, "Let Us, [Father, Son, and Holy Spirit] make mankind in Our image, after Our likeness..." Who was God talking to here? He was talking to the rest of the Trinity. Holy Spirit included. God the Father who created us, who chose us before the foundations of the world to make us in His image, who loves us, who guards us, and protect us was talking to God the Son who gave Himself for us so that we could be born again and so that this world wouldn't be our home because we were created for another. Who lives to make intercession for us and is building a home for us and coming back to get us. As well as talking to God the Holy Spirit who, when we receive Jesus as our Lord and Savior, comes to dwell inside of us.

So what is this Holy Spirit that many have been convinced is something to be scared of or avoided? John 14:16-17 describes Him this way: *"I will ask the Father and He will give you another advocate who will never leave you. He is the Holy Spirit who leads you into all truth. The world cannot receive Him because it isn't looking for Him and doesn't recognize Him. But you know Him because He lives with you now and later will be in you."* (v 25) *"I'm telling you these things now while I am still with you but when the Father sends the advocate as my representative, that is, the Holy Spirit, He will teach you everything and will remind you of everything I have told you."*

The Holy Spirit is the one who is able to help us discern truth. How desperately is that needed now? When lies are being propagated even from the pulpit, we need the Holy Spirit. And He doesn't just teach us *some* truth, it says He teaches us *all* truth. We have, as believers, living inside of us Someone who can point out at any time when we are believing a lie! Then, it says, He teaches us *everything* and, when we can't remember, He will remind us. So not only do we have inside of us all that we need to discern the truth from a lie, we have inside of us the One who knows everything, has the ability to teach us anything, and then, when in our human, infinite minds we can't remember, He has the ability to bring it back to our remembrance.

But the Holy Spirit goes farther, still. "The Spirit of God, who raised Jesus from the dead, lives in you."[86] Can you comprehend that truth? The Holy Spirit actually raised Jesus' body from the dead and He lives in the heart of every believer. So, inside of us lives that which can resurrect even the deadest of things: our marriages, our finances, our health, our children's lives, our dreams. Oh, what has been forfeited when we move in fear or ignorance in regard to the Holy Spirit and all that He is and desires to be to us…

The Holy Spirit also comes to us with fruit.[87] He comes to us with gifts.[88] Yet again, often times we partake of one while being afraid of the other. My pastor, Mike Glenn, said recently to our congregation in a message regarding the Holy Spirit, "Many of you have thwarted your inheritance because you are afraid of the Holy Spirit. You won't even pray to be healed."

It isn't hard to see how masterfully the enemy has played the hand of deception against this beautiful third person of the Trinity, God, the Holy Spirit. This is God inside of us! God Himself dwells in us. This advocate, as scripture calls Him, which actually means *intercessor, counselor, comforter*, is all these things to us and for us.

I do not know what I would do without the Holy Spirit. One of the many ways that I engage the work of the Holy Spirit in my life is to ask questions. I am always inquisitive with the Lord, especially when I have a huge reaction to a comparably small action. And I usually think, *okay something's going on that I need to pay attention to in my heart.* For instance, one time I was riding down the road to go meet Philly and he said something on the phone that I had this huge reaction to. I stopped my

---

[86] Romans 8:11 (NLT)

[87] Galatians 5:22-23

[88] 1 Corinthians 12:8-10

mind and said in my heart, "Lord, I need you to explain to me what's going on in my heart because something isn't right…" Immediately, I felt like the Holy Spirit gave me the revelation of what was going on.

When we read the Word, He is able to help us understand it. He convicts us, scripture says, of sin, of judgment, and of righteousness.[89] When you feel that tug on your heart that is pulling you off in a direction, different than the one you were headed, that's the Holy Spirit. He is convicting you, He's tugging you, He's leading you.

He is our counselor. When we need wisdom and guidance and discernment in our decision making or our conversations He can give us exactly what we need to move or to stand still or to speak. He is also our comforter in those seasons of indescribable grief, in those moments of pain that we cannot express with words. He comforts in a way and gives us a peace, scripture says, that passes all our understanding.[90] The Spirit of God took up His home in our human forms to lead us, to guide us, to direct us, to convict us, to be an advocate for us.

He is the One who gives us access to the fruit of patience when ours is inadequate; to self-control when we want to grab for what we want; to gentleness when we want to push our way through life. He is the One who places in us His gifts of healing and prophecy and wisdom and praying in a prayer language that can communicate the perfect will of the Father. And He is the same power that raised Christ from the dead and He has chosen to dwell in us. Wow! Oh what this beautiful Holy Spirit gives. May we enjoy all the benefits of God in us. May we pray for a fresh filling every day so that those who come in contact with us come in contact with the God in us… what a privilege… what a holy, holy privilege…

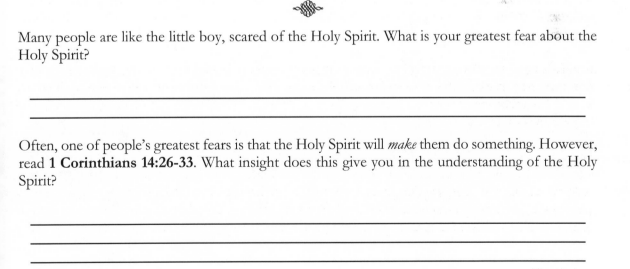

Many people are like the little boy, scared of the Holy Spirit. What is your greatest fear about the Holy Spirit?

_____

_____

Often, one of people's greatest fears is that the Holy Spirit will *make* them do something. However, read **1 Corinthians 14:26-33**. What insight does this give you in the understanding of the Holy Spirit?

_____

_____

_____

---

[89] John 16:8
[90] Philippians 4:7

Tuesday

The Trinity is such a huge theological concept to grasp that we often just throw our hands up and say, "This is too big for me," and keep moving.

However, I want you to stop one minute. Right here. Consider this question: Does it *really* resonate with you that the Holy Spirit is God? Not a piece of God or part of Him, but God Himself? Like the old hymn says, "God in three persons, blessed Trinity."

_____

_____

_____

Now consider this: If the Holy Spirit is God, what does that mean for you if He lives in you?

_____

_____

_____

_____

Take each one of these scriptures below individually and consider what this means for your life and your daily living if the Holy Spirit is God Himself.

"And if the Spirit of Him who raised Jesus from the dead is living in you, He who raised Christ from the dead will also give life to your mortal bodies because of His Spirit who lives in you." **Romans 8:11 (NIV)**

_____

_____

_____

Do you not know that you are God's temple and that God's Spirit dwells in you?" **1 Corinthians 3:16 (ESV)**

_____

_____

_____

"But when He, the Spirit of truth, comes, He will guide you into all the truth; for He will not speak on His own initiative, but whatever He hears, He will speak; and He will disclose to you what is to come." **John 16:13 (NASB)**

_____

_____

_____

"However, you are not in the flesh but in the Spirit, if indeed the Spirit of God dwells in you. But if anyone does not have the Spirit of Christ, he does not belong to Him." **Romans 8:9 (NASB)**

_____

_____

_____

Wednesday

On Monday we talked about fears regarding the Holy Spirit. Often one of the greatest hindrances to the movement of the Holy Spirit in our life and the fullness of all that He has available to us is the fear of seeming or looking foolish.

So, now, let's look at the flip side of that coin.

Take a look at the passage below:

"If I acted crazy, I did it for God; if I acted overly serious, I did it for you. Christ's love has moved me to such extremes. His love has the first and last word in everything we do."
2 Corinthians 5:13-14 (MSG)

How does it say we need to be willing to act for God?

_____

It is important to remember that true surrender to Christ is being willing to look foolish in the eyes of the world. Few things seem as foolish as the Holy Spirit. It is this same Holy Spirit that can lead us to do things that, in the natural, seem crazy. He can invite us to give when we don't think we have anything to give. He can direct us to leave the familiar and take a step of faith when everyone else is telling us we are crazy. He can speak through us with discernment and words of knowledge. He can pray through us with groans and spiritual language. He can convict us from doing things that in the eyes of the world look normal.

So the ultimate question in regards to your life and the Holy Spirit is: are you willing to surrender completely to even looking foolish to others at the cost of missing the fullness of the Spirit of God dwelling in you?

_____

_____

_____

_____

_____

Thursday

Let's look closer today at what missing the fullness of the Spirit of God dwelling in us might look like. Think about some of the seemingly crazy or foolish things you have heard people do in the name of Christ – whether in the Bible or in modern day – that ended up producing something powerful in their lives that only God could have done. Write them below.

_____

_____

_____

_____

In each of those situations, how did God bless and honor their obedience?

_____

_____

_____

If those people hadn't been obedient, they would have missed out on the blessing, the fruit of the fullness of the Spirit in them. So, yes, He comes in us with salvation, but He also brings with Him all kinds of beautiful gifts and fruits that self-sufficiency can cause us to miss.

What might you be missing by your unwillingness to look like a fool for the cause of Christ? Know that there is a big difference in being a fool for Christ and acting and living foolishly.

_____

_____

_____

What could happen in your life if you radically surrendered to all that the Holy Spirit had for you? In your family? In your church? In your city? In your nation? In this world?

_____

_____

_____

Friday

~❋~

Recently Philly and I were at a dinner with some people we dearly love. However, in the middle of that dinner I realized that without Jesus these people would not be with us in heaven. It just crashed over me as we broke bread together. I have prayed for them for years. But it has given me a new fervency in how I pray for them and how I pray for opportunity to reach them. Ask the Lord to begin to fill you with boldness to share the gospel. This also comes with us being willing to look foolish for the cause of Christ. You cannot become a sharer of the gospel if you are more concerned with how people perceive you. That is why we need to be refilled every morning with the Holy Spirit and continue to ask the Lord to strip us of anything that would cause us to resist the fullness of all that He has.

Read **Acts 1:8**. What did the Holy Spirit bring when He came?

_____

And what did it then lead the disciples and those in the upper room to do?

_____

_____

The Holy Spirit brings a power into our lives that is not found anywhere else. It also creates in us a boldness to be messengers of the cause of Christ. What happens when you think about sharing the gospel with someone? What thoughts go through your mind? How do you feel? Why do you think this is so hard?

_____

_____

_____

_____

Having the fullness of the Holy Spirit isn't for us to keep to ourselves. It's a gift for us to constantly seek to pass on. Two of the greatest evangelists of our time are Billy Graham and James Robison.

Both of them have recorded their evangelistic journeys in their memoirs: "Just as I am" and "Living Amazed." These are both such powerful reads that I highly recommend them for a closer look into what it truly looks like to witness "to the ends of the earth."

Saturday Surrender

"On one occasion, while He was eating with them, He gave them this command: "Do not leave Jerusalem, but wait for the gift my Father promised, which you have heard me speak about.""
Acts 1:4 (NIV)

Oh what a gift, what a privilege it is to have direct access to our heavenly Father and to have His Holy Spirit alive, active, and dwelling in us. But to truly walk in and experience everything He has for us, we must first surrender to Him.

Surrendering doesn't turn us into some puppets on a string, being forced to do things. It opens up a new place of freedom, of boldness, of authority, to pray differently, live differently, and share the beauty of the gospel differently.

Who would want to miss out on that?!

Talk to the Lord today about what might be in your way, hindering true surrender and what getting to that place would look like. Even ask Him to give you a deeper understanding of what your heart – and even the hearts of those around you – may miss out on due to your lack of surrender.

Sunday Sabbath

"The Lord replied, "My Presence will go with you, and I will give you rest.""
Exodus 33:14 (NIV)

Songs for Your Sabbath
Michael Ketterer, *Spirit Lead Me*
Phil Wickham, Michael Crawford, Chicago Mass Choir, or Nederland Zingt, *(Spirit of the Living God) Fall Fresh On Me*

Just as God promised Moses His presence and rest in Exodus, we have access to His presence still, today, and the sweet rest that only He can provide.

So nestle into the peace, the safety, the fullness of His presence this Sabbath. Know how much of an honor it is that our Father in heaven would choose to bless us with His presence… and there is so much available to us there – all we have to do is simply ask…

Lord, what a privilege it is to have Your Holy Spirit in me. Show me anything that may be holding me back from the fullness of Your Spirit in me and let my heart be increasingly sensitive to His leading. Fill me with everything that He has. I don't want to miss anything. May I walk in a new level of freedom, boldness, and authority in You, Father with the power of Your very Spirit alive in me.

Week 45

When the Word and Spirit Meet

Monday

Read: John 4:1-30

Good Monday morning.

Her life was a train wreck. Bad decision after bad decision. Man after man. Marriage after marriage. Divorce after divorce. Shunned by the neighbors. An outcast drawing water. Jesus loves train wrecks. In fact, He seeks them out. The gospels are full of them. This meeting with one, He would not miss…

She had a water jug and He needed water so He asked her for some. Jews didn't do this kind of thing — talk to Samaritans, that is. Samaritans were beneath them, dogs to their culture. He never did "culture" well. Politically correct would have never defined Jesus. Nor would racist. Nor would religious. Jesus busted up into the gods of that culture just like He busts up into the gods of ours today.

She is shocked at His request. She knows who she is. Life has defined her. She has let it. She points out His lack of understanding of what is appropriate in settings like these. He points out that if she knew who was asking her for water, she would be asking Him, the fount of Living Water. She mocks Him. He moves in deeper. "Anyone who drinks this water will soon become thirsty again. But those who drink the water I give will never be thirsty again. It becomes a fresh, bubbling spring within them, giving them eternal life."[91]

He's got her now. Anything to get rid of the shame of her story. Anything to not have to travel these dusty roads in the heat of the day after all the others and all alone. "Please, sir," the woman said, "give me this water! Then I'll never be thirsty again, and I won't have to come here to get water."[92]

---

[91] John 4:14 (NLT)
[92] John 4:15 (NLT)

He goes deeper still and asks about her husband. She deflects. Oh, how the human soul is so good at deflecting from our deepest places of pain. She brings up religion. The difference between His and hers. Jews do it one way. Samaritans do it another. Jesus… well, Jesus does it the real way, the way He designed. "But the time is coming — indeed it's here now — when true worshipers will worship the Father in spirit and in truth. The Father is looking for those who will worship Him that way. For God is Spirit, so those who worship Him must worship in spirit and in truth."[93] This encounter with Jesus transforms this Samaritan woman. So much so that she becomes the first female evangelist by an encounter with Jesus, the Spirit and the Truth.

I grew up Pentecostal. That heritage has afforded me the beauty of seeing the fullness of the Spirit of God on display in its Biblical form. I am now, and have been for many years, a member of a Baptist church and have enjoyed the impenetrable truth of God's word. The danger in both of these environments is when the other is excluded. When it is only Spirit and no Truth or only Truth and no Spirit. Jesus was saying, "I am both."

We're all broken like this woman at the well whether we want to admit it or not. And brokenness needs both the power of God's truth and the healing balm of His Spirit. To say that the Holy Spirit and His power and gifts were only for a season leaves the church "forfeiting its inheritance" as my pastor said recently. Nowhere in scripture does it say that God's Spirit has ever ceased to move or operate as it began. In fact, Paul even goes on to define the gifts and give us a beautiful model in which they can and should operate in a healthy and thriving church. However, a heart that makes the "gifts of the Spirit" the only way to encounter God will soon move to living off of their own experience and can quickly begin to distort the truth of God's word into a gospel based on their feelings and not on truth. In as much, a heart that makes God's word the soul focus and calls those things of the Spirit witchcraft and evil not only risks great error, but spends their life missing the beauty of what the anointing and gifts of the Spirit afford every believer.

I want to be clear that moving past what we've always been taught isn't easy. As a person raised in a Spirit-focused denomination (and not always the Holy Spirit, I might add), I have had to jump over prejudices and error from my own upbringing to minister effectively to the many denominations God allows me to minister to as well as to receive and enjoy all of the beauty and anointing that resides in my Baptist church. Philly, being raised in a Baptist church, has also had to jump over prejudices and error from his upbringing to allow Himself to enjoy many of the things of the Spirit that He has been exposed to.

But when we do, when we allow both Spirit and Truth to meet inside of us, when our heart and head are allowed to converge and encounter the power and beauty of all that Jesus is, oh, the things God can do! Just like in Samaria, entire cities can be transformed and human hearts can come alive in ways that earthly water can never fill.

---

93 John 5:23-24 (NLT)

Read **John 14:6** and **Colossians1:4-5**.

What do these speak to you about the "Truth?"

_____

_____

_____

_____

Tuesday

According to Strong's Dictionary, the word "good news" is also the "gospel," which literally means "God's good news;" this is also the entire Bible.

Read **John 1:1-5**.

If Jesus is the Word in the flesh, and the Word gives life to everything that is created, then, in light of all that is expressed about the Word, what does reading the Word of God do to our life and our heart and our circumstances?

_____

_____

_____

_____

Where should our faith also be, according to **1 Corinthians 2:4-5**?

_____

_____

How true is this for you?

_____

_____

Wednesday

What is the Holy Spirit for the believer in Christ according to **Ephesians 1:13-14**?

_____

_____

Read **1 Corinthians 12:1-11**.

What does verse 7 say about why the manifestation of the Spirit is given?

_____

_____

_____

What are the different gifts found in the Spirit of God?

_____

_____

_____

_____

Now look at **1 Corinthians 12:12-29**.

When God is asking us to earnestly desire the most helpful gifts, what is He asking of us and what is He saying about His gifts?

_____

_____

_____

_____

_____

_____

Thursday

What does **John 10:10** say that the enemy is perpetually trying to do?

_____

With that in mind, how could he be stealing, killing, and destroying by having God's people not live in both the truth of His Word and in the power of His Spirit? In our personal lives? In the body of Christ? And in the world at large?

_____
_____
_____
_____
_____
_____

Friday

What does **Luke 24:27-32** reveal about both the Word and the Spirit?

_____
_____
_____
_____

Fear is the greatest motivator for people resisting either.

One feels they will look foolish. However, risking looking like a fool is better than missing the fullness of Christ's Spirit. Other's believe they will have to give up their "experiences."

But experience should never trump the Word of God. In fact, "The grass withers and the flowers fade, but the word of our God stands forever." Isaiah 40:8 (NLT)

Saturday Surrender

"If I acted crazy, I did it for God; if I acted overly serious, I did it for you. Christ's love has moved me to such extremes. His love has the first and last word in everything we do."
2 Corinthians 5:13-14 (MSG)

Yesterday, I mentioned our potential fear of looking foolish when leaning into either the Word or the fullness of the Spirit.

Could it be that what is in question is our surrender? Surrender makes it okay if we look crazy and okay if we speak words of life that are very serious. But we do it all because we don't want to miss one thing Jesus has for us in this life! I'm not saying we move about in foolishness without using discernment. Discernment and wisdom are a believer's best friend.

Our willingness to lay down our pride automatically shows our willingness to let God take control and do exactly what He wants to do in and through us. Ask Him today to begin to cultivate in you a heart that doesn't think twice when it comes to potentially looking foolish in the eyes of man — whether that is speaking Truth to a world that no longer wants to hear it, or moving in all the fullness of God's Spirit — because being obedient in the eyes of our heavenly Father is what's most important anyway.

Sunday Sabbath

"But seek first the kingdom of God and His righteousness, and all these things will be added to you."
Matthew 6:33 (ESV)

Songs for Your Sabbath
Kari Jobe, *Breathe On Us*
Chelsea Moon with the Franz Brothers, *How Firm a Foundation*

It's really that simple.

We simply keep our gaze ahead and above — on God's Truth and Spirit.

So, this Sabbath, be intentional to do just that: refocus your heart on the truth of God's Word and the role of His Spirit in your life. How does the gospel, God's good news, impact your daily life? If you don't have an answer to that question, you might want to start there as you're recalibrating your focus.

Does your pursuit tend to lean more towards experiencing the Spirit or diving into the truth of the Word? We should know the beauty of both and not be intimidated by a fear of what we might not know or understand. Why? Because God's Spirit will lead us into all truth.

Father, thank You for access to both Your Truth and Your Spirit. Thank You for how they don't operate independently of each other but that they were created to complement each other — always leading me straight to Your heart. Please show me anything in me that may be hindering me from fully experiencing both and forgive me for allowing anything to come between my heart and Yours.

Week 46

Taking On Our Goliaths

Monday

Read: 1 Samuel 17

Good Monday morning.

Recently, when studying the story of King David, I was captured by this moment… David is sent by his father to take some food to his three oldest brothers who are fighting in the Israelite army against the Philistines. He was also tasked with bringing a report back to his father. When he gets there, David comes across a giant named Goliath. Goliath is taunting and mocking the armies of the Israelites. Upon seeing and hearing this, David is shocked. He can't believe someone would dare mock the armies of the living God. He also can't believe the reaction of the Israelites. They are running scared. The nation that had all of the promises of God was being pushed around by a giant bully.

But David wasn't afraid. Why? Because his entire life had been preparation for this moment. The bears he killed protecting the sheep were preparation. The lions he destroyed were preparation. While being a faithful shepherd, out in the fields worshiping the Lord, the Lord had prepared him to face a giant named Goliath.

Saul notices the tenacity of the young fellow and is willing to let David face the giant. He even gives David his armor. Honestly, every time I read that section I wonder, "Saul, why in the world didn't you face that giant yourself? People follow the leader. Their fear could only be a product of yours." The armor is a joke. (Note here, you don't need to ever go into battle thinking another man's armor will save you. We put on our *own* armor.) David goes with what he knows. He is a slingshot kind of boy. With nothing but five stones, though he won't even need all of those, David goes out to meet this mocking giant.

Read again what he tells Goliath in 1 Samuel 17:45-47.

Did you notice where David ran? Not away. No, he runs straight into the battle. And as he does, scripture says he takes one stone and slings it and down Goliath goes, dead. But that isn't where the story ends, though it is often where it quits being told. Do you remember the very last thing he did to Goliath? He didn't just kill him, but he then went and cut off his head.

That is a powerful statement that doesn't need to be lost in where we are going this week. So let me ask you, "What are the Goliaths in your life that God is telling you to destroy?" We all have Goliaths – things that mock us or try to torment us... they can be our fears, our unbelief, our unforgiveness, our jealousies, our addictions... we can have all kinds of Goliaths. But if we listen to them to the point that we believe them, then we will forget who we are, who we are in Christ.

David was in a transition season from shepherd boy to king. He knew it even if King Saul didn't. But Goliath had to be dealt with in order for David to get to where the Lord had called him. And we need to know that there may be things in our lives that have to be dealt with before we can get to the next place that God is inviting us to. However, the beautiful thing about our Goliaths is that, just like David, we don't face them alone. David told Goliath, "Today the Lord will conquer you" – we don't battle in our own strength. We fight from a place of faith, we fight from a place of victory because we are fighting from the promises and partnership of God. We fight from a place that isn't by our might or by our power, but is by His Spirit.

Yet, so many times we try to do it alone... we try to fight from a place of self-sufficiency, we try to fight from a place of control where we want to manipulate and control life so that it'll work out the way we think it should. We fight from a place of desperation. But we end up either exhausted or we end up with broken relationships because we're not fighting from the strength of the Lord. And the reason God doesn't allow it to work this way is because if we can win the battle ourselves then we could take the glory. But do you know what? God will not share His glory. The reason God could trust David to be king is because David let Goliath know that when I've cut off your head, when all your men have been fed to wild animals and birds, the world will know that there is a God in Israel! When we, with the power and strength of the Holy Spirit and the Lord fighting with us, defeat the Goliaths in our lives, people will take notice. And then we will have a choice of whom to honor: our own strength or the power of the living God.

Friends, God is always moving in our lives and He's always desiring to take us from strength to strength.[94] And, often, in order to get to the next place of glory, a Goliath has to be slayed. So I encourage you, get curious with the Lord this week and ask Him if there are any Goliaths standing in the way of the next place, the next season, the next vision, that He is desiring you to go. If there are, know that God is able to get rid of them and be willing to partner with Him however He needs you to. I will tell you this: when you do, people will know there is a God in Israel.

Like David in this piece of his story, we can find ourselves in transitions between seasons. Is that

---

94 Psalm 84:7

where you might find yourself right now? If so, what season are you leaving and/or moving into? If not, think back to the last transitional season you walked through.

_____

_____

_____

_____

_____

Whether it was/is planned or not, transitions always mean change – not only in our situations and circumstances, but in our hearts. And even then, it may not always mean change for the better, unfortunately.

Describe what change(s) happened in you during your last season of transition or what you may even sense is changing in you now.

_____

_____

_____

_____

Tuesday

❧

The enemy is a master at putting giant Goliaths in our paths. They block our view of where we're heading. What are some people or situations in your life that seem immovable? Too big?

_____

_____

What does **Psalm 24:1** say belongs to the Lord?

_____

And what do we learn about our God in **Isaiah 40:28-31** and **Jeremiah 10:12-13**?

_____

_____

_____

These passages of scripture and so many more point to how *big* God is. Once we begin to wrap our minds around the bigness of our Creator, what does (or what would) that do to our perspective of those other seemingly "too big" things we're dealing with?

_____

_____

_____

_____

May your prayer today be to have an even deeper understanding of how big, how mighty, how powerful the God of heaven and earth is!

Wednesday

Now, let's go back to that powerful last line in **1 Samuel 17:51**. It is vital to remember that Goliath's head also needs to be cut off. That means that sometimes we have to handle our Goliaths in an extreme way. But Corinthians tells us God's love has moved us to extremes.[95] That means when we live out of a deep and abiding love relationship with Jesus Christ, we are okay if we have to be extreme in some areas of our lives. Others may be going to see that movie, but we don't need to. Others may be able to have a computer in their bedroom, but we can't. Others may be able to "get by," albeit deceptively, with a mediocre relationship with Jesus Christ, but that isn't going to work for us. *Extreme is our only option.* But, when we have truly encountered His love, we are more than okay with acting extreme or being viewed as extreme because it doesn't feel extreme. It feels like simply, deeply loving the One who gave us everything.

Read and write out **2 Corinthians 5:13-14** in the MSG translation, if you have access to it.

_____

_____

_____

_____

What are some of the ways in which you've seen God's love for you? A breathtaking sunset? The right encouragement at the right time? His provision in a time of need?

_____

_____

_____

---

[95] 2 Corinthians 5:14 (MSG)

How has being aware of those moments of His love affected and maybe even changed you?

_____

_____

_____

_____

Pray this week and ask God to open your eyes to clearly see all the ways He loves you this week. Write them down. Remember, the more we look, the more we see. The more we thank Him for what we've seen, the more He will show us. It is a powerfully beautiful cycle.

Thursday

Take another look at the passage in 2 Corinthians we talked about yesterday. A byproduct of having a love relationship with God is the calling, the leading, to do some extreme things.

Noah built the ark.
John the Baptist wore animal skins and lived off of locusts and honey.
A group of men lowered their sick friend from a hole they cut out of a roof to get him to Jesus.
Abraham almost sacrificed his son.
A woman broke her jar of incredibly expensive perfume to pour on Jesus' feet.
Joseph forgave his brothers for selling him into slavery.

I'm going to say it again, as followers of Jesus, *extreme is our only option.*

What are some "extreme" ways you have seen others serve the Lord? How has that impacted you?

_____

_____

_____

_____

Now ask yourself, what are some of the "extreme" or even countercultural things you have done or may be sensing the Lord leading you to do in response to His love?

_____

_____

_____

_____

_____

Friday

With the idea of a "Goliath" being something that needs to be dealt with before we can move into our next season, what might be one, or a few, of those for you? A habit? A mentality? A fear? An unhealthy relationship?

_____

_____

_____

What do you think about your "Goliaths?" Have they become your comfort? Does their presence make you angry? Does it seem as if they are even mocking you? Do they make you afraid?

_____

_____

_____

Ask the Lord what He is asking you to do with this Goliath. Seriously, ask Him. Also ask Him how you may need to get extreme with it. Then just listen. Come back to this space as you hear Him speak.

_____

_____

_____

_____

Saturday Surrender

"Humble yourselves before the Lord, and He will exalt you."
James 4:10 (ESV)

This is not an easy topic - Goliaths. Often because we have become friends with them. So, the very thought of cutting off their head can cause us great anxiety. But remember, we can do nothing separate of Christ. Nothing. It isn't about what you can do; it is, however, about what you are willing to let go of.

It's also important to remember that David's heart was not seeking personal gain or glory in defeating Goliath. His desire was to bring glory to the God of Israel, where it belongs.

As you are seeking the Lord to help you destroy the Goliaths in your life, may you trust that He is more than big enough and may you also be mindful to surrender your motives and purposes to Him. Glory and credit for any and all success goes completely to the God of the universe.

Sunday Sabbath

**"The eternal God is your refuge,
and underneath are the everlasting arms.
He will drive out your enemies before you,
saying, 'Destroy them!'"
Deuteronomy 33:27 (NIV)**

Songs for Your Sabbath
Casting Crowns, *Oh My Soul*
Chris Tomlin, *How Great is Our God*

You and Jesus have done a lot of battling your Goliaths this week. Take some time today to rest in His everlasting love and settle into His arms. Thank Him for how He fights on your behalf. Let Him know how much you love and worship Him. Enjoy His sweet, sweet presence this Sabbath…

Lord, thank You for not only helping me identify those things keeping me from moving where You want me, but also for going before me into battle and killing my Goliaths. I ask that whatever extreme measures I may need to take would be revealed to me in order to assure complete destruction of anything that would try to keep me from my destiny. May all of the victory I experience point to the power that belongs to You and You alone. And may the revelation of Your love be the conduit for me loving you to what may feel to the world as extreme, but to me be a joy.

Week 47

A Note of Thanksgiving

Monday

Read: 1 Corinthians 1:4-9

Good Monday morning.

Thanksgiving. We know this word so well. We celebrate it as a day and are encouraged to practice it as a lifestyle. The word is made up of two words, "thanks" and "giving." In its most basic definition it is "the act of giving thanks." So can we talk a few moments about this most simple yet profound act?

As we enter this Thanksgiving season, I am reminded of what Paul wrote in 1 Corinthians 1:4, *"Every time I think of you, and I think of you often, I thank God for your lives of free and open access to God given by Jesus."* Can I tell you today that after all of these weeks together I'm thankful for *you*. I may never get to meet you in this lifetime. But, one day, we'll have an uninterrupted season in our heavenly home to enjoy an ocean view, I hope… or mountain if you prefer… we'll get to have a cold Coca-Cola that won't have calories or lose its fizz, and a long conversation that won't be rushed by the confines of time and schedules. I also want to give thanks to you for affording me the privilege of having access to your heart over this year through these devotionals. You're not reading this book and participating in these daily devotionals because of me. You're doing it because you want a word from the Lord each day, just like I do; so I thank God for you and I pray His richest blessings on you in this next season of your life, that you would feel and know Him in a new way, and that you would see Him in the smallest details of your story.

Paul goes on to say, "Just think, you don't need a thing. You've got it all." I'm also thankful for the fact that God will supply all of our needs according to His riches in Christ Jesus. So whatever need you and I may have in this season, whether it's a need of mended relationships, healing in our emotional, mental, or physical selves, or a material or visional need — whatever it is — it has already been supplied. Thus, ultimately, we don't need a thing because we have Jesus.

"All God's gifts are right in front of you as you wait expectantly for our master, Jesus, to arrive on the scene for the finality." God places gifts in each one of us to use for the advancement of His kingdom on the earth. Scripture says "His callings and gifts are without repentance;" meaning even if we run from them those giftings will still be inside of us. You can be in prisoner and still be a preacher. Just ask Jim Bakker.

And we are to live in full operation of our gifts as we wait in the expectant hope that there is a finale to this book, this play, this story, of our lives and that God has written the final chapter and Jesus will one day show up to take us home.

What more could we ask for? If that were it, if the fact that this world is not our home and salvation secures us an eternity with Jesus was all there is… it would be enough. But there's so much more to be thankful for. David said, "I would've lost hope unless I would believe I would see the goodness of the Lord in the land of the living."[96] We can even be thankful that we get to see God's goodness in this life now! We don't have to wait for eternity. Jesus has already laid out His gifts for us to use and His supply has already gone before every need.

There is much to be thankful for in this season. I am thankful for you. I am thankful that God has us — our needs and our desires — and that Jesus is coming one day to get us. May our hearts express this thankfulness and so many others in this season. To those around us, may we tell them how thankful we are for them; and to our Father, from whom every good and perfect gift flows, may we tell Him how thankful we are for Him, too.

Take time to write out the top ten things you are most thankful for in this season.

_____

_____

_____

_____

_____

_____

_____

Think about the five people you are most thankful for during this season. I encourage you to write them a note of thanksgiving this week.

---

[96] Psalm 27:13

Tuesday

❧

What does **Ephesians 5:4** tell us our mouths should be full of?

_____

Read **1 Thessalonians 5:18**.

What are the most challenging areas of your life right now where it is hard to be thankful?

_____

_____

_____

_____

What could being thankful, in spite of what you are going through, do to both you and your circumstances?

_____

_____

_____

_____

Wednesday

❧

Why is thanksgiving needed in our prayer life? Refer to **Philippians 4:4-7** and **Colossians 4:2**.

_____

_____

_____

Getting our minds on God creates the opportunity for our perspective to be clear on our circumstances - that is why thanksgiving is so powerful in prayer. Most of the time we want to focus on our petitions, but thanksgiving gets our eyes on Christ and what He has done and is able to do.

What does thanksgiving in our prayer life, then, produce?

_____

_____

_____

Read **Revelation 7:9-12**. What does this passage of thanksgiving to God make you feel? What does it speak to your heart about this moment to come?

_____

_____

_____

_____

Thursday

Remember the account of Jesus feeding the 5,000 men we read last week? Look back at **John 6:11-14** to refresh your memory.

What was the last thing He did with the bread before sharing it with the multitude?

_____

What connection, then, might we be able to draw between thankfulness and provision?

_____

_____

_____

Where do you need provision in this season and how could you begin to approach God with a heart of thanksgiving in that area?

_____

_____

_____

_____

Friday

Read **Luke 17:13-19**. How many come back to give thanks?

_____

What does Jesus connect with this leper's thankfulness and his wholeness? So, could it be that our thankfulness is a direct reflection of our faith in God?

_____
_____
_____
_____

God is a detailed God.

I shared with you that I believe developing an eye that looks for God in the smallest details of our story creates a heart of thankfulness and I truly believe, in return, has God so delighted that He does even more. However, even if my theology is flawed and God does the same detailed love for all of us, I can say with confidence that many do not see it and the disconnect can only be one thing alone: our faith — believing that He loves us enough to do those detailed things which, in return, cannot help but illicit our thanksgiving. Thus connecting, once again, our faith and our thankfulness.

A person who doesn't believe in God's goodness or detailed love is not going to be a person who can see those detailed love moments.

Saturday Surrender

"Enter His gates with thanksgiving, and His courts with praise! Give thanks to Him; bless His name!"
Psalm 100:4 (ESV)

Where is your focus? Is it on your stuff or your Savior? As children of God in intimate relationship with Him, know that we don't have to fight _for_ our victory; we fight _from_ a place of victory!

So why shouldn't we, then, continually offer up our thanks to our mighty Victor?

You wrote Tuesday about circumstances that might affect your ability, or desire, to express your gratitude. Ask God today to help shift your focus off of what is in your way and onto His magnificent goodness — surrender your perspective and I *promise* He will honor your obedience.

Sunday Sabbath

"Don't worry about anything; instead, pray about everything. Tell God what you need, and thank Him for all He has done."
Philippians 4:6 (NLT)

Songs for Your Sabbath
Lakewood Live, *You Are Good*
Don Moen, *Give Thanks*
Darlene Zschech, *Worthy is the Lamb*

It's so simple, yet it tends to be so incredibly difficult: assuming a posture of gratitude when everything in us says there's no time or no need.

Over the course of this past week you've become aware of or have been reminded of the value in turning our hearts to thanksgiving rather than fear or control.

And so, this Sabbath, as you're settled in your quiet place, I encourage you to take this time to intentionally express thanks to your heavenly Father for whatever comes to your mind — and I encourage you to do it out loud. Let your heart feel and your ears hear all that you are especially thankful for in this season.

Father, I thank You. I thank You for Your goodness, for Your grace, for Your salvation and for Your presence in my life. I ask that You would help me to maintain a heart focused on You and all I have to be thankful for —not just in this season but always. May my posture of gratitude be so evident that it draws others to You.

Week 48

Celebrating Jesus' Arrival by the Hope of His Coming

Monday

Read: Isaiah 2

Good Monday morning.

There are days that the brokenness of this life settles in on me in ways that can take my breath. It can make a brilliant sunrise look muted. It can make the captivating cackle of a little one feel annoying. It can even cause the majesty of the mountains or the power of the Pacific ocean as it crescendos its crash with the roar of a thousand trumpets to be silenced and missed. Yes, life can do that. For many, the holiday seasons bring the pain of their story to light in a new way. My prayer in this season for us, however, is that the hope this season brings will collide with the reality of our circumstances and force our hearts to encounter what only Jesus can do: bring unexplainable, inconceivable, and inexpressible joy!

The Advent season, what these weeks between Thanksgiving and Christmas are called, is about us understanding that every promise in the Word, the promises that move our hearts from despair to hope, finds its *yes* and its *amen* in Jesus Christ. It does that by revealing to us His birth and the miracle and gift that it was to our hearts — that the King of heaven would come down and take on human form in a way so humble many would refuse to believe this could be the Messiah, so that those who would believe could walk in the forgiveness that His death would bring and the saving grace that it would afford us. This season also invites us to focus on the beautiful promise of His return which is what makes this life, at moments, endurable and gives us a hope that even the darkest days should not be allowed to steal.

The first week of Advent focuses on the power of the prophecies about this Jesus we love… His birth, His anointing, His betrayal, His death, and the fact that He would be crucified. It also tells of His resurrection and return to His rightful throne in heaven, and the fact that He will rule and reign there… all of these things prophesied before Jesus ever arrived.

Did you know that Jesus fulfilled every prophetic announcement of the over 300 that are recorded in the Old Testament? Peter wrote it this way, "He was foreknown before the foundation of the world but was made manifest in the last times for the sake of you."[97] Those prophetic announcements of Him made it clear that He was known before time. God brought Him into time because we would need Him so desperately.

For you math people (this would be Philly, not me) this very fact alone, that He fulfilled all Old Testament prophecies, make it clear He was the prophesied Messiah. The statistical odds of this are breathtaking. If He had only fulfilled 48 prophecies, the odds of that happening are one in ten to the 157th power (10^{157}). For those of you without a math mind, that's a 1 with 157 zeros behind it. Yet, He fulfilled **all**! Undeniable proof of this, our Messiah. Which also provides an undeniable gratitude that life has a meaning far beyond what we see, feel, hear, or touch. Why? Because we were made for another world. We are spirits living in a natural world, not natural men living in a spiritual world as the enemy likes to get us to believe so often.

It's interesting that Advent starts in reverse it seems. It starts with the awe-inspiring anticipation of the fact that one day, that sky that we gaze at all throughout our often ordinary days is the same sky that will split open and for the first time allow our faces to rest upon our Savior's face and in one singular moment we will be made like Him. This weak and frail semblance of a casing will be stripped away for the vibrant, alive, soul that is inside of us.

With this crazy imagination I have, I've often wondered if God's children would, right before that sky splits open, have this shimmer of something run through us that would let us know our Bridegroom is about to appear. I remember when I married Philly there was this quaint little church I had driven by for a few years and told the Lord, "If I ever get remarried I want to get married there." When I called to see if the church was available, the date I desired was the only available date for weeks before it or after it. I took that as a sign.

The church had no foyer, you simply walked in one of the two front doors and you were in the sanctuary. So, for a few moments, after my matron of honor had gone inside, it was just me and my heavenly Father. He had told me a year earlier that He would give me away this time. So as I stood outside, with that red door yet to open in front of me, the sun peeked around the corner of the church and flooded my face with its warmth as if my heavenly Father was saying, "I'm about to give you away." Everything in my heart was so alive because I knew that in just a moment my bridegroom was on the other side of that door and I was going to see him. Yes… just wondering… if it might be that way when Jesus, my bridegroom comes for me.

As hard as it is to believe on this side of that door, one day He is coming back. And for those who have chosen to live this life in a love relationship with Jesus, we are going to get to spend the rest of our lives with the One our hearts were created for.

---

[97] 1 Peter 1:20 (ESV)

In the New Testament, Luke said it this way, "And there will be signs in sun and moon and stars, and on the earth distress of nations in perplexity because of the roaring of the sea and the waves, people fainting with fear and with foreboding of what is coming on the world. For the powers of the heavens will be shaken. And then they will see the Son of Man coming in a cloud with power and great glory. Now when these things begin to take place, straighten up and raise your heads, because your redemption is drawing near."[98]

Ever thought of the fact that of all the things in this world, creation is the one thing that knows what Eden was like? Why wouldn't it groan for the return of such perfection? So it rages its seas. It shakes its foundation. The hurricanes ravage. The earthquakes shatter, leaving hearts filled with fear of what will happen next and where. But, oh, the hope! Right in the middle of the chaos, the clouds will hold our Bridegroom! And our redemption from the brokenness, the persecution, the bigotry, the bitterness, the poverty, the divorce, the death… all of that will finally be redeemed!

Now *that's* a good way to start this Advent season...

We've come a long way this year. Now, as it nears its end, I think you can start asking your own heart questions. First, pray before you read the passage given each day. Then, write down in your journal any thoughts, questions or prayers that come to your mind as you read that passage. Then, take those thoughts, questions, or prayers back to the Lord in a prayer as you finish up your time each day.

Don't be afraid.

Don't avoid this.

This is part of spiritual growth and learning how to hear God for yourself and invite Him into your time in the Word. Remember, Jesus Himself is the Word. So as you read it you are, in a way, drinking Him in.

May these next few weeks be a gift to your heart as you celebrate this Jesus that so wildly loves you and is so excited about coming back to get you.

(Read all of these passages this week from the MSG or New Living Translation, if you can.)

---

[98] Luke 21:25-28 (ESV)

Read **1 Peter 1:1-2.**

_____
_____
_____
_____
_____
_____
_____
_____

Tuesday

Read **1 Peter 1:3-5.**

_____
_____
_____
_____
_____
_____
_____
_____

Wednesday

Read **1 Peter 1:6-7.**

_____
_____
_____
_____
_____
_____

Thursday

Read **1 Peter 1:8-12**.

Friday

Read **1 Peter 1:13-21**.

Saturday Surrender

Read **1 Peter 1:22-25**.

_____

_____

_____

_____

_____

_____

_____

_____

_____

Sunday Sabbath

"The people who walked in darkness
have seen a great light;
those who dwelt in a land of deep darkness,
on them has light shone."
Isaiah 9:2 (ESV)

Songs for Your Sabbath
Fernando Ortega, *Come Thou Long Expected Jesus*
Andrea Crouch, *Soon and Very Soon*

How fitting is this, that each Sunday of Advent, traditionally a candle is lit. Oh what joy and assurance we have in the promise of our Savior's return — the Light of the world shines so brightly on us!

I'm sure switching gears in our weekly structure came as something of a surprise to you. If you truly leaned into it, though, I'm also sure you probably even surprised yourself with how deep you were able to dig in on your own.

And, so, as you're in your quiet place this Sabbath, think back on the progress your heart has made this week and also over the course of this past year.

I don't know about you, but when I taste the sweet fruit of growth, I crave it even more, I'm eager to experience what's next. Well, if you're a follower of Jesus, you and I have experienced His beautiful saving power — and that should make us all the more eager to encounter Him in eternity!

Be mindful of that today, friend, and let your heart find its way to a posture of eager expectation for even more of Him...

Father, thank You for making a way to have restored access to Your presence. Thank You that as this holiday season begins, even in the mess that is mine, that one day all of this trouble will be gone and I will be with You. What a wonderful hope to think about. I ask that You would continue to cultivate in me an ever-increasing desire for Jesus' return. If there are things I am holding onto tightly here, reveal them to me so that my prayer can be, "Even so come Lord Jesus."

Week 49

He Really is Coming Back!

Monday

Read: Isaiah 11

Good Monday morning.

For almost two years I did an intense study in the book of Revelation. I, like you I'm sure, avoided it for many reasons or read it quickly as if really understanding it was impossible. However, the very beginning of the book starts out with these words, "Blessed is the one who reads aloud the words of this prophecy, and blessed are those who hear, and who keep what is written in it, for the time is near."[99] This passage makes it all too clear that the enemy of our hearts has been a master at convincing us that reading about the return of our Savior, Jesus Christ, is somehow too much for us to handle or understand. But what I discovered from my own study was that my heart had an even greater understanding of the mercy and grace of God and an even greater desire for His return.

This second week of Advent, we focus yet again on the beautiful hope of the return of Jesus. As a believer, this fact that one day this life will be over and we will finally be home, brings the greatest hope possible for the hardest days. Yet, I dare say many of us rarely spend time pondering the thought that this life isn't the end and that one day Jesus will return. This is another reason I am grateful for this Advent season, to recalibrate us to the fact that we are simply travelers passing through…

When Paul wrote to the Thessalonians, he said this: "He died for us so that, whether we are awake or asleep, we may live together with Him. Therefore, encourage one another and build each other up, just as in fact you are doing."[100] Is there anything more encouraging or hopeful than the fact

---

[99] Revelation 1:3 (ESV)

ay we will be with Jesus? C.S. Lewis says it this way in his book, *Mere Christianity*, "If we ...lves with a desire that nothing in this world can satisfy, the most probable explanation ...e were made for another world."

fact that we search for things to try to satisfy us, that we try to quench a holy hunger with ...re morsels of stale bread, is proof that we were created for a world far beyond the one in which ...e dwell. Our home is with Him and the hope of this painfully beautiful life is that one day we're going to see Him face to face and in that moment we will be made like Him. Oh, the thousands of ways and times in a day this reality comes to my heart and makes me ache in the deepest places of my soul for His return while also igniting me to make sure others know and are ready too.

Isaiah's prophetic voice trumpets to us again in chapter 11. Jesus arrived to us via the lineage of Jesse. Jesse was the father of King David. When Matthew records Jesus' genealogy, Matthew describes Jesus as the Son of David. So, after Isaiah so perfectly describes His heritage, he then lovingly describes His character. Wise. Understanding. A Counselor. Mighty. Knowledgeable. Fear of the Lord. Righteous. Just. He covers His arrival, His years on the earth, and finishes with His return.

Part of the hope of this return is that one day the demonic evil that Satan has relentlessly and, at times, catastrophically spread will finally be judged. An end will one day come to all remnants of evil and sin having any access to the atmosphere and our lives. Can you imagine? A world without sickness, without child abuse, without murder and hatred and division, without broken marriages or death… one day it will all be over.

The challenge for many is that this also makes clear that sin will not remain before a holy God. Sin will one day be judged. I know it's hard to wrap our minds around how this loving God can allow anyone to be separated from Him. However, we must first realize that this was never His plan. Adam and Eve *chose* sin. In Eden, in the middle of perfection, they *chose* self-sufficiency. But God, in His extravagant love *gave* Jesus. Why? Because sin cannot dwell where God is. That's why when Adam and Eve chose their sin they had to be removed from the presence of God, but they were also removed because God did not want them eating from the Tree of Life, because then they — and we — would live forever in a sin state, preventing even Jesus' death from saving us and affording us eternity back with our Father.

Scripture tells us, "But do not overlook this one fact, beloved, that with the Lord one day is as a thousand years, and a thousand years as one day. The Lord is not slow to fulfill His promise as some count slowness, but is patient toward you, not wishing that any should perish, but that all should reach repentance."[101]

The reason He is slow, the reason that He waits, is because He's patient toward us, not wanting *anyone* to be separated from Him. He waits, and waits, and waits yet again so that everyone that is

---

[100] 1 Thessalonians 5:10-11 (NIV)

[101] 2 Peter 3:8-9 (ESV)

willing will repent. But just like He didn't snatch the fruit from Adam and Eve, He won't snatch our will to choose something other than Him. He woos, He pursues, He pushes, He reveals, He loves, He surrounds, He invites, He gives sacrificially all in an effort to lead our hearts to repentance. And He waits to come back yet to judge us according to the way that we should be judged, because He's so patient with us; He doesn't want anyone to perish. God doesn't want one person to be lost. So He waits, and then He waits, and then He waits some more. But He will not wait forever. And when He does return, it is then all sin, past and present will be judged. It has to be. And as a believer we will want it to. Because heaven is about being with Jesus and finally being free from all sin. Until then there remains the opportunity to accept Jesus as Savior so that no one has to know separation from Him, but so that we can enjoy the hope of being with Him forever.

Peter prophesies it this way in 2 Peter 3:10-13 (ESV), *"But the day of the Lord will come like a thief, and then the heavens will pass away with a roar, and the heavenly bodies will be burned up and dissolved, and the earth and the works that are done on it will be exposed. Since all these things are thus to be dissolved, what sort of people ought you to be in lives of holiness and godliness, waiting for and hastening the coming of the day of God, because of which the heavens will be set on fire and dissolved, and the heavenly bodies will melt as they burn! But according to His promise we are waiting for new heavens and a new earth in which righteousness dwells."*

This advent season, in the middle of our messiness and pictures that look a lot different from our Christmas cards, our hearts have the promised hope of eternity. One day this world will pass away, God will come and judge us based on the decision we have made about Him. For those of us who have chosen Him, this Advent season is a reminder of the hope that we have that awaits. This world does not have the last word — Jesus, Emmanuel, the One who came to set us free, His love does. And of that, it brings a glorious hope that we will spend eternity with Him. That is the beauty of this Advent season. May we celebrate that blessed hope this week.

Read **Matthew 24:1-32**.

_____

_____

_____

_____

Tuesday

Read **Matthew 24:33-51**.

_____

_____

_____

_____

Wednesday

✦

Read **Matthew 25:1-13**.

_____

_____

_____

_____

Thursday

✦

Read **Matthew 25:14-30**.

_____

_____

_____

_____

Friday

✦

Read **Matthew 25:31-46**.

_____

_____

_____

_____

Saturday Surrender

Read **Matthew 26:17-30**.

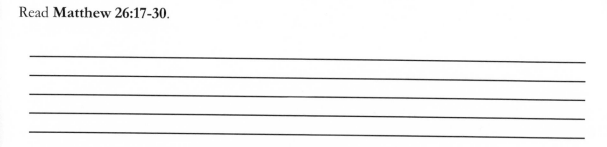

Sunday Sabbath

"**Do not let your hearts be troubled. You believe in God; believe also in Me. My Father's house has many rooms; if that were not so, would I have told you that I am going there to prepare a place for you? And if I go and prepare a place for you, I will come back and take you to be with Me that you also may be where I am. You know the way to the place where I am going.**"
John 14:1-4 (NIV)

Songs for Your Sabbath
Big Daddy Weave, *The Lion and the Lamb*
The Singing Contractors, *What a Day That Will Be*

Are you excited now? Nothing makes this life more endurable than knowing that it is not our home. That our heavenly Father is preparing our real home. On the days when your discontent may feel overwhelming, speak peace to your troubled heart, reminding it that you are not forgotten, but instead, you are being planned and prepared for, in your real and heavenly home.

❧

Dear heavenly Father, forgive me for the times I've been so wrapped up in life that I have failed to remember that one day You are coming back for me. If there is anything in this season that would have my heart disconnected from Yours, I ask that You reveal it to me and I be willing to repent or let go of anything I need to. I thank You for the reminder this week of Your patience, will one day return and that sin will not be present forever. Thank You for how ...'ve been with me. And help me share the truth of who You are with others in this season where all the world is hearing about You.

Week 50

Messiah of the Mess

Monday

Read: Luke 2

Good Monday morning.

It's been said that the season between Thanksgiving and Christmas each year has many of us encountering depression on a scale larger than any other season. Interesting fact, in the very season where the very angels declared to scrappy shepherds, "I bring you good news that will bring great joy to all people!" Luke 2:10 (NLT), people are suffering depression. This third week of Advent comes wrapped to us in that word: *joy.* Yet for many of us, that may be the least prominent adjective in our vocabulary right now. In fact, you may have already started panicking about what Christmas day would look like before you even turned the calendar to December.

For many, as you imagine Christmas morning, you're the first one up, coffee in hand, deep breath just exhaled and head leaned back in a silent prayer that the chaos that is life doesn't explode at the dinner table. Or maybe you're imagining the coma that follows Christmas dinner when you can steal away for a few moments without the beeping of electronics or entanglement of tissue paper to catch your breath and figure out how to survive the rest of the day without strangling an in-law. Or maybe you're thinking about how you'll collapse when the last relative leaves and you'll scroll through Facebook only to realize that out of all of your "friends," you, my dear, are the only one that had a screwed up Christmas. Or it could be that you are fearing that moment when you lay your head on your pillow at the end of Christmas Day and your mind rummages through all the "what ifs," "what weres," "what weren'ts," and "what could have beens" and you simply wonder when will anything in life ever be, well… normal? And angels want to talk about joy?!

But God allowed Isaiah to see this one coming centuries away. So He prophesied the joy Jesus would bring when he said in Isaiah 61:

The Spirit of the Lord God is upon me,
  because the Lord has anointed me
to bring good news to the poor;
  He has sent me to bind up the brokenhearted,
to proclaim liberty to the captives,
  and the opening of the prison to those who are bound;
to proclaim the year of the Lord's favor,
  and the day of vengeance of our God;
to comfort all who mourn;
to grant to those who mourn in Zion —
  to give them a beautiful headdress instead of ashes,
the oil of gladness instead of mourning,
  the garment of praise instead of a faint spirit;
that they may be called oaks of righteousness,
  the planting of the Lord, that He may be glorified.

That is what the birth of our Savior brought: hope to the brokenness of our story. And that brings joy… great joy.

Truth be told, normal is a highly over-rated — albeit ridiculous — word. Normal doesn't change lives and help heal wounds or turn the other cheek. Nor does normal have a *Southern Living* Christmas. No, normal has, well… ordinary. It has paper plates with poinsettia leaves at best and tacky napkins at worst. Normal doesn't do extravagant. And just like Jesus' arrival railed against the status quo and ridiculous quest for normal, it is this same arrival that lets us know how well He does with our mess. And let's be honest, few things reveal how messy a family really is like the holidays.

It is recorded in Luke 2, but allow me to summarize it for you this way, the detailed fulfillment of this messy Christmas.

Jesus' dad, too, had to go home for Christmas Day — and not by choice, I might add — which is probably like many of us. So there Joseph goes with pregnant wife and, not pregnant by him. Want to talk about *messy*? Then, he gets pregnant wife to his hometown, the place where his ancestors are from, and nowhere is there an actual room for his child to be born. It's uncertain whether the Messiah was born in a stable next to a "no-vacancy" inn or the bottom floor of a family's house where the animals stayed at night; what is certain is that the Creator of heaven and earth moves into earth via a borrowed manger. Sound like a mess? Is this the way the King of Kings and the Lord of Lords should arrive? Shouldn't there be a parade? A celebration? A few relatives at least? No, Jesus arrives in the middle of a mess. The first Christmas isn't much different than many of ours. A lot of stink and whole lot of noise. No, there was nothing normal about Jesus' arrival. Nothing normal about the Savior arriving in a stall.

Yet, it is this very messy arrival that is *the* hope and *the* joy of this Christmas season. A joy that can't be measured by feeling, but instead is measured by that inward stillness as silent as any night could be. An arrival that came for even the greatest pain of our mess, the mess we are in today or the one that waits up the road. Jesus is the Master of Messes. In fact, He doesn't want your life to be normal, He wants it to be extraordinary. So, in this Christmas season, before you succumb to the despair of the "what could have beens" or "should've beens," surrender, instead, to the confident trust that because of the first Christmas every other Christmas has been redeemed!

That, my friend, can move you to joy… to great joy.

⁕

Read **Psalm 16:11**.

Tuesday

⁕

Read **Matthew 11:2-5**.

Wednesday

Read **James 1:1-3**.

_____
_____
_____
_____
_____
_____
_____
_____
_____

Thursday

Read **Romans 15:13**.

_____
_____
_____
_____
_____
_____
_____
_____
_____

Friday

Read **Psalm 30:5**.

_____
_____
_____
_____
_____
_____
_____
_____
_____

Saturday Surrender

Read **Hebrews 12:1-2**.

_____
_____
_____
_____
_____
_____
_____
_____
_____

Sunday Sabbath

"Jesus looked at them intently and said, 'Humanly speaking, it is impossible. But with God everything is possible.'"
Matthew 19:26

Songs for Your Sabbath
Planetshakers, *Joy*
The Christ Church Choir, *Joy to the World*

The Prince of Peace comes to bring His presence to your holiday season. Don't miss the hope He wants to speak in the hubbub of the holiday. Stop. Be still. Listen. He will speak.

Heavenly Father, I am grateful You are the Messiah of the mess. That nothing in my life or this season is lost on You. Thank You for the hope Your birth has provided for me. May I live in that joy. I ask, Father, that I would begin to make professions of faith and rejoicing knowing that when I do, it changes my very atmosphere. May this Christmas season be transformed by the joy in me. In Your precious name I pray.

Week 51

The Giver of the Gift

Monday

Read: Luke 1:26-33

Good Monday morning.

Near the end of each year, I buy a new calendar and start recording all of the kids' activities, ministry deadlines, and travel responsibilities for the next year — a calendar that is defined by Jesus' birth. Ever thought about that? How much His birth changed everything? History is divided by it: AD and BC. The very book that He wrote is the number one seller of all time. And His arrival marked what "love" really means — because "God so loved the world…," this very same world that denied Him then, resists Him now, and continually tries to redefine Him. Yet, He knew that to come He would have to die… could there be a greater love than this…?

A few years back I was asking God to allow me to show one of my bonus-daughters specifically how she was seen by me and, in return, loved by Him. There was a particular gift that I really felt would express this to her for a myriad of different reasons: a beautiful yet dainty heart necklace. I made the decision, however, not to get it for her when she shared that her grandparents were getting her a necklace. As Philly and I looked around the store for an alternative at the same price, my heart was aching over not being able to get her what I truly wanted to. But we settled on a small pair of earrings that I knew she would like.

Christmas morning arrived and when she opened the little jewelry box that had been wrapped by the seller at the store out of our eye-sight, her eyes lit up. But my heart was still sad. Then she pulled out the item, it was the necklace. What?! We had bought the earrings. But it was the exact necklace that I had wanted to give her inside that box. I was stunned!

She noticed my shock so I finally said, "I don't know what happened. Those were supposed to be earrings. The necklace is what I wanted to get you, but when you said your grandparents were getting you a necklace, I changed to earrings."

"Oh, Denise, I love it," she said, still beaming, "They didn't get me a necklace."

I was floored. My heavenly Father knew exactly every desire of my heart to love this child and, in return, He loved me. I shared the whole story with her in more detail later and she said, "That's like what you always say, that is God loving me in my details." That mere statement alone did as much as the necklace to my heart. God was also allowing me to see that what I had deposited had taken root and had impact.

Isaiah, again, records the love of God in Isaiah 7:10: "Again the Lord spoke to Ahaz: 'Ask a sign of the Lord your God; let it be deep as Sheol or high as heaven.' But Ahaz said, 'I will not ask, and I will not put the Lord to the test.' And he said, 'Hear then, O house of David! Is it too little for you to weary men, that you weary my God also? Therefore the Lord Himself will give you a sign. Behold, the virgin shall conceive and bear a son, and shall call His name Immanuel.'" This word *Immanuel* means "God with us."

Friends, God is with us. He is with us in the Christmas season to lavish His love on us. A love that extravagantly gave us Jesus. That detailed love didn't end there; that detailed love is bigger than our biggest messes and as detailed as our heart's smallest desire. His birth echoed through the ages His immeasurable and matchless love.

But what about in those moments when His love might not feel like love? I have often wondered if that is how Mary might have felt in the passage you read today?

Sure, this angel said this miraculous seed was because she was found to have favor in the sight of God, but angel or not I have to wonder if for a moment she felt anything but favored. Even on our best days, the whole immaculate conception still seems inconceivable. Yes, there are moments that God's love doesn't feel like love. That's why we can't look at life through "our thoughts and our ways." Remember…?

We cannot see all that God is doing in His gifts of love. It's hard to see wine when the water is dried up. It's hard to see the healing when the pain is so great. And it's hard to feel love when it arrives in a way that feels unloving. But Mary simply said, "I am the Lord's slave,"…"May it be done to me according to Your word."[102] She received the gift of love because she trusted the Giver of the Gift.[103]

Friends, He is Immanuel, God with us, in the moments when we see His detailed love and in the moments we can't. He came so that we could do life, the understood and the misunderstood, with Him. Creator stooped to creation. King collided with ordinary. Lion of Judah became a lowly Lamb. That is what love does. And Love did that just for you… Merry Christmas.

---

[102] Luke 1:38

[103] Giver of the Gift by Denise Hildreth Jones, Jonathan Pierce, Phil Naish

Read **1 John 4:7-12**.

_____

_____

_____

_____

_____

_____

Tuesday

Read Psalm **103:1-14**.

_____

_____

_____

_____

_____

_____

Wednesday

Read Psalm **103:15-22**.

_____

_____

_____

_____

_____

_____

Thursday

❧

Read **Psalm 136:1-9**.

_____

_____

_____

_____

Friday

❧

Read **Psalm 136:10-22**.

_____

_____

_____

_____

Saturday Surrender

❧

Read **Psalm 136:23-26**.

_____

_____

_____

_____

Sunday Sabbath

"For God so loved the world that He gave His one and only Son, that whoever believes in Him shall not perish but have eternal life."
John 3:16 (NIV)

Mary's statement to the angel regarding her acceptance of the Holy Spirit's gift is evident that Mary was willing to trust God with everything. My prayer this week is that your encounter with the love of God will create a desire in your heart to do the same. In all of the giving of gifts may your heart be exceptionally tuned to the Giver of every good and perfect gift.

Giver of the Gift
Shine down on us now
Let us know the warmth of your embracing love
Shower down on us
A miracle that we can see
Bestower of Peace
You knew that we'd believe in Giver of the Gift.

Songs for Your Sabbath
Mary Did You Know
Amy Grant, *Breath of Heaven*

Heavenly Father, thank You for this season to stop and reflect on You — on Your arrival then and Your return anytime now. What a sweet recalibration this has been to get my mind focused on what this season truly is about. Thank You for the ultimate Gift You gave me in Jesus and thank You for the Giver that You are.

Week 52

Preparing for New Year

Monday

Read: Matthew 5:6

Good Monday morning.

This is our very last Monday of the year together... can you believe that?! 52 Mondays we've been together... and I have some thoughts to share with you, for you to prayerfully consider, as we close out this year and as we head into a new year.

One of my favorite parts about a new year is going into it with a time of intentionality. I steal away with the Lord in a different kind of way. I have some intentional fasting, I have some very focused prayer time and some very purposeful time of study. What I long to come away with after that season is what my friend and mentor, Dr. Albert Lemons, calls a *focus of heart* -- which is something a season like that truly provides.

I especially appreciate the role of fasting inside of this season. Fasting takes away the distraction of food by denying that flesh part of me which, thinking back to Genesis, got us into this mess in the first place. If you remember, the tool that the enemy chose in the garden was food. So, it's an intentional way to look back at what the enemy propagated in the very beginning of our stories in Genesis and still propagates to our hearts today: that we would live from this place of self-sufficiency, of self-desire, of self-satisfaction, and self-preservation.

So, what fasting at the first part of the year does is it offers us the privilege of pushback on self and moves us towards surrender. In fact, what I've discovered in my own personal story is that when I set aside this first part of the year to the Lord in such a focused way, those "flesh" things that dwell inside of me simply fall away and my hunger for Jesus grows.

"Blessed are those who hunger and thirst for righteousness, for they will be filled."[104]

This is so true. God takes this hunger and thirst that we are offering to Him in a season like this because we truly long for more of Him and He fills it every time. Do you know, not one time in one of these seasons has God failed to speak to me. He has given direction, He has given strategy. He has given a word to me often for that year for my heart. He has refined and sometimes redefined Philly's and my "I musts" — the "I musts" that we need to focus on over the course of the next year.

But more than anything, He has given freedom from distraction of my flesh to be able to focus on the heart of my Father's love for me.

I'll be honest with you, I often go into those seasons reluctantly. But I can tell you this honestly as well: I have never left those seasons wanting them to be over. It's a bittersweet ending. On one hand, I'm really wanting food and I'm really wanting a cold Coca Cola, but at the same time I don't want the sweetness to end. I don't want my attention to get back on the stuff and things of this world because I have really enjoyed my time of focused attention on the Lord.

So I encourage you this year. I encourage you to get a book on fasting. I encourage you to pray about fasting. I encourage you to set aside a specific time in the beginning of this new year to really allow the distractions of self to be pushed aside for the privilege of entering a season of focus of heart to encounter the heart of your Father in a way that could potentially transform this new year.

Each day this week I'm going to help guide you into different practices and things to be mindful of as you enter into this next year. You don't have to have a solid answer for everything right now, but I definitely encourage you to be especially mindful of each day's topic and question in order to get the most out of an intentional time of prayer and fasting.

Prayerfully ask God how He wants you to enter this new year or what He may want you to do. What do you hear Him saying?

_____
_____
_____
_____
_____
_____
_____
_____

_____

104 Matthew 5:6 (NIV)

Tuesday

Take the time to plan specifically what your fast will look like. Planning it helps you in times when you want to give up or quit.

It can be one meal a day for three days or all the way up to a 21-day Daniel Fast where you have no bread, no meat, no sweets.

Ask the Lord, He will tell you.

_____

_____

_____

_____

_____

_____

_____

Wednesday

Listen for a word or phrase or a passage of scripture that comes up multiple times during this season. Write it down to remember it. Write out what you think God may be speaking to you with it. Then come back at the end of the year and see how it may have changed or stayed the same.

_____

_____

_____

_____

_____

_____

_____

Thursday

What are some specific scriptures you want to pray during this new year?

_____

_____

_____

_____

Friday

Who are some specific people you want to pray for during this new year?

_____

_____

_____

_____

Saturday Surrender

What are some things you desire to see God do in this next year?

_____

_____

_____

_____

Sunday Sabbath

"But He answered, 'It is written, "Man shall not live by bread alone, but by every word that comes from the mouth of God."'"
Matthew 4:4 (ESV)

Album for your New Year
Michael O'Brien's, *Be Still My Soul, I Want to Know You More*

If thinking ahead to an intentional time of focus on the Lord and His plans for you for the next year feels like work or stresses you out, let me offer a different perspective. This is a sweet time. It is not punishment. It is an invitation. An invitation to encounter your Father in the beginning of this new year to set your heart for all it will hold.

Father, thank You for Your Word, Your rest, and Your love. Thank You for Your desire to have a love relationship with me. Thank You that You have good plans for me. Father, I ask that in the beginning of this new year You allow my heart to focus on You in a new way. I ask that the stuff of this past year that has consumed me, ensnared me, or simply overwhelmed me be removed and that a new and fresh filling of Your Spirit would saturate me as we walk into this new season together. I am grateful that there is not one piece of this journey that I travel alone. I cannot wait to see what You will reveal and do in this New Year!

Made in the USA
Middletown, DE
24 November 2019